T0265566

THE PHILIP ROTH WE DON'T KNOW

# The Philip Roth we don't know

## Sex, Race, and Autobiography

*Jacques Berlinerblau*

UNIVERSITY OF VIRGINIA PRESS

*Charlottesville and London*

University of Virginia Press
© 2021 by the Rector and Visitors of the University of Virginia
All rights reserved
Printed in the United States of America on acid-free paper

First published 2021

9 8 7 6 5 4 3 2 1

Library of Congress Cataloging-in-Publication Data

Names: Berlinerblau, Jacques, author.
Title: The Philip Roth we don't know : sex, race, and autobiography /
    Jacques Berlinerblau.
Other titles: Philip Roth we do not know.
Description: Charlottesville : University of Virginia Press, 2021. | Includes
    bibliographical references and index.
Identifiers: LCCN 2020058638 (print) | LCCN 2020058639 (ebook) |
    ISBN 9780813946610 (hardcover) | ISBN 9780813946627 (ebook)
Subjects: LCSH: Roth, Philip—Criticism and interpretation.
Classification: LCC PS3568.O855 Z575 2021 (print) | LCC PS3568.O855
    (ebook) | DDC 813/.54—dc23
LC record available at https://lccn.loc.gov/2020058638
LC ebook record available at https://lccn.loc.gov/2020058639

*Cover art*: "Philip Roth, 1984." David Levine. (© Matthew and Eve Levine)

*To Rubin Berlinerblau (1929–2019)*

So you're going to redeem Lonoff's reputation as a writer by ruining it as a man. Replace the genius of the genius with the secret of the genius. Rehabilitation by disgrace?
   —PHILIP ROTH, *Exit Ghost*

"Lucidity," he said, "is more important than happiness, because there isn't any perpetual happiness, but there can be perpetual lucidity."
   —PHILIP ROTH, "His Mistress's Voice"

# CONTENTS

# Art Is Slimy/Reverse Biography

*And as he spoke I was thinking, the kind of stories that people turn life into, the kind of lives that people turn stories into.*
    —PHILIP ROTH, *The Counterlife*

In October 2017, the #MeToo movement burst onto social media, igniting a multinational, multi-industry reckoning about sexual misconduct. Seven months later, on May 22, 2018, Philip Milton Roth passed away at the age of eighty-five. There is, obviously, no causal relation between these two events; the former did not precipitate the latter. Then again, the types of concerns that #MeToo raises about male misbehavior and privilege might precipitate the demise of Roth's literary legacy. By which I mean to say that among younger readers—readers attuned to our age's sensitivities about gender, race, and class—this author is a really, *really* hard sell.

Roth's fictional protagonists can outrage and "turn off" the current generation in myriad ways. When Mickey Sabbath in *Sabbath's Theater* plots to seduce a woman forty years his junior, he reflects thusly: "He could not let her get away. . . . The core of seduction is persistence. Persistence, the Jesuit ideal. Eighty percent of women will yield under tremendous pressure if the pressure is *persistent*."[1] Tonally, Sabbath reminds us of David Kepesh in *The Dying Animal*. He is a professor who serially preys upon his students. Reflecting on one of his lovers with whom he has had sexual relations for decades, Kepesh remarks, "Carolyn the undergraduate flower you pollinated, Carolyn at forty-five you farmed."[2]

When they're not sounding like epaulet-bearing brand ambassadors from "rape culture," Roth's men find other ways to alienate vast swaths of today's readership. They indulge in racist banter.[3] They mock multiculturalism. With especial verve, they lampoon feminists and feminism.[4] After decades of teaching Roth to college students, I find more than a few losing patience with him. Some appreciate his awesome talent, obviously. But with each passing year, more and more appear impervious to his charms.

It certainly doesn't help that many of Philip Roth's fictional bad boys greatly resemble Philip Roth; some of his characters actually bear his name. This tendency to write fictionalized autobiography—a tendency that he denied until his death—imbues debates about his work with a certain ferocity. Roth criticism often gets *personal*. His detractors, be they women's studies majors or even professional literary scholars, frequently associate the misogyny of the author's characters with the author himself.[5]

If a readership skeptical of white male privilege needed any other reason to dismiss, or "cancel," Roth, let's never forget his lofty cultural stature.[6] This cisgendered, heterosexual genius was garlanded with every imaginable major literary prize save the Nobel.[7] Many of his twenty-eight novels were greeted by fanfare, hype, and scrutiny likely unknown to any previous American author.[8] His name was a virtual watermark on the pages of the *New York Times*, *New York Review of Books*, *New Yorker*, and other high-toned places. He started his career in the mid-1950s as a Jewish "outsider." Yet, like so many of his industrious coreligionists, he eventually scaled the fence, and soon the peak, of his gentile profession. In the mostly white, mostly male, preserve of American letters, few writers attained Philip Roth's wealth and prestige.

One might imagine that this establishment novelist, deemed "too-testosterone-y" by graduate students, and assailed by critics for the "super-abundance of cock" in his prose, might fare badly among those with a #MeToo sensibility.[9] And, in truth, he often does! We shall encounter pre- and post-#MeToo feminist critics who lament the manner in which Roth writes about women, love, masculinity, and eroticism.

Yet it is simplistic to suggest that anyone who is sympathetic to #MeToo's intervention might be allergic to Roth's prose. This movement is not an orthodoxy. Those who concur with some, or all, of its goals have discovered characters and/or ideas that intrigue them in his fiction. What I'm about to show is that there are unexpected, and unnoticed, conceptual synergies in how both approach aesthetics. The relation between Roth and #MeToo, I will argue, is more complicated than either his admirers or critics recognize.

Once we understand that relation, new possibilities for studying his work will emerge. And maybe, just maybe, a younger generation of readers might be persuaded to engage with his art.

## The #MeToo Reckoning

In 2006, the activist Tarana Burke coined the phrase "Me Too."[10] Ms. Burke did so in order to draw attention to sexual violence experienced by young women of color. A decade later, on October 15, 2017, her slogan reemerged.[11] The "Me" and the "Too" were conjoined, hashtagged, and primed for the staggering amplification of solidarity and outrage that social media enables.

The scholar Carly Gieseler notes that within just ten days, the handle had "spread to eighty-five countries, with 1.7 million tweets."[12] On Facebook, 12 million people had posted about these two words within twenty-four hours.[13] Women of color, however, were no longer the focus of this viralizing phenomenon. Rather, the first revelations and reactions centered on the mostly white actresses whose suffering at the hands of the Hollywood mogul Harvey Weinstein had just fully come to light. (Alyssa Milano, who reintroduced the term "#MeToo," apologized for the inadvertent appropriation. Ms. Burke appeared to accept.)[14]

According to one writer, #MeToo is "an attempt to get people to understand the prevalence of sexual harassment and assault in society."[15] The movement, in the words of the *New York Times*, is "a national reckoning over harassment and gender discrimination, toppling powerful figures in nearly every industry."[16] Media icons such as Matt Lauer and Charlie Rose grabbed a lot of the headlines. But of all the industries in which powerful figures were exposed (and sometimes toppled), it was the misbehavior of the creative class that consistently produced the most riveting story lines.[17]

Philip Roth's name was everywhere in this new conversational intersection between #MeToo and the arts.[18] "What are we to make," asked Erin Vanderhoof in a reflection on Roth's "dirtbag" aesthetic, "of literature's towering male figures in the #MeToo era?"[19] Katy Waldman saw the occasion of his death as an "inflection point"—a prompt to ponder the "gendered blindness" of a more patriarchal literary era.[20] Upon his passing, the *New Yorker* gathered some of his closest friends for a dialogue entitled "Philip Roth in the #MeToo Era."[21] Elsewhere, Meghan Daum cheekily praised Roth for writing fiction that provided women with a bestiary of toxic men.[22] The title of her piece says it all: "In the Age of #MeToo, Philip Roth Offers an Unlikely Blueprint for Feminists." When asked about Roth's alleged misogyny, the writer Chimamanda Ngozi Adichie commented, "I read his women and roll my eyes but there is a truth there, because there are many men like his men."[23]

Upon first glance, Roth's consistent inclusion in these discussions is baffling. An artist streaks across the #MeToo Radar Screen because of an alleged sexual misdeed. The accusation is made through a journalistic exposé, a revelation on social media, or some fusion of both. Roth, for his part, was eighty-four years old in 2017, when #MeToo's "viral roar" was first heard.[24] He announced his retirement from writing in 2012.[25] He thus lived most of his life well before the digital era's facility for effectively drawing attention to male misbehavior.

In the decades prior, when print media ruled, little was known about his private life. Occasionally former lovers published accounts about him. In a few of these portrayals, as we shall see, the author comes off as likable, though colossally self-absorbed.[26] There were, however, some unflattering reports, most notably his ex-wife Claire Bloom's *Leaving a Doll's House* (1996).[27] There, Roth is depicted as manipulative, emotionally abusive, and occasionally mentally unwell. But neither in Bloom's memoir nor anywhere else was he publicly accused of the types of crimes that have been discussed in the #MeToo reckoning.[28]

Which is to say that to the best of our knowledge, he did not rape numerous women as Harvey Weinstein was convicted of doing.[29] He did not allegedly drug and rape multiple victims, a crime that a jury convicted Bill Cosby of committing against Andrea Constand in 2018.[30] He did not have unlawful sexual intercourse with a minor, a felony to which Roman Polanski pled guilty in 1977.[31] He did not molest his seven year-old stepdaughter, a charge leveled against Woody Allen.[32] He did not physically or sexually assault women, as the authors Junot Díaz and David Foster Wallace are alleged to have done.[33] He did not masturbate in front of female colleagues without their consent, an indecency which the comedian Louis C.K. admitted was true.[34]

To the best of our knowledge, Philip Roth did none of the things that justifiably raise the concerns of #MeToo. He wrote, however, a lot of fiction about men who *did* do things like that. In another one of those #MeToo-themed engagements with his work, the *New York Times* asked him about the present moment in which "so many women [are] coming forth and accusing so many highly visible men of sexual harassment and abuse."[35] Roth riposted that he spent his career writing about the "lunacy" that overtakes men "hungry in the grip of carnal fervor."[36] He was, therefore, not surprised by any of this.[37] "None of the more extreme conduct I have been reading about in the newspapers lately," he summed up dryly, "has astonished me."[38]

Roth was not astonished by what the #MeToo moment illuminated. That's because men behaving shabbily toward women was part of his subject matter. Nathan Zuckerman in *My Life as a Man* is attracted to his twelve-year-old stepdaughter. A few years later, after her mother's suicide, he runs away to Italy with his now-teenage lover.[39] In the same book, the novelist and troubled genius Peter Tarnopol assaults his former wife so viciously that she nearly dies. Violence against women is also intimated in *Sabbath's Theater*. Mickey Sabbath looks a young woman in the eye and declares, "I have never said anything more seriously to anyone: I killed a wife."[40] Rape is attempted— and played for laughs—in the infamous finale of *Portnoy's Complaint* ("I had the edge, and forced her body down beneath me—and shot my tongue into her ear. . . . 'Oh I am going to fuck you, Jew girl,' I whispered evilly").[41]

In Roth's fiction, many male protagonists behave monstrously. Let us recall, however, that #MeToo scandals occur in the *nonfictional* world. Insofar as no allegation of impropriety has surfaced, why is Roth's name such a fixture in these discussions? In order to answer that question, we need to understand how intellectuals influenced by #MeToo reflect on the arts.

## Bringing the Artist Back In

The essayists, journalists, and scholars who examine the intersection between #MeToo and the arts are a diverse cohort. They could not easily be described as a school of thought. Nor does the charge that they espouse a "victimology paradigm" and emit an "inquisitorial whiff" seem warranted to me.[42]

I do notice some key methods and assumptions that most, but not all, of these writers share when assessing novelists, filmmakers, comedians, musicians, and others accused of sexual impropriety. To begin with, they spend a great deal of time discussing the accused artist, who is usually, but not always, a heterosexual male (I will assume a heterosexual male perpetrator throughout this analysis).[43] This focus on the accused may seem like an obvious move. In the study of aesthetics, however, it actually upends scholarly conventions.

By concentrating on the artist and his deeds, the #MeToo critics are revolting against what used to be a tacit Golden Rule of cultural analysis. The unspoken edict prohibited us from studying anything but the art itself. In the words of the *New York Times'* A. O. Scott, the only thing that "mattered was the work."[44] Scott argues that this "separation of art and artist" was a "cultural habit" rather than "a philosophical principle."[45] He underestimates, though, *how* philosophical this premise was for professors in the humanities.[46]

Scholars of literature are rarely trained as biographers, or interested in writing biographies. Sure, we can tell you when an author we research was born, died, etc. We might know that our author once studied glassblowing in Zurich. But this pales in comparison to what we know about his or her body of work. Many of us are theorists deploying very sophisticated—and to outsiders, utterly incomprehensible—tools of textual analysis. These approaches have names like "New Criticism" and "reader-response theory," or fly under a postmodern banner that reads "Death of the Author."[47] Contrary to Scott's claim, these theories provide us with highly philosophical reasons for concentrating on the fiction, and the fiction alone.

#MeToo interventions expose how ill-equipped most humanists are to ponder the *interplay* between an artist and that which he creates. We're not biographers; our training itself shunts our attention away from any sort of inquiry into the artist himself. This blinds us to understanding how sexual misbehavior is connected to creativity. It's the type of investigation we pass off to an ethicist, a neuroscientist, or a district attorney. This is "business as usual" for a literature professor—and there's nothing intentionally sinister about it. The problem is that it gives immoral artists a free pass.

#MeToo theorists identify another reason why we tend to ignore the misdeeds of an artist—and it has little to do with obscure academic literary theory. Some argue that the problem stems from a misplaced cultural worship of male "genius." We delink the art from the artist because we love to link sublime art with transgression. Stefania Marghitu uses the term "*auteur* apologism" to describe "the separation of the art from the artist, underpinned by the claim that a problematic identity is a prerequisite for creative genius."[48] The latter, as Rachel Cusk observes, "does everything we are told not to do: He is violent and selfish. He neglects or betrays his friends and family. He smokes, drinks, scandalizes, indulges his lusts . . . all to be unmasked at the end as a peerless genius."[49]

In a bravura meditation on David Foster Wallace (accused of physically and psychologically abusing his girlfriend), Megan Garber ruminates on how much we overlook antisocial and even criminal behaviors in the name of spectacular talent: "Genius cannot be reasoned with. Genius is the answer and the question. It will be heard. It will be respected. Even when it kicks and stalks and climbs up the side of the house at night."[50] Garber provocatively refers to genius as "its own kind of infrastructure," implying that the category is built to aid and abet male misbehavior.[51] By questioning the *category* of "genius," these thinkers have launched a preemptive strike against an age-old excuse for the misconduct of creative folk.

## The Art Cannot Stand Alone

A feature of #MeToo-tinged analysis of the arts that we just observed might be called "bringing the artist back in." Once he is reinserted into the analytical frame, these theorists ponder the *relation*, or lack thereof, between his immoral acts and what he creates. Sometimes a "genius's" creation obscures his immoral deeds. Bill Cosby's crimes never did square with the domestic saint he portrayed in *The Cosby Show*. As Sarah Stewart-Kroeker remarks, this disconnect is what made his case so unsettling: "Bill Cosby . . . perturbs less because of a continuity between his personal life and his character than because of its discontinuity: the rapist who plays the loveable family man."[52]

In other cases, by contrast, the transgressions of male geniuses surface in their texts. Once Louis C.K.'s bouts of unsolicited self-exposure became known, observers noticed similar acts depicted in his (recalled) movie *I Love You, Daddy*.[53] Once allegations of Woody Allen's pedophilia were aired, critics reevaluated his film *Manhattan*, where an underage woman is the hero's love interest.[54] The singer R. Kelly apparently had his girlfriend, Kitti Jones, reenact onstage a scene of sexual bondage, a "cage girl" ritual he subjected her to in their home.[55] These examples, as one legal scholar put it, show how art "embodies and perpetuates the artist's harmful conduct."[56]

It emerges from all this that, in the #MeToo moment, the art *cannot* stand alone. If a writer's biography includes acts of sexual misconduct, then the critic must make that information a part of his or her interpretation of the creative product. But how big a part? Here there is considerable diversity of opinion. It might be concluded from all the sound and fury surrounding #MeToo that its mantra is *Immorality Trumps Aesthetics, Every Time!* In other words, if Twitter alleges that a male acted inappropriately toward a woman, then his work will be "canceled." For a few critics, and social media trolls, yes, this reductive and simple formula obtains. But some of the most insightful reflection stimulated by #MeToo does not necessarily subordinate art to morality.

The position is more nuanced. It's not that *Immorality Trumps Aesthetics*, but that immoral conduct and aesthetics must be intertwined by us, the conscientious audience. This means that once we learn incriminating information about an artist, our understanding of his *art* changes radically. "We can't watch or listen to or read the great work without remembering the awful thing," writes Claire Dederer.[57] Although Dederer is outraged about the behavior of what she calls "monstrous men," she shows no desire to censor them.[58]

True, Dederer might have elsewhere called Roman Polanski (who "statutory raped" a thirteen-year-old girl) a "fucking moron."[59] Yet Dederer never challenges his work's right to exist. Instead, she reflects on what his cinema *now* says and means to her as the mother of a teenage girl.[60] Dederer signals that *our* evaluation of Polanski's art can never be totally separated from his ethical failings. His misdeeds and his films have become enmeshed; one is a prism for the other. Amanda Hess makes a similar point and also eschews any gesture toward censorship. She urges us to linger on the "connections between art and abuse."[61] By repressing the old impulse to separate one from the other we would "see the works more clearly . . . understand them in all of their complexity, and . . . connect them to our real lives and experiences—even if those experiences are negative."[62]

So, it's not that I won't ever again listen to Michael Jackson's "Wanna Be Startin' Somethin.'" It's just that every time I hear it, the allegations of pedophilia leveled against him in the documentary *Leaving Neverland* infiltrate my thoughts, as do rumors about the abuse he himself suffered as a child.[63] It's all entwined forevermore. Precisely as Hess suggests, the entire experience of listening to Jackson's music becomes different, more tensile.

We honor art we love in fairly primal ways. We clap. We stand. We roar. We whistle. We imitate. We purchase more of the art. We rave to our friends. Perfectly fine, all of that. But #MeToo encourages more freighted reflections on what art is, who artists are, and how we ourselves engage with both. I don't think Philip Roth would want us to do otherwise. And with that in mind we are ready to examine those "conceptual synergies" mentioned earlier.

## Art Is Slimy

With this basic sketch rendered of how the #MeToo reckoning has reflected upon the arts, we can return to a question we asked above: why does Philip Roth's name keep popping up in these discussions, even though there has yet to be an allegation of sexual misconduct made against him?

One reason was floated by Roth himself earlier, namely that toxic males are a staple of his prose diet. To borrow a line from Roxane Gay, this author "practically revels in the unlikability of his men."[64] Roth serves up "crazy cuntstruck" fellows who are, in one critic's estimation, "unapologetic mixes of brainy sophisticate and borderline sexual predator."[65] Perhaps #MeToo analysts keep returning to his work for the unmediated access to masculine grotesquerie that it provides.

This is certainly one reason, but permit me to advance a less obvious suggestion. As I see it, Philip Roth and the #MeToo theorists we just encountered share a lot of core beliefs about art. Does it mean Philip Roth is a "Pro-#MeToo Writer"? Well, not really. A far better candidate would be Chimamanda Ngozi Adichie, to whom I'll return in a moment and whose talent is far too capacious to wedge into such a reductive category. For now, let's look into those conceptual synergies between Roth and #MeToo.

We've discussed how #MeToo theorists dismantle the Wall of Separation between the life of the artist and the art he creates. They reason that a creative product should not be disarticulated from the immoral actions of the person who brought it into being. Herein lies a striking parallel with Roth.

In his *fiction,* Philip Roth does, at first, build a Wall of Separation between art and artist. And then he blasts through it, Wile E. Coyote–style—plunger detonator, flaming wire, dynamite sticks, all that. Many of his novels depict artists who, although they initially believe otherwise, gradually come to learn that their art can *never* be disarticulated from their existence. There is, they learn, no wall. His art often scrutinizes the *delusion* that artists maintain about their art's originality and sovereignty from their own lives. We'll see many examples of this, but for now let us focus on just one.

Early on in *The Anatomy Lesson* the writer Nathan Zuckerman avers: "Life and art are distinct. . . . [W]hat could be clearer?"[66] But the joke's on Zuckerman. By story's end, he is in excruciating physical pain. During his hospital convalescence, he prays that none of the afflictions he has just endured will end up being the subject of one of his novels. He pleads to himself: "Just don't make me write about it after. Not everything has to be a book."[67] A few sentences later he concedes: "everything *can* be a book. And doesn't count as life until it is."[68] The *delusion* was that this mythical wall would prevent him from writing about his own experiences.

*The Anatomy Lesson,* a book published in 1983, *is* the book that emerged from all that pain Nathan Zuckerman underwent. If that sounds a bit dizzying—for who wrote this book, Philip Roth or Nathan Zuckerman?—then please recall that Roth is a master of what is known as "metafiction." That literary genre often features a fiction writer in the process of writing the very fiction we are reading.[69] Talk about bringing the author back in! Metafictional works like *My Life as a Man, The Ghost Writer, The Counterlife,* among others, demonstrate that an author *always* writes from experience. Roth was intent on arguing that life bleeds into art (and denying, as we shall see, that *his* life bled into *his* art).

In another parallel to #MeToo interventions, the creative men he depicted in his storyworlds were "geniuses." Sometimes they were young geniuses who had hit a rut (e.g., Peter Tarnopol and Nathan Zuckerman in *My Life as a Man;* Nathan Zuckerman in *The Ghost Writer*). Sometimes they were middle-aged celebrity geniuses grappling with fame (e.g., Nathan Zuckerman in *Zuckerman Unbound*). Sometimes they were graying, washed-up geniuses whose "magic" was "lost" (Simon Axler in *The Humbling;* Mickey Sabbath in *Sabbath's Theater;* Nathan Zuckerman in *Exit Ghost*).[70] Naturally, they all had very messy, often abusive, romantic relationships with much younger women.

These geniuses thrived on the mistreatment of women and others. Roth mined this insight in novel after novel. "What set of aesthetic values makes you think," sniffs Judge Leopold Wapter in *The Ghost Writer,* that "the slimy is more truthful than the sublime."[71] The angered judge is reprimanding young Nathan Zuckerman for selling out his people. At age twenty-three, the young genius had the audacity to draft a short story based on a nasty family dispute.[72] Nathan's elders howl that if published, it will reflect badly not only on the Zuckermans, but on the Jews. "Kikes," his irate father intones, "Kikes and their love of money. That is all our good Christian friends will see."[73] The ordeal plunges young Nathan into a psychic swoon. So much so that he proceeds to draft *another* unspeakable story-within-the-story. This one is about the Holocaust martyr Anne Frank, who is romantically active and brooding in the Berkshires in 1956.[74] Nathan has just met a young woman who reminds him of her.

In *The Ghost Writer,* for the umpteenth time, Roth correlates a writer's creativity with a particular type of willingness to transform personal experience into art. This willingness inflicts pain on others, be they women, one's family, one's coreligionists, and so forth. Yes, Judge Wapter, art is slimy. That's because the artist's process is slimy, not sublime. If this is so, then we must rethink some platitudes. Maybe art doesn't emanate from a noble region of the soul. Maybe its provenance is vile. Maybe it's born of the suffering one inflicts on others, alongside one's own.

We are now positioned to understand those synergies between Roth's oeuvre and #MeToo to which I alluded earlier. Both reduce the Wall of

Separation to rubble. Both affirm that there is robust transit between art and life. Both have a rather jaundiced view of "genius." Both encourage readers to dwell on the complexity of the artistic process. Both linger on sexual transgressions. Both reflect on how the sins and excesses of the male "genius" slither their way into the male genius's creation.

But there are crucial differences as well. A glance at Chimamanda Ngozi's Adichie's short story "Jumping Monkey Hill" brings them into sharp relief. First published in *Granta* in 2006, the tale suggests to me that Adichie had read her Roth.[75] Its heroine is an aspiring Nigerian writer named Ujunwa Ogundu who is invited to a two-week African writers' workshop at a resort near Cape Town. Immediately upon her arrival the inchoate genius is leered at by the conference convener.[76] Edward is his name, and this gate-keeper is rumored to have connections to all of the leading literary agents in London.[77] When Edward is not eyeing and micro-aggressing the female participants, he lectures the assorted scribes about what "real" African literature is all about.[78]

All workshop participants are required to write a story while in residence. In a Rothian flourish, "Jumping Monkey Hill" includes drafts from the piece that Ujunwa is composing during the days she is avoiding Edward's stares. Ujunwa decides to give her protagonist a "common" name, Chioma (Ujunwa toys with giving her an "exotic" name, Ibari, but decides against it).[79] The story within the story recounts how Chioma has her breasts groped at an interview for a bank position.[80] Thereafter, she takes another job on a trial basis. Her trial, so to speak, involves visiting the home of a wealthy business-man with a female colleague, named Yinka. The businessman asks Yinka to sit on his lap, which she promptly does. After enduring rounds of cringe-y come-ons, Chioma has had enough. She walks out of an unjust and absurd situation—as so many Adichie heroines do—effectively forsaking income she desperately needs.[81]

Ujunwa reads this demoralizing fiction about Chioma's #MeToo's encounter aloud to the workshop participants. Edward weighs in deri-sively: "It's never quite like that in real life, is it? Women are never victims in that sort of crude way, and certainly not in Nigeria. Nigeria has women in high positions. The most powerful cabinet minister today is a woman."[82] The gatekeeper insists that this is not a common story: "The whole thing is implausible. . . . This is agenda writing, it isn't a real story of real people."[83] To which an anguished Ujunwa stands up, laughs (even as she is tearing up inside), and reveals that the entire "fiction" had actually happened to her, save one minor detail.[84] As she walks away, shaken, "she wondered whether this ending, in a story, would be considered plausible."[85]

Adichie's wicked little tale assembles many of the themes and techniques we have been tracking in Roth's work: art/life loops, male sexual misbehavior, emerging genius writer, story within the story, use of metafictional devices. But in terms of moral tone, there is a sharp difference. Adichie's work is sensitive to sexual harassment and sexual assault in a way that Roth's is not.[86]

Roth shows us how *men* convert their mistreatment of women, of family, of community, into art. Adichie reverses field: she shows us how women who are mistreated by *men* convert their experience of trauma into art. Roth may be a theoretical forerunner of #MeToo. But he does not share its ethical investments.

## The Question of Auto/Biography

Chimamanda Adichie would later reveal that "Jumping Monkey Hill" was based on an actual incident from her life.[87] A most un-Rothian admission that was! Save one or two exceptions, Roth vehemently denied that he wrote autobiographically.

His denials are pervasive. His denials are unpersuasive. His denials create real difficulties for Roth scholars. I'll have much more to say about this in chapter 3, but to orient the reader to my own view on the matter, I submit the following: his denials are absurd. Philip Roth relentlessly grafted Philip Roth into his own storyworlds. He didn't write *a little* autobiographically. He wrote *a lot* autobiographically. He stuffed his novels with nakedly personal details, turning his life into his stories. He gleefully made it difficult for his readers to figure out where his fiction ended and where he began. And yet: when confronted about this, he would position himself behind that Wall of Separation separating art from artist—the very Wall his fiction demonstrated was just a hedge.

He maintained this position even though he wrote five novels and one short story about a fictional character named Philip Roth.[88] This style is known as "autofiction"—a postmodern cousin of metafiction.[89] In her study of the genre, Marjorie Worthington offers a basic definition of autofiction as a form in which "the author appears as a fictionalized character." Autofiction need not be autobiography; it is *fiction*. But in Roth's autofiction, a staggering amount of source material is based on his own life. Roth's autofiction, and his metafiction, dwell on the subject of art/life loops. Acquaintances of Roth found themselves roped into these loops—and were none too happy. We'll deal with his romantic partners—and the associated #MeToo dilemmas— later. At present, I draw your attention to the complaint of the novelist Alan Lelchuk, a onetime friend of Roth's, after having read *The Professor of Desire* (1977): "Correct me if I am wrong, but didn't we make an agreement or pact, some seven or eight years ago in a Yaddo study, that we would not write about each other's lives in fiction? . . . I have been extremely upset at reading the half-portrait of myself in TPOD. Real characteristics of myself I prefer to use myself. And as to the unpleasant invented ones, why didn't you attach them to a completely invented figure, instead of one clearly recognized as yours truly?"[90]

Lelchuk, to his great dismay, has noticed resemblances between himself and the story's predatory lush, Ralph Baumgarten. This poet convinced Wendy, a seventeen-year-old "high school girl shopping for a paperback for her English class," to disrobe in front of him and David Kepesh.[91] Does Philip not, asks Lelchuk incredulously, comprehend how portrayals of this sort will endanger his career?[92]

Roth ripostes with nuclear-powered gaslight. "You know better than most," he sighs, "how angered and bored I was when people assumed that PORTNOY was a self-portrait." "But the fact remains," he continues, "that Portnoy is not me . . . and Baumgarten is hardly you, and anyone reasonably intelligent who knows me and anyone who knows you, understands that easily enough."[93]

In light of the #MeToo issues we've discussed, Roth's autobiographical bent raises a delicate question: what is the relation between all that male rage-y prose and all those scenes of predation on the one side, and Roth's personal experiences with women on the other? To procure an answer to this question, as well as other biographical queries, would require the services of a professional biographer. Here, things get dicey. As Alan Lelchuk phrased it in his payback novel about Roth (whom he calls Ziff): "SOMEONE HAS POINTED OUT THERE'S BEEN NO BIOGRAPHY OF ARTHUR ZIFF."[94]

Put bluntly, there's a lot about Roth's life we don't know and many reasons we don't know it. Our lack of a biography is astonishing given that he has been in the public eye since 1959, when *Goodbye, Columbus, and Five Short Stories* won the National Book Award.[95] By 1969, with *Portnoy's Complaint* scandalizing all and sundry, Roth was a "literary celebrity."[96] Yet only now, in 2021, are biographies on the horizon.

We do possess a *literary* biography, Claudia Roth Pierpoint's 2013 *Roth Unbound: A Writer and His Books.* The author, a friend (not a relative) of Roth's, conversed with her subject about his art/life loops. Only a few revelations about gender-related matters arise—but they are not untantalizing (see chapter 3). She confirms what was previously suggested by scholars, namely that Roth based many female characters on his former wives and lovers. That material begs #MeToo-ish introspection. *Roth Unbound* either sidesteps these issues or can't overcome its subject's skilled stonewalling.

In her introduction, Claudia Roth Pierpoint mentions her eight years of "easy camaraderie" with Roth.[97] "Camaraderie" is another reason why accurate biographical information is hard to come by. The author shared his deepest reflections on his life almost exclusively with confidantes. The many Friends of Philip who were granted access to him were very intelligent and talented people. Still, they were *friends*. When it came to his own public image, Roth never really embraced the idea of "critical distance."[98]

Nor did the Arts and Culture Establishment. Consider this remark from David Remnick, editor of the *New Yorker*, to his *camarade* Roth: "Just know these pages are as open as can be to you. I suspect an editor of the New Yorker . . . is not supposed to have a favorite living writer. Indecent, indiscreet, unfair, vulgar. Too bad."[99] Remnick's invitation made me think about #MeToo's skepticism about "genius." In 1998, when he handed Roth the keys to the kingdom, weren't there other writers, some of whom were not men, who equally deserved this cherished platform?

But let's get back to the absence of a biography. "I work now for Blake Bailey. The pay's not so good," Roth joked in 2012.[100] He was referring to the *second* individual he had appointed to chronicle his life. Bailey, a professional biographer, consulted with his subject while he was alive and "became very fond of him."[101] Roth revealed that he "had never been as truthful with anyone before."[102] A piece about Bailey in—where else?—the *New Yorker*, describes him as possessing "as good a temperament as any for telling Roth's story."[103] To his credit, Bailey recognizes that Roth had an agenda and was using him to write "his biography by proxy."[104]

Then again, Bailey's handpickedness raises some obvious concerns.[105] In a 2012 interview Roth mentioned he selected Bailey to make sure that, of the many biographies that will appear after he dies, "one of them's correct."[106] Roth continues: "Once Blake Bailey has got what he needs, I've asked my executors—my agent, Andrew Wylie, and a friend who's a psychoanalyst—to destroy them after my death. I don't want my personal papers dragged all over the place. No one has to read them. All my manuscripts are already in the Library of Congress and have been there since the seventies."[107]

The statement is remarkable. Is Philip Roth—*of all people!*—saying there is a correct version of his life? (see chapters 5, 6, and 7 for the absurdity of this proposition). Does he forget that maybe 90 percent of the personal correspondences in the Library of Congress are letters written *to* Philip Roth, not *from* Philip Roth? Is scholarship, or humanistic inquiry, or even professional biography possible if one person, and one person only, gets to view and then comment on the significance of an archive before it is set aflame?[108]

Let's recall that Roth was not averse to dumping official biographers. Before there was Blake Bailey, there was Ross Miller. In 2004 it was announced that Professor Miller of the University of Connecticut and, naturally, a close friend of Roth's, would be entrusted with the access necessary to write the biography.[109] Five years later, Roth abruptly relieved him of his duties.[110] To make sense of this bizarre spat would take a separate chapter (readers can consult the reportage of the late, great Roth scholar Derek Parker Royal).[111] In a recently released memoir by another of Roth's confidantes (Benjamin Taylor's *Here We Are: My Friendship with Philip Roth*), Miller gets roughed up again.[112] Neither Roth, nor his circle, ever really embraced the concept of critical distance. But critical distance is what the study of Philip Roth needs.

## Obsessional Themes

The present book is not a biography. Rather, it is inspired by #MeToo analysts who prompt us to think more carefully about the interplay between an artist's life and his or her art. One significant cultural shift precipitated by #MeToo is that it has licensed and mainstreamed this once controversial move.

The present book is a *reverse* biography. Scouring the master's fiction, I will look for what Philip Roth called a writer's "obsessional theme[s]."[113] Once I draw these out, then biographers can explain *why* Roth was obsessed by them. As for "obsessional themes," Roth conceded that writers can't recognize them.[114] They are based on an "enduring grievance" that the novelist cannot fully grasp.[115] To my mind, this is Philip Roth's begrudging way of sanctifying the role of the critic. He might have granted access to his thoughts solely to his closest friends. He might have mocked English professors ("shut down all the literature departments").[116] He might have acted as if he was the best interpreter of his fiction (he once interviewed himself about *The Great American Novel*).[117] But some ombudsman in his soul grasped that there are certain self-truths that are not evident to an author.

In this book, I'll go trawling for Roth's obsessional themes. Many of his preoccupations center around sex, gender, race, and the privileges of white males. These will be discussed in chapters 1–4 and will mesh with the discussions of #MeToo above. Some of his preoccupations, by contrast, have little to do with those issues (see chapters 5–7). Roth was infatuated with the "self." He spent a lifetime chronicling how wobbly, labile, and unstable our personalities are. He also made radical suggestions about literature's supremacy, its unique capacity to illuminate truth. This author, then, had sexed and unsexed obsessions. Identifying the latter may provide one way of selling him to the current generation, where he is often seen as just another White Guy who prose-ogled women's bodies.

In order to discover these thematic through-lines, my approach will be a little different from that of the vast and formidable community of Roth scholars. Each question I pose will be answered by recourse to *every* piece of fiction he published. My data set consists of his fifty-three fictional products: twenty-eight novels and twenty-five short stories. This body of work comprises nearly 8,500 printed pages accumulated across nearly sixty years.[118] I will dwell on his lesser-known works, some of which are so obscure (e.g., the 1960 short story "The Good Girl") that even specialists are unaware of them. The examination of these fifty-three texts will be cross-pollinated with correspondences from the manuscript drafts and letters to Roth in the Library of Congress and reams of Roth scholarship (cited in my endnotes). Last, I will sprinkle my inquiry with insights gathered across a quarter century of teaching fiction.

This "longitudinal" analysis (1952–2010) will rummage through six decades of literature. Intriguing patterns will emerge. I will chart some of these in the detailed tables that comprise the appendix of this volume. This unusual step is necessary to counteract a certain "impressionism" that prevails in some discussions of his work. For example, everyone "knows" that Franz Kafka and Henry James were Roth's chief literary influences.[119] But when I and two colleagues conducted a soon-to-be-published analysis of every author Roth ever cited, a different writer came up, as did lots of other intriguing facts.[120]

I write this book as neither friend, nor foe, nor fan of Roth, but as a scholarly critic alive during the #MeToo moment. What will emerge in this study is an artist rife with contradictions. What will emerge are the often unnoticed, racial, sexual, and philosophical hang-ups of a great American writer. What will emerge is a novelist who transits between fiction and his own lived reality with such abandon that it is sometimes hard to figure out what dimension this man believed he actually inhabited. Ideally, what will emerge is a Philip Roth we did not know well, or knew incorrectly, or knew not at all.

# PART I

# Race, Gender, Sex, and Autobiography in Roth's Writing

# Roth and Race

Well, ain' dat somethin'. De Jew, he wanna buy de bess playuh we done got!
And how much you wanna pay, Jew?
     —PHILIP ROTH, *The Great American Novel*

In the U.S. census I am, *for good or bad, counted as Caucasian.*
     —PHILIP ROTH, *The Counterlife*

The main rot in the minds of "academic" liberals like yourself, is that you take your
own distortion of the world to be somehow more profound than the cracker's.
     —LEROI JONES, "Reply to Philip Roth"

Fans and scholars alike tend to believe that Philip Roth wrote sporadically and sympathetically, though perhaps not entirely unprob-
lematically, about Black people.[1] The assumption is based on two
well-known works. The first is the 1959 novella "Goodbye, Columbus." Its
Jewish protagonist, Neil Klugman, behaves protectively toward an African
American kid who marvels at postimpressionist paintings in the Newark
Public Library.[2] Neil shows a lot of concern for "the small colored boy"; he
even dreams about him.[3]

Then there's *The Human Stain* (2000), whose plot revolves around a Black,
non-Jewish scholar who passes as a white Jew. While not without its critics,
this novel won the PEN/Faulkner Award. Like "Goodbye, Columbus," it is
often lauded for its thoughtful engagement with America's racial dilemmas.[4]

On the basis of those two texts, one might surmise that Roth was yet
another Jewish liberal, doing his small part to extend the hand of friendship

to another oppressed minority. If so, the author would be following in the footsteps of many twentieth-century Jewish intellectuals, artists, and activists who made common cause with African Americans.[5] This partnership between Blacks and Jews, often called the "Grand Alliance" or "Grand Coalition," "is the stuff of legend, as it were."[6] In recent years scholars have questioned how stable and robust this partnership actually was.[7] In any case, the idea that Roth depicted African Americans sporadically, thoughtfully, and sympathetically is widespread. I will refer to this way of thinking as the "Alliance Paradigm."

Yet a study of Roth's *entire* fictional corpus reveals a much more complicated state of affairs. For starters, Roth did not write sporadically, but *consistently*, about African Americans. To help the reader grasp how consistently Roth engaged this subject in his fiction, I have tried to take stock of every available proof text.[8] A glance at table 1, in the appendix, demonstrates that references to Black people or Black issues are present in twenty-six of his twenty-eight book-length works of fiction. No fewer than ten of his short stories touch upon the theme as well.[9]

If a researcher were to scrutinize all of these texts, it would become evident that Roth's representation of African American characters can be neither sympathetic nor thoughtful. From "The Box of Truths" (1952), until his finale, *Nemesis* (2010), we encounter: (1) a steady flow of minor characters who are Black, (2) disparaging comments about the Blacks of Newark, (3) racist banter uttered by white gentiles, (4) racist banter uttered by white Jews, (5) caricatures of Black English, (6) asides on the physiognomy of Black bodies, especially those of women, and, (7) occasional references to prominent African Americans.

What we are about to see is surprising. Roth's sketches of African American (and African) characters are not infrequently racist. This reeks of a double standard; he railed against anti-Semitism *in the very same stories in which he indulged in racist depictions*. What is also surprising is that the patterns, and even some texts to which I'll draw your attention, remain almost completely unremarked upon. This component of his writing has seldom been flagged by Roth scholars and critics.

These considerations will prompt me to suggest that we abandon the Alliance Paradigm. Roth's African American portraiture, I will argue, makes better sense when contextualized within the complex, shifting relationship between Blacks and Jews in the United States. Roth's fiction often reflected the antagonisms between these two supposed "allies," albeit in a one-sided manner. What emerged were numerous representations of Blacks that are thoughtless and occasionally quite disturbing.

## Fellas

As just noted, Roth's representation of an African American boy in "Goodbye, Columbus" has generally been interpreted as well-meaning.[10] He depicts a youth who has the precocity to hang around a library all day, peruse Gauguin's paintings, *and* drop F-bombs.[11] That's one likable kid!

In the same narrative, our Jewish protagonist, Neil Klugman, is often symbolically twinned with the boy.[12] The scholar Elèna Mortara has pointed out that when "Goodbye, Columbus" first appeared in the *New Yorker* in 1959, the accompanying illustration was of an African American child.[13] As far as liberalism back then went (or could go), this was the type of story that challenged American racism.[14]

Roth may have issued the same noble challenge in "Defender of the Faith" (1959).[15] The story is narrated by Nathan Marx, a Jewish drill sergeant. He is frustrated by a trainee of dubious sincerity who plays the Jewish Card in order to gain religious accommodations. When Marx confers with a certain Captain Barrett about the matter, his white gentile superior expounds as follows: "Marx, I'd fight side by side with a nigger if the fella proved to me he was a man."[16] A few sentences later Captain Barrett asks, "You're a Jewish fella, am I right, Marx?"[17] Two "fellas"—one Black and one Jewish. These fellas are coupled in Captain Barrett's thoughts, likely because our author wants to spotlight a broader linkage in the white Christian mind-set.

The same linkage is seen in *Letting Go.* A working-class white woman by the name of Theresa Haug recounts a story about a boy who is hit by a car and taken to "the Jewish hospital."[18] "They made a Jew out of him," she observes, implying that he was forcibly circumcised.[19] After giggling she adds, "He was a nigger, so must be."[20] Later in the work, the woman with the un-kosher surname chuckles again as she wonders "what it was like to do it with a Jew."[21] While contemplating that erotic possibility, "she remembered the story of the little nigger boy they had taken to the hospital back home."[22]

That white Christians are wont to connect these two minority groups is a grim American truth Roth is eager to expose.[23] In *I Married a Communist,* we learn that when Ira Ringold was in the armed forces, "someone in the mess hall called him a Jew bastard. A nigger-loving Jew bastard."[24] Ira reveals that the culprit was "a southern hillbilly with a big mouth."[25]

White gentiles in Roth's works don't always speak about Blacks *and* Jews; sometimes they reflect solely on Blacks. In *When She Was Good* (1967), two families, the Bassarts and Sowerbys, are discussing the pros and cons of living in Chicago. Lloyd Bassart exclaims, "They've got a big colored problem down there, and I don't envy them."[26] To which his nephew Roy responds: "It isn't Negroes, Uncle Lloyd. You people think everything is Negroes—and how many Negroes do you actually know? Really know, to talk to? . . . I knew one who I used to talk to a lot. . . . He was a darn smart guy too. I had a lot of respect for him."[27] Roy's cousin Ellie Sowerby chimes in: "I know a girl who dates a Negro. . . . She's probably a red."[28] The assembled white folks then debate the possibility of befriending Blacks (some in favor), and dating Blacks (less enthusiasm for that).[29]

Which brings us to *The Great American Novel*.[30] The entire tale is recounted by Word Smith, an octogenarian baseball writer who traffics in odious stereotypes.[31] He introduces us to a train conductor named George who, while "scratchin' his woolly head," comments, "Well, suh, day don' say nuttin' 'bout dat in de schedule."[32] A few pages later Ernest Hemingway enters the storyworld and describes Melville's *Moby Dick* as follows: "Five hundred pages of blubber, one hundred pages of madman, and about twenty pages on how good niggers are with the harpoon."[33]

Elsewhere, Smith (and Roth) return to literary minstrelsy. We are told that Aunt Jemima, of flapjacks fame, is a cunning businesswoman who owns an entire Negro baseball league.[34] One might expect that an accomplished entrepreneur like her wouldn't speak like this: "howdydo, Reverend! Ain't we honored, though!"[35] In Smith's other reminiscences, racial slurs drop freely from the mouths of white baseball players who speak of "coons" and "spades."[36]

About three hundred leaden pages into *The Great American Novel,* Smith recounts a tale featuring the long-serving manager of a feckless baseball team known as the Ruppert Mundys. Ulysses S. Fairsmith is a fervent Christian, scarred by the memory of having tried to bring the gospel to Africa twenty years prior.[37] Clad in his "khaki short pants, half-sleeved shirt, and pith helmet," he dreamed of Christianizing the indigenes by introducing them to the delights of baseball.[38] Roth goes all in here, devoting some sixteen pages to recounting a religious mission gone terribly wrong.[39] The section is deeply offensive, often to the point of unreadability. The account includes references to "the primitive interior of Africa," "savage women," and "black devils."[40]

Upset about a rule preventing them from sliding into first base, the mercurial tribesmen revolt against Fairsmith. The missionary and his nephew are readied to be slaughtered and eaten by the men whom they tutored in America's pastime.[41] During the ensuing cannibalistic ceremony, Roth describes the ritualistic "deflowering" of virgins with baseball bats.[42]

One would have to deploy considerable ingenuity to read these asides as anything other than gratuitous racist jokes.[43] What rankles about these descriptions is the obvious delight the author seems to have taken in creating them. As he told Joyce Carol Oates about the vibe he adapted while working on *The Great American Novel*: "I tried to put my faith in the fun I was having. *Writing as pleasure*."[44]

A final example of how Roth's white gentiles talk about Blacks can be found in the autofictional novel *Deception*. The work is comprised of chapter-length "fragments of conversation" between "Philip" and others.[45] One exchange is with a Czech writer named Ivan. He is convinced that his wife, Olina, is having an affair with Andrew, a Black neighbor. There is almost no racial stereotype that Ivan doesn't deploy: "It's that nigger that does it. I don't say 'black person' I say 'nigger.' . . . [H]e gives her an orgasm on his black prick. . . . He's a typical pimp type. . . . Doesn't know how to spell, writes like a child. This half-illiterate black guy. . . . Black guy doesn't work. Lives off her unemployment benefits. . . . I couldn't kiss ever again that mouth that sucked that long black prick."[46]

Unhinged Ivan soon casts aspersions on "Philip's" talent as a writer and accuses him of also having slept with his wife.[47] "Philip" responds to Ivan by (1) denying that he is having an affair with Olina, and (2) taking offense at Ivan's criticism of his writing ("So, my books stink too").[48] "Philip" does not raise any concerns about Ivan's racist diatribe. A few pages later, "Philip" rants about an anti-Semitic incident he endured in London.[49]

## Cracks/Malignancies

We just encountered a slew of white Christians who served up some choice racial invective. Our interest now shifts to how Roth's Jewish characters engage with Blacks.

Ira Ringold in *I Married a Communist* is nothing like any of the white gentiles we just encountered, nor like any of the Jews we shall meet below. His Communist convictions motivate him to actually seek out working-class Black people. Young Nathan Zuckerman accompanies Ira to Newark's Black Third Ward and observes, "I'd never before imagined, let alone seen, a white person being so easygoing and at home with Negroes."[50] I have a question, though: if Nathan Zuckerman is recounting this story a little before the year 2000, why does he continually refer to Blacks as "Negroes?"[51]

In any case, Ira engages in street-corner political banter with a group of Black men.[52] While his exchanges with them reveal him to be confident of his Communist platitudes, he is ultimately respectful.[53] Elsewhere, he displays the well-known condescension of the know-it-all comrade. This is evident as he harangues Wondrous, the cleaning woman who works in his wife's Greenwich Village townhouse. Ira scolds her: "I don't know how a Negro woman can get it into her head that the Democratic Party is going to stop breaking its promises to the Negro race."[54] He gets so mad that he threatens to throw a dish. To which Wondrous responds: "Do what you want, Mr. Ringold. Ain't *my* dish."[55]

Yet, as far as Roth's depictions of Jews speaking with, and reflecting on, Blacks, Ira is the least offensive of them all. In the 1962 *Letting Go* our secular Jewish narrator, Gabe Wallach, introduces us to an acquaintance named Blair Stott. Of this man, Wallach says that he wore two masks: "Alabama Nigger and Uppity Nigger."[56] The description comes absolutely out of nowhere. It's hard to tell why Gabe Wallach (or Roth) has taken the time to drop a slur like this into his narrative, unless Gabe wants to confess his racial hang-ups to us. Such a confession, however, would seem to have no connection to the story line.[57]

Blair speaks what Roth imagines Black English sounds like. Thus, he uncorks sentences like this: "we is all of us taking a deserved rest, for we expended a prodigious, a fantastic, a burdensomely amount of laboriousness and energy."[58] African American characters often talk this way in Roth novels. "Who you supposed to be?" snarls a Black drug dealer in *Zuckerman Unbound*.[59] In *The Anatomy Lesson*, we meet a cleaning woman, Olivia, described as "a small, bottom-heavy, earthbound stranger, the color of bittersweet chocolate."[60] Surprised to see Nathan Zuckerman in her place of work, Olivia exclaims: "Who you!' . . . My God, you like t' scared me to death. My heart just flutterin'. You say you Nathan? . . . Well, you a good-lookin' man, ain't you?"[61]

The convoluted ways Blacks figure in the Jewish mind is insightfully explored in *Portnoy's Complaint*. During his therapy, Alexander Portnoy reveals that he had Communist sympathies in his adolescence.[62] As an eighth-grader he was lauded for his "courageous stand against bigotry and hatred."[63] The middle-schooler led a protest when African American singer, Marian Anderson, was not permitted to perform in Convention Hall.[64] As an adult, Alexander works as the "Assistant Commissioner for the City of New York Commission on Human Opportunity" in the mayor's office, where he defends the civil rights of indigent minorities.[65]

Liberal Alex inveighs against his parents' racism. He excoriates his mother's insincere and patronizing attitude to Dorothy, the African American maid.[66] As for his father, an insurance salesman, he offers this description:

> He lurks about where the husbands sit out in the sunshine, trying to extract a few thin dimes from them before they have drunk themselves senseless on their bottles of "Morgan Davis" wine; he emerges from alleyways like a shot to catch between home and church the pious cleaning ladies, who are off in other people's houses during the daylight hours of the week, and in hiding from him on weekday nights. "Uh-oh," someone cries, "Mr Insurance Man here!" and even the children run for cover—the *children*, he says in disgust, so tell me, what hope is there for these niggers' ever improving their lot?[67]

The coarseness of his father incenses Alex: "And I tell you, if he ever uses the word nigger in my presence again, I will drive a real dagger into his fucking bigoted heart!"[68]

It's ironic that at the very moment Portnoy is decrying irrational hatred for others he is indulging in it as well. His 274-page oration reveals an individual teeming with resentment toward Poles, Irishmen, Puerto Ricans, Chinese, Italians, gays, women, all gentiles, and, of course, Blacks.[69] Such sentiments, needless to say, are surprising coming from liberal Alex.[70] Norman Podhoretz, in a controversial essay, once confessed that "we white Americans are . . . so twisted and sick in our feelings about Negroes."[71] Via Alex, Roth demonstrates the contradictions of racial liberalism; he manages to draw our attention to a real crack and malignancy in the Jewish American psyche.

More evidence of how some Jews really feel about Blacks surfaces in a short piece entitled "On the Air."[72] John Updike, Roth proudly recalls, once described it as "a truly disgusting story."[73] The narrative, such as it is, centers on one M. Lippman, a Jewish talent agent, intent on convincing Albert Einstein to host a radio show.[74] "Mostly I represent colored," Lippman informs Einstein in a meandering letter.[75] He references two tap dancers he works with ("Buck and Wing"). Lippman boasts that he is helping these young men "to raise themselves into a respectable life."[76]

Then we hear Lippman's inner thoughts: "Who were Buck and Wing when he found them? . . . They were two dumb nigger kids giving ten-cent shines outside his shoe store."[77] Later on Lippman muses: "All he had set out to do was to take two little jigaboos who could already tap-dance better than they could walk, and teach them to do it without saying 'shee-yit' every word. And to get the lice off them."[78] By the time we learn that Lippman taught them "to eat a piece of watermelon with a knife and a fork," the story has vindicated Updike's verdict.[79]

The fictional Jews in these Roth tales are every bit as bigoted toward African Americans as their white gentile counterparts. The question is, why?

## "The Late City of Newark"

To understand this bigotry, we must first recognize the *urban* dimension of the Black-Jewish encounter.[80] These groups may have shared, as Julius Lester once observed, similar experiences as despised others in "the broad context of Western civilization."[81] But they also shared tight spaces and limited resources in neighborhoods from Boston to Chicago. Their ordeal in the Occident made them (abstract) allies in victimhood. The encounter in cities, by contrast, led to concrete antagonism amid all that concrete. Their physical closeness, or what the scholar Hasia Diner calls "spatial propinquity," placed them side by side.[82] The conditions of inequality between them drew them apart. Roth sketches this conflict "of two peoples occupying overlapping ghettos."[83] Yet his analysis is one-sided.

*The Professor of Desire* features a memorable cameo from one Mr. Barbatnick, a sweet and thoughtful Holocaust survivor. Over a breezy summer dinner, he analyzes the anti-Black racism of some of his Jewish acquaintances thusly: "What's eating them . . . is that they owned homes, some of them, and businesses, and then came the colored, and when they tried to get out what they put in, they took a licking."[84] In *The Counterlife* Bill Goff discusses the circumstances that led to the closing of his business in Albany, New York: "Colored people started to come in. How could I turn them away? That's not my nature. But my Christian customers of twenty and twenty-five years, they didn't like it. They told me right out, no bones about it, 'Look, Goff, I'm not gonna to sit here and wait while you try ten pairs of shoes on some nigger. I don't want his rejects either. So one by one they left me, my wonderful Christian friends.'"[85]

Such testimonials are well known to urban sociologists. As the Great Migration sent African Americans northward in the early and middle decades of the twentieth century, they followed what one scholar called "the path of least resistance."[86] This path led them to Jewish neighborhoods—neighborhoods which, unlike those of other white ethnic groups, did not greet them with "firebombs, guns, or clenched fists."[87] As I and others have noted elsewhere, this made Jews quite unique among white ethnics.[88]

In many cases (e.g., the Boston suburbs, Brooklyn in the 1960s and 1970s) Jews moved out rapidly upon the appearance of Black residents.[89] As a result, they did indeed, as Mr. Barbatnick surmised, watch their financial circumstances decline. Or, as Cornel West once put it, "Blacks are seen as the cause of Jews losing the value of their investment in housing."[90] In other cases, such as Harlem, Jews vacated the neighborhood as residents, but remained as shop owners, landlords, teachers, and so forth.[91] The consequences of sharing this space with Blacks under conditions of such inequality are on full display in James Baldwin's famous 1967 essay "Negroes Are Anti-Semitic Because They're Anti-White."[92]

And then there's Newark. Roth's protagonists often sing a lament which goes like this:[93] The Jews of Weequahic thrived in their quasi-paradisiacal slice of Newark from roughly the 1930s to the 1960s. Paradise would be lost when Blacks moved near.[94] After the Newark riot of July 12, 1967, the entire city became dangerous and uninhabitable. Those Jews who didn't flee to the suburbs lived or worked in a broken, crime-filled hovel.

In *The Anatomy Lesson,* Nathan Zuckerman returns to postriot Newark.[95] His birthplace, he sighs, is now "the burnt-out landscape of a racial war."[96] The depressed writer concludes that Newark is "occupied now by an alien tribe."[97] In *Zuckerman Unbound,* a Jewish character excoriates the novelist Nathan Zuckerman for portraying Newark nostalgically in his novels: "Newark! . . . What do you know about Newark, Mama's boy! I read that fucking book! . . . Moron! *Moron!* Newark is a nigger with a knife! Newark is a whore with the syph! Newark is junkies shitting in your hallway and everything burned to the ground! Newark is dago vigilantes hunting jigs with tire irons! Newark is bankruptcy! Newark is ashes! Newark is rubble and filth!"[98]

Roth again turned to Newark in his so-called "American trilogy" of the late twentieth century.[99] The same remonstrance surfaces: Blacks have destroyed it all. Lou Levov emotes about his factory as follows: "But they took that city and now they are going to take that business and everything that I built up a day at a time, an *inch* at a time, and they are going to leave it *all* in ruins!"[100] By the end of this novel, Lou mourns "the late city of Newark."[101]

Another result of sharing urban spaces with Blacks, as far as Roth's Jews are concerned, is street crime. A character named Herbert Grossman in

*The Counterlife* exclaims: "You can't even walk to the store. You go out to the supermarket in broad daylight and blacks come out and rob you blind."[102] In *Patrimony,* Roth reveals that his own father was mugged by a Black teenager.[103] Murray Ringold's wife is murdered during a robbery in Newark in *I Married a Communist.* At his life's end, Murray blames her death on his prideful desire to not abandon his hometown: "I wasn't going to move out of the city where I had lived and taught all my life, just because it was now a poor black city full of problems."[104]

That Blacks are bent on the physical annihilation of the Jews is a paranoid delusion of militant religious settlers in Israel.[105] In *The Counterlife* a group of extremists prophesy the future of diaspora Jews as such: "The American Goy will . . . permit the resentful Blacks to take all their hatred out on the Jews, and afterward they take care of the Blacks. And without the nosy Jews around to complain that they are violating black civil rights."[106]

These portrayals are problematic. As Larry Schwartz pointed out, Roth is "disturbingly uncritical about race and its legacy in Newark."[107] What Roth's characters—and likely Roth himself—can't see, alleges Schwartz, is that Newark was a "'Jim Crow' city as completely and thoroughly segregated as any in the South."[108] His fiction fails to capture the unyielding structural racism that thrust Blacks into Jewish neighborhoods in the first place.

Nowhere in Roth's urban opera do we hear about the skulduggery of the Federal Housing Administration, the practices of "redlining" and "blockbusting," or the manner in which municipalities abandoned neighborhoods once Blacks settled there.[109] As Jun-Suk Hwang observes, the author "casts black Newarkers as irrational instruments of destruction, not as its victims."[110]

We can't blame Roth for not transposing the findings of urban sociology into fiction. We can, however, accuse him of violating his own precepts. When it comes to Newark, he indulges in a type of blanching nostalgia which he elsewhere mocked. He called it "a pastoral." That's a feel-good illusion, a "womb-dream," that an individual or group has about itself.[111] As regards his hometown, "Roth the hard-edged, thoughtful, and ironical realist, becomes a conservative 'utopian.'"[112]

## The One-Man Freedom Ride

*The Human Stain* (2000) is markedly different from anything Philip Roth had previously written about persons of African ancestry. Gone are Buck and Wing grunting "shee-yit." Gone is the focalization of Black-Jewish dilemmas through the minds of Jews *only*. Studying Roth's archives in the Library of Congress, I was always struck by how few correspondences he maintained with people who were not white-identified. My guess is that in researching *The Human Stain*, Roth read about, and/or thought about, and/or spoke with, and/or listened to, Black people more than at any other moment in his career.[113]

In the 1940s, Coleman Silk, a light-skinned African American teenager from East Orange, New Jersey, realizes that he can pass as a white Jew.[114] The star student and boxer maintains this fake persona during his stint in the navy. Thereafter, he never relinquishes the disguise.[115] Like a character in the Langston Hughes's poem "Passing," Coleman soon "crossed the line to live downtown."[116] He moves to bohemian Greenwich Village, attends NYU, pursues a doctorate in classics, and goes on to a successful academic career.[117] Along the way, he forsakes his family and breaks his mother's heart.

Living in a nearly all-white world, he performs his new ethnic/religious/racial identity to perfection.[118] (As one bemused scholar noted, this is one of the only Black passing narratives in which the passer seems to derive *pleasure* from the whole ordeal).[119] Neither his white Jewish wife, Iris Gitelman, nor their four children ever uncovers the secret.[120] In fact, Coleman performs white Judaism so well that his murderer is likely a local anti-Semite![121]

When I teach *The Human Stain* to my "Blacks and Jews" class, most of my students initially find Coleman to be a loathsome sort. They consider him a fraud who trims his sails to the horizon of white privilege.[122] Roth *does* put this interpretation into play. By the time Coleman was murdered, his brother hadn't spoken to him for a half century. His despondent mother upbraided him, "Coleman Brutus. You're white as snow and you think like a slave."[123]

Nevertheless, Zuckerman, who narrates the story (and Roth, who writes it), is quite sympathetic to Silk's act of self-reinvention.[124] This presents a huge ethical and commercial challenge. After all, publishing a novel about a self-hating Black man who finds peace and fulfillment in being white and Jewish is a risky endeavor. Roth devotes a great deal of time to explaining the rationale of a person whom many construe as worthy of contempt.

In order to do so, one crucial move must be made. The author must negate the idea of self-hatred; a non-race-based motivation for Silk's metamorphosis must be identified. Roth thus emphasizes that Coleman did not pass as white because he loathed his own ancestry.[125] Rather, he simply sought liberty from *any* identity: "All he'd ever wanted, from earliest childhood on," Zuckerman observes, "was to be free: not black, not even white—just on his own and free."[126]

Of course, we'd *expect* a person like Coleman (and one enthralled by him like Zuckerman) to insist he had no racial hang-ups whatsoever. So Roth corroborates the point through an independent witness. Coleman's estranged sister, Ernestine, shares that "Coleman never in his life chafed under being a negro" (again, why is an African American using the term "Negro" in the summer of 1998?)[127] Nor, she testifies, did he ever demonstrate "the slightest evidence" of envying white people.[128] The point is that Coleman did not pass because he hated being Black, or because he craved privilege, *but because he simply didn't want to belong to any group.*[129] In one of the novel's most memorable lines, he is described as "the greatest of the great *pioneers* of the I."[130] The man retains a sense of individualism and "singularity" that verges on the maniacal.[131] Zuckerman ponders his "savagery" of purpose—a savagery that has "nothing to do with wanting to be white."[132]

Roth establishes Silk as an individualist who despises group membership (but not blackness per se). Now the moral ground is cleared for him to build a towering monument to one of his grandest themes. Later, I will argue that Roth was positively obsessed with the question of what a self *is* and how it transforms into something new. Silk's self-determination, so to speak, is what mesmerizes Zuckerman and Roth.[133]

The idea that Coleman is playing the *role* of a white person—and thus demonstrating how arbitrary and absurd the concept of race is—intrigued scholars. Michele Elam refers to his passing as "a performative doing."[134] She thus warned against reading Coleman's behavior as merely "racial self-hatred."[135] Then again, not everything about Coleman Silk's one-man freedom ride struck critics as laudable.

For some, neither Silk nor Zuckerman (and perhaps neither Roth) seemed to fully grasp how impossible the quest to abandon one's socially ascribed race actually is. Brett Ashley Kaplan has pointed to a glaring problem in Roth's celebration of the "I" over the "we."[136] The "we," especially as it pertains to race, "cannot be jettisoned by sheer acts of will."[137] This reminds me of a comment the literary critic Henry Louis Gates Jr. once made: "Racial recusal is a forlorn hope. In a system where whiteness is the default, racelessness is never a possibility."[138] It is likely that Roth, begrudgingly, realized this as well. Silk didn't "escape" a "we" as much as he chose the different "we" of Judaism. He died for it nonetheless. This might be Roth's concession that in a racist society identity is indelible.[139]

My students often ask a pointed question. Namely, if Coleman were so courageous and pioneering, why did his odyssey of the "I" steer him to the relatively serene harbors of white, upper-middle-class Judaism? In his bold expedition to a new self, why did this adventurer set up camp in such a safe space?

### Reverse Racial Biography

If I were to compose a reverse racial biography of Philip Roth, I would divide his life into three periods, each with its own orientation to his Black compatriots.[140] Before I describe these stages, let me note that one belief appears to have stayed constant throughout all three: Roth and his fictional Jews saw themselves as unambiguously *white*.

A character in *The Counterlife* chortles at the very idea of "Black Jews" from Ethiopia migrating to Israel.[141] In a 1959 essay, Roth reminisces about spending his summers on Bradley Beach. What surprised him were the Syrian Jews, who "stand around being dark."[142] "They were supposed to be Jews," exclaims Roth, "but I never believed it. I still don't."[143] As one of this chapter's epigraphs indicates, for this author Jewish Americans were Caucasians—"us whites," as Ira Ringold puts it in *I Married a Communist*.[144] Roth's facile embrace of this notion places him at some distance from other major Jewish American writers like Bernard Malamud (in "Angel Levine") or Grace Paley (in "Zagrowsky Tells") who were more curious about this association. It also indicates that Roth did not think carefully about Sephardic Jews and Afro-Jews, nor even his own eastern European ancestors whose racial assignment as "white" in the United States only became commonplace in the mid-twentieth century.[145]

As for my racial biography, I would propose thinking of Roth's life in the following stages.

The "Liberal/Communist" phase stretches from the 1940s to the early 1960s. My surmise would be that young man Roth, like many of his characters, toggled between mainstream liberalism and fringier Marxist-inspired ideologies shaped by his eastern European forebears. All those approaches harbored hidden racist assumptions, obliviousness to white privilege, and patronizing attitudes toward Blacks. Simultaneously, however, liberals and Communists tended to be curious about, and positively inclined toward, African Americans.[146] Jewish attitudes toward Blacks were precisely as convoluted as those of Alex Portnoy in *Portnoy's Complaint*.

These idealistic men of Roth's generation had to contend with their Unrelenting Jewish Fathers. Hardscrabble, minimally educated fellows, raised in the working class, like Mr. Patimkin ("Goodbye, Columbus"), Jake Portnoy (*Portnoy's Complaint*), Lou Levov (*American Pastoral*), and Herman Roth (*The Plot Against America*), were decidedly *not* Communists. They were New Deal liberals whose enthusiasm for FDR's policies did not necessarily extend to racial sensitivity. Their attitudes toward Blacks were pervaded by either apathy or prejudice. Whether the real Herman Roth and his cohort were anything like these fictionalized patriarchs deserves further scrutiny.

These tensions and contradictions within midcentury Jewish thought surface in "The Box of Truths." Written in 1952, the story lingers on a "negro" waiter.[147] He is described as "pygmy-like" and a "black mass."[148] After observing his "wrinkled mahogany forehead," the narrative voice relays this about our protagonist—a drunk, assumedly white writer who has just had his manuscript rejected: "In his watery eyes he saw floating, resignation; he saw age written around his mouth. He saw a person."[149] This triumphant recognition of "personhood" amid the racist depictions encapsulates the contradictions of racial liberalism I have been charting above.[150]

The decades from the mid-1960s to 2000 constitute the second period of my proposed racial biography. I would refer to it as the era of the "Broken Alliance"—and the era that belies the assumptions of the Alliance Paradigm.[151] Here, Roth's prose on Blacks gets considerably coarser. The insensitive asides about Blair Stott in the 1962 *Letting Go* foreshadowed troubling depictions ahead. In works of the 1970s such as "On the Air" and *The Great American Novel,* the author hit new lows. From there, he went on to chronicle Jewish rage about the fate of Newark, a predicament for which Blacks are held singularly responsible.

A biographer might wonder why the "Liberal/Communist" and "Broken Alliance" phases are so different in tone. One obvious answer is to be found in the broader context of Black-Jewish relations. Scholars see the 1960s as the moment in which the so-called "Grand Alliance" collapsed.[152] We needn't rehearse the argument that the Alliance was fragile and overhyped well before that.[153] What we can say is that by the end of the 1960s, Black/Jewish "unity" fractured.

The flashpoints are well known: the 1967 Six-Day War that coincided with the Black Power movement's globalist awakening;[154] the Student Non-Violent Coordinating Committee's "vitriolic articles criticizing the Jewish state" as a white settler colony;[155] the 1968 Ocean Hill–Brownsville strike that paralyzed

New York City. From there it was a slow, miserable descent to an endless, looping conversation about "Black anti-Semitism" and "Jewish racism." Such recriminations abounded in the 1979 "Andrew Young Affair," the fallout over Jessie Jackson's 1984 "Hymie Town" remark, Jewish neoconservative assaults on Affirmative Action, and the Crown Heights Riot of 1991.[156]

Black and Jewish intellectuals, I repeat, had already been sniping at one another throughout the Grand Alliance era (see the brutal exchange in 1964 between Roth and the poet LeRoi Jones as a minor example).[157] But by the end of the 1960s, the conflict was visible. So visible, I would surmise, that Roth felt emboldened to traffic in slurs and stereotypes in his prose.[158]

My final period of "*Slightly* Somewhat More Thoughtful Engagement" commences with the publication of The Human Stain in 2000. This novel marks the first time that Roth flipped his racial script and wondered what Blacks made of Jews. In one scene, a Dr. Fensterman offers the Silk family a bribe.[159] The Silks reject it, amused by the *chutzpah* of it all. Coleman's father nevertheless recognizes that "even audaciously unsavory Jews like Dr. Fensterman, were like Indian scouts, shrewd people showing the outsider his way in, showing the social possibility, showing an intelligent colored family how it might be done."[160] Suddenly, the author shows us the reasoning of *Blacks* confronted with problematic *Jews*.

The third phase was not without its unsettling moments. In The Plot Against America (2004), Philip's artist brother relishes drawing Black people. One of whom is a "Negro bellhop . . . one not picturesquely grooved and crannied quite like Edward B., though from an artistic point of view no less of a find—very dark with strongly African facial features of a kind Sandy had never before gotten to draw from anything other than a photo in a back issue of National Geographic."[161] This description dismays for a variety of reasons, foremost among which is that it appears in a chapter called "Loudmouth Jew." There the Roth family emotionally implodes under the weight of the anti-Semitism they encounter in Washington, D.C.[162]

The act of gazing at Black bodies without any awareness of what this operation entails occurs again in Exit Ghost (2007). A biographer by the name of Richard Kliman is discussing a chorus of female African American singers he gawked at during a funeral.[163] He starts by describing their physiognomy in great detail: "the ones with the enormous cans, and the little balding gnarled ones looking a hundred years-old."[164] That Kliman immediately goes on to rail against Christianity, America, "slavery and cross," again displays the contradictory racial psyche of Roth's characters.[165]

At the conclusion of *Everyman* we overhear a dialogue with an African American gravedigger.[166] He too, like Everyman, our assimilated Jewish protagonist, lacks a name. In their anonymity, Black and Jew are twinned again. The differences, however, are striking. Unlike the Jewish Everyman who is estranged from his sons, the gravedigger has Arnold, to whom he is teaching the craft.[167] Unlike the Jewish Everyman, he has a companion, Thelma, who lovingly cares for him. As their conversation develops, we learn that this dignified individual dug the graves that Everyman's parents now occupy.[168] He will likely shovel the dirt for Everyman's plot as well.

Whether the Black man who prepares the interment for the secular Jew is meant to be read symbolically is up to the reader. As will be the possibility that Philip Roth himself was trying to bury a lifetime of mostly unfortunate prose about Blacks.

## · 2 ·

# Old Men, Young Women

You've taught me so much, and you're the best friend I have. I just can't . . .
It's so not . . . *normal.*

    —LISA HALLIDAY, *Asymmetry*

Ordinary people are profoundly disturbed by these age differences. Look, is
this a good thing, this kind of talk?

    —PHILIP ROTH, *The Counterlife*

When we first meet Alice, a twenty-five-year-old editorial assistant in Lisa Halliday's 2018 novel *Asymmetry*, she is aimlessly sitting on a Manhattan park bench, slogging through a novel.[1] Her afternoon drudgery is interrupted by the flirtatious advance of Ezra Blazer, a famous writer nearly a half century her senior. The septuagenarian comes on to Alice brazenly, while slurping a Mister Softee ice cream cone no less![2] A fairly serious sexual and emotional affair ensues. The affair, apparently, stops ensuing when old-man Ezra is admitted to the Emergency Room with chest pains.[3] It is at this moment, as our epigraph suggests, that Alice is poised to terminate their relationship.

Ezra Blazer bears a tidy resemblance to Philip Roth.[4] Much about him, from his fondness for baseball, to his rapacious erotic appetite, leads us to surmise that *Asymmetry* is based on the famous novelist. In subsequent interviews, Halliday mentions that—yes!—she just happened to have a romantic episode with the great Man of Letters. "I really did want to share with the reader," she told *New Yorker* editor David Remnick, "some of what I loved about Philip, what I loved most about him."[5] In penning this novel, Halliday has thus made what one wag calls "a valuable addition to the burgeoning corpus of first-hand accounts of what it's like to have sex with Philip Roth."[6]

*Asymmetry,* with its depiction of carnality between a young, entry-level female editor and an elderly, wealthy guy who showers her with gifts, great novels, and cash is not only about Roth, but Rothian in its romantic dynamics.[7] That's because "age-dissimilar" romance, as scholars refer to it, is a salient theme in his oeuvre.[8] To a degree that is not widely recognized, this writer crafted stories in which a man loves and/or has sex with a much younger woman (the reverse scenario, involving a considerably older woman, also surfaces, but rarely).

Table 2, in the appendix, summarizes another of those "obsessional themes" discussed in my introduction.[9] Intergenerational eroticism rampages its way through twenty out of twenty-four novels starting from *The Breast* (1972), gaining ground speed toward the advent of the millennium in works like *Sabbath's Theater, The Human Stain,* and *The Dying Animal.*[10] Despite the frequency of the old man/young woman motif, no scholar has subjected it to extended analysis. This is likely because critics are more likely to scrutinize the problem of how the author depicts women in general. This takes the focus off of those women who enter into relationships with men old enough to be their fathers or grandfathers. By concentrating just on the latter phenomenon, we will be able to isolate some core elements of this author's thought. These insights are not just about so-called "manthers" and "cougars," but about the nature of erotic attraction itself.

Roth and his fiction have often been branded as misogynistic (see chapter 3). His decades-long interest in a type of romance which Alice in *Asymmetry* declared "not . . . *normal*" does, on occasion, display the superficiality and sexism that aggravates his critics.[11] This having been said, I'd like to show that some of his portraits of age-dissimilar love are crackling with the thoughtfulness and bleak insights that make him a writer worthy of our scrutiny.

### "The Purest Form of Eros"

The unlikely romance depicted in *The Human Stain* occurs between a seemingly Jewish professor of classics and a seemingly illiterate school janitor. The professor/grandfather/lover in question is seventy-one years old. His name is Coleman Silk.[12] His partner, Faunia Farley, is thirty-four.[13]

The narrative action in *The Human Stain* commences when Coleman gets embroiled in a campus Political Correctness maelstrom. While taking attendance aloud, the professor off-handedly refers to two absent students as "spooks."[14] As it turns out, the truants, whom he never previously met, were African American. In an ironic (or just?) twist for a person denying his own African heritage (see chapter 1), Silk gets sent up on charges of racial insensitivity. He resigns in fury from Athena College, whose sinking fortunes he once reversed after a long and successful stint as its dean.[15]

During his forced retirement Coleman strikes up an affair with Faunia, a school janitor who moonlights at the local dairy farm. This woman, at first glance, seems victimized beyond repair. Sexually abused by her stepfather, physically battered during her failed marriage, mourning the death of her two children by fire, Faunia appears mute and incapacitated by her hardships.[16] Yet as the narrative develops, we learn otherwise. Faunia emerges as resilient, thoughtful, and complex; Roth portrays this character as cryptically heroic. She's also a great talker.

What makes *The Human Stain* a gripping read is the raw intensity of the encounters between Coleman and Faunia. Their association is deeply sexual. Courtesy of Viagra, Silk experiences erotic thrills historically not available to men of his age. Faunia, for her part, has no issues or hang-ups about being "with a man as old as her grandfather."[17] During one of their assignations she laments that Silk is too *young* for her. "Do you have a friend in a wheelchair you can introduce me to?" she inquires.[18]

Their relationship, however, is not *merely* sexual. Earlier in *The Human Stain*, Nathan listens to Coleman describe Faunia and observes to himself, "He's found somebody he can talk with."[19] Sure enough, throughout the novel these lovers *speak* incessantly to one another, and with brutal honesty at that.[20] Coleman's infatuation is based not upon sexual attraction per se, but the ability to converse authentically and truthfully with his multidimensional partner. Coleman is aroused by Faunia because he can *talk* to her. And because she's a great listener.

I want to linger a bit on this equation between eroticism, words, and conversation. This linkage is a staple of Roth's conception of romance, and not scrutinized nearly enough. Marcus Messner in *Indignation* loves Olivia Hutton's gorgeously written letter to him so much that he first kisses it.[21] Then he licks "the ink of the signature."[22] Then he has to restrain himself from ingesting the paper.[23]

In *Deception* a character named "Philip" is accused of favoring talk and "postcoital intimacy" over physicality.[24] One of his colleagues remarks: "You only enter into life to keep the conversation going. Even sex is really at the edge. You are not driven by eros—you are not driven by anything. Only by this boyish curiosity. Only by this gee-whiz naïveté."[25] Later in *Deception* a former student, whom Philip seduced when she was nineteen, recollects that "Philip" was "the fatherly lover who listened."[26] In the same novel a character exclaims, "All the time I thought you loved me for my body when in fact it was only for my sentences."[27]

The literary critic Debra Shostak has noticed that while a great deal of *Deception* is composed of "pre- or post-coital" dialogue, there are no descriptions of flesh, eroticism, the sweat of bodies, etc.[28] The lovers in each scene, she observes, "are transposed to pure language."[29] Her point can be soldered to our own about Coleman's attraction to Faunia: their sexual activity is a portal to meaningful conversation. In terms of male stereotypes, the reversal is intriguing. Coleman Silk and "Philip" in *Deception* are shown to be driven not solely or even mostly by a desire for epic fornication, but for *greater emotional intimacy* with women.

Female characters, perhaps less surprisingly, often exhibit the same motivation. An adulterous woman in an obscure Roth story ("Psychoanalytic Special") speaks of her latest partner as "the most beautiful *after*-lover."[30] Pamela Solomon, the twenty-four-year-old paramour of Ira Ringold in *I Married a Communist*, revels (at first) in pillow talk with a man twelve years her senior: "Pamela liked these conversations. They excited her. It made her feel strong to talk freely like that."[31] The central role that conversation plays in Roth's thinking about sex is evident in Maria Zuckerman's melancholy reflection in *The Counterlife*: "Most people have sex cut off from love, and maybe it appears we had the opposite, love cut off from sex. . . . That endless, issueless, intimate talk. . . . [T]o me it was the purest form of eros."[32]

In each of these cases, the erotic acts described are both a cause *and* effect of increasingly truthful and frank discussions. The emphasis on dialogue may help us understand why consensual romances between old men and young women draw no moral condemnation from Roth. If earnest conversation is what makes a human sexual relationship meaningful to *both* partners, then why should anyone cavil about a couple of decades of difference in chronological age?

In *The Human Stain*, we glimpse an intergenerational (and interclass) union rooted in earnest speech acts. What is interesting for our purposes is how Roth invests this relationship with an undeniable dignity. The affair is portrayed as emotionally serious and morally credible because it is grounded in authentic dialogue. As we are now about to see, not every old man/young woman coupling in Roth's fiction rises to this lofty standard.

## *Sabbath's Theater*: Because They Must

There is a certain type of Roth connoisseur for whom the 1995 *Sabbath's Theater* is the real thing—the Roth novel for those in the know. Roth himself shared this high valuation of the 450-page work: "I'm particularly partial to a book called *Sabbath's Theater,* which a lot of people hate. Now, that's not the reason I like it. . . . But I think it's got a lot of freedom in it. That's what you're looking for as a writer when you're working. You're looking for your own freedom. To lose your inhibition to delve deep into your memory and experiences and life and then to find the prose that will persuade the reader."[33]

*Sabbath's Theater* is uninhibited all right! This "pornutopia," or "tour de fuckfest," is stuffed to the gills with detailed descriptions of its hero's erotic escapades.[34] Across his sixty-four years, Mickey Sabbath has hooked up with women of many different ages. These experiences can range anywhere from his lengthy extramarital affair with Drenka Balich (who is fifty-two years old), to the maid he encounters and promptly sodomizes while crashing at his friend's house when in town for a funeral.[35]

Our interest is with Sabbath's disastrous three-week fling with a coed by the name of Kathy Goolsbee—"a freckled redhead with the shiksa overbite."[36] One day, out of the blue, the undergrad calls the home of Sabbath, who teaches at Athena College. Although Kathy simply requests an extension on her project, Sabbath interprets her communication as a come-on. The arthritic puppeteer muses: "When you feel a strike like that at the end of the line, you don't have to be much of a fisherman to know you've hooked a beaut."[37]

Maybe it is a come-on. For a reason which is never fully explained, Kathy seeks instruction in the art of writing erotica. Sabbath, naturally, stands at the ready. The link between words and eroticism is again evident in this coupling. Phone sex is on the syllabus, and our old man records these conversations surreptitiously. Actually, Sabbath has amassed shoeboxes full of secretly taped material of women talking about, and having, sex with him (sometimes he plays these in the background as he frolics with his lover Drenka). Words again. Needless to say, readers in the #MeToo era are not likely to view the unauthorized capture and repurposing of intimate acts as an innocuous quirk.

Sabbath himself worries that having an archive like this lying around might be a tad risky. Pondering the possibility of ditching his incriminating stash, he protests:

> That would have been like burning the flag. No, more like defiling a Picasso. Because there was in these tapes a kind of *art* in the way that he was able to unshackle his girls from their habit of innocence. There was a kind of art in his providing an illicit adventure not with a boy of their own age but with someone three times their age—the very repugnance that his aging body inspired in them had to make their adventure with him feel a little like a crime and thereby gave free play to their budding perversity and to the confused exhilaration that comes of flirting with disgrace.[38]

Sabbath doesn't only want to have sex with these women (and record the proceedings for posterity); he wants to reprocess the sex into a teachable moment! He aspires to instruct these young women in the theory and practice of shamelessness, a subject in which he surely possesses an advanced degree.[39]

But Kathy Goolsbee—note the ghoul in the name, as David Brauner points out—may not be as hooked as Sabbath initially thought.[40] She, too, keeps her own taped version of the tutorial with her professor. Through an oversight on Kathy's part (which Sabbath insists was not an oversight) the salacious materials are leaked. Needless to say, the following transcript is not what Mickey Sabbath, a lowly adjunct professor, wanted to wind up as an "action-item" on the desk of Dean Kakutani:

> Go ahead. Fuck it with your finger.
> I want it to be you, though.
> Tell me what you want.
> I want your cock. I'll get it really, really hard.
> Want me to stick it in you?
> I want you to stick it into me hard.
> A nice stiff cock inside you?[41]

And on and on it goes *for twenty pages*.[42] Roth included this exchange as a running footnote under the main body of the text. Why he did so is not clear to me. There is nothing funny, original, lyrical, profound, or aesthetically intriguing about Kathy and Sabbath's joint masturbation sesh. It's just not an interesting conversation. Roth wrote scenes, by contrast, in which

Faunia and Coleman delighted and devastated one another when they spoke during and after sex. Give us better wordy smut, Mr. Roth![43]

Kathy swears that she played no part in the unfortunate chain of events that resulted in the aforementioned texts falling into the hands of the women's studies department. Sabbath is of the opinion that his student divulged these materials on purpose. As she apologizes in the front seat of his car, an enraged Sabbath threatens the young woman. Kathy exits his vehicle so quickly that she almost falls out the door. Her panic is understandable since her professor has just told her he killed his first wife and would like to kill her as well.[44]

Roth's exploration of the old man/young woman theme in Sabbath's Theater does little to bring profound insights and questions to our attention. Unlike Coleman Silk in The Human Stain, Sabbath's taste in young women is indiscriminate. Whereas we understood *why* Coleman fell for the inscrutable Faunia, little makes us comprehend what in particular it is about Kathy that renders Sabbath willing to risk his teaching job and marriage to be with her. Sabbath, as best I can tell, likes this young woman because she is nubile and willing to engage with his repugnant body (and soul). Given his satyr-like proclivities, it is also plausible that Sabbath likes her simply because she possesses female genitalia.

All of which is to say, Roth underperforms in Sabbath's Theater. As a fictionalist, his job is to illuminate the complexities, nuances, and quiddities of age-dissimilar romance. True, Roth teases us with three complicated ideas. Namely, that an older man like Sabbath might construe his sexual encounters as (1) works of art in and of themselves, or (2) a course of study which confers timeless erotic wisdom upon young women, or (3) rooted in the erotic power of words. The novel never develops those themes. In the absence of that analysis, it seems that Roth is basically telling us old men sleep with younger women because if they *can,* they *must.* Which is not strikingly different from what some men themselves believe to be true, should they ever see fit to reflect on the matter.

As for Kathy's perspective, Roth does a lackluster job in making her interest in Mickey Sabbath credible. Alice in Asymmetry is awed by Ezra Blazer's fame, fiction, and even the swagger of his park pickup move. Eerie Faunia in The Human Stain seems genuinely drawn to the trampled-upon, debased Coleman Silk. But at no point in Sabbath's Theater does Roth help us understand what it is about hobgoblin Sabbath that so intrigues the redheaded woman with the shiksa overbite.

## Dying Animals

Professor David Kepesh, narrator of the *The Dying Animal*, is, at first glance, a poster child (or poster man-child?) for toxic masculinity. A reviewer in the *New York Times* complained about "his sentimental, unreflecting idealization of sex, his callous incuriosity about women as anything other than sexual objects."[45] Whether this assessment is accurate is something we shall return to forthwith. For now, all we can say is that Kepesh is exceedingly useful to our inquiry. Like other Rothian protagonists, this old man serially targets young women, undergraduates in particular. But unlike so many other Rothian bad boys, he gleans wisdom from his transgression.

Now nearly seventy years old, the scholar starts his story by sharing his time-tested techniques for seducing coeds, or "student-mistress[es]," as he likes to call them.[46] "They come to my first class," the lecherous professor explains, "and I know almost immediately which is the girl for me."[47] Once the mark has been selected, the predator knows that he cannot pounce until "they have completed their final exam and receive their grade and I am no longer officially in loco parentis."[48]

The prey, when Kepesh was sixty-two years old, was a twenty-four-year-old undergrad by the name of Consuela Castillo. We do not learn much about her personality. She's not a talker. Most of his descriptions of Consuela concern her body, her bodily fluids, and her erotic performances. Kepesh describes her genitalia in such lush detail that one critic proposes Consuela's name is a play on the words "cunt" and "swell."[49]

The *Dying Animal*, with its dry, clinical descriptions of sex acts ("I began coming, she abruptly stopped and received it like an open drain. I could have been coming into a wastepaper basket") and chilly objectification of women's bodies, is not likely to ingratiate itself to readers who sympathize with the #MeToo movement.[50] They do not usually explore fiction in order to learn about how old geezers in positions of authority lure young women into their beds. That spider-and-the-fly plotline, after all, is like the *nonfiction* that brought the movement into being in the first place.

Yet given Kepesh's unexpected character development, I think we should cut Roth a little slack. To begin with, Kepesh does get his comeuppance. *The Dying Animal* is recounted six and a half years after Consuela broke up with Kepesh. Their split occurred because he blew off her graduation party and a chance to meet her family. Maybe Kepesh wishes he had just attended the celebration, hugged Mom and Dad, and returned to New York for more mind-blowing sex with Consuela. The loss of her as a lover caused him three years of excruciating psychic misery.

The resulting swoon was not pretty: "I played Beethoven and I masturbated. I played Mozart and I masturbated. I played Haydn, Schumann, Schubert, and masturbated with her image in mind."[51] Throughout the breakup period the aging man is seized not only by bouts of jealousy, but by crippling existential angst.[52] The professor spends his evenings agonizing over imagined male suitors vying for Consuela's hand. Kepesh cries out: "This need. This derangement. Will it never stop? I don't even know after a while what I'm desperate for. Her tits? Her soul? Her youth? Her simple mind? Maybe it's worse than that—maybe now that I'm nearing death, I also long secretly not to be free."[53]

Aside from rehearsing his classical piano repertoire and pleasuring himself, Kepesh spends a lot of time ruminating. This brings us to another reason why I think that readers concerned about #MeToo issues might engage with this book. It is undeniably true that Kepesh, like Mickey Sabbath, displays some weapons-grade sexism. It is undeniably true that Kepesh, like Sabbath, is an automaton of the erection—a man propelled by his genitals. Kepesh, however, possesses an extra analytical gear which Sabbath clearly lacks.

As the novel progresses, an unraveling Kepesh shows himself to be deeply reflective, even self-critical, about age-dissimilar romance. The trigger is not only the breakup, but Consuela's eventual diagnosis of breast cancer. The entire 156-page novel is a monologue he delivers about Consuela to, presumably, another young lover. As he speaks, he is keeping a "vigil by the phone," anxiously awaiting her call about her deteriorating condition.[54]

What emerges from his fevered oration—for the first and only time in Roth's writing—is an *explanation* of why women and men find themselves in these types of relationships. Here is Kepesh, theorizing grandly about what his lover felt:

> It was the true beginning of her mastery—the mastery into which my mastery has initiated her. I am the author of her mastery of me. . . . But the age I am has great significance for Consuela. These girls with old gents don't do it despite the age—they're drawn to the age, they do it *for* the age. Why? In Consuela's case, because the vast difference in age gives her permission to submit, I think. My age and my status give her, rationally, the license to surrender, and surrendering in bed is a not unpleasant sensation. But simultaneously, to give yourself over

intimately to a much, much older man provides this sort of younger woman with authority of a kind she cannot get in a sexual arrangement with a younger man. She gets both the pleasures of submission *and* the pleasures of mastery. . . . To have gained the total interest, to have become the consuming passion of a man inaccessible in every other arena, to enter a life she admires that would otherwise be closed to her—that's power, and it's the power she wants.[55]

Kepesh's reference to power is germane. Older men in these situations are traditionally accused of "punching down," of using their wealth, status, experience, and so forth, to take advantage of weaker young women. Kepesh proposes something different. In his view young women relish the combination of powerlessness *and* power, submission *and* mastery that a relation with an older man provides. These types of romances are often criticized because it is alleged that there exists a massive power differential between the lovers. But Roth collapses that distinction, countering that women experience *both* power and powerlessness when cavorting with "old gents." The pleasure for the young woman lies in the *transit* between the two states.

For the old gent, however, there can be no pleasant fore and aft between power and powerlessness. Submission is, apparently, not an option for a man. This fact of life is conveyed to Kepesh by his poet friend George, who tries to console his miserable chum: "Look, . . . see it as a critic, see it from a professional point of view. You violated the law of aesthetic distance. You sentimentalized the aesthetic experience with this girl—you personalized it, you sentimentalized it, and you lost the sense of separation essential to your enjoyment."[56] By falling for Consuela, argues George, Kepesh has become "powerless."[57] In George's reckoning, a man must be emotionally estranged, separated, from a sexual conquest *in order to enjoy it.*

As the scholar Velichka Ivanova points out, "Kepesh preserves his masculine integrity by maintaining coldness and distance from his sexual partner."[58] The sex is gratifying to our narrator *because,* not in spite, of the emotional distance. To be cruelly aloof is to be liberated. When we think of toxic masculinity, this is precisely what we have in mind: men who shut down their humanity—which includes their moral capacity, empathy, etc.—in pursuit of erotic conquest. For George, and for Kepesh before his awakening, a man who courts a young woman must emotionally stay afar. This is how power is maintained. This is what it means for a man to be "free." I would concur, then, with the opinion of those critics who argue

Roth is exposing, not celebrating, the unseemliness and irrationality of being a man.[59]

When all is said and done, Kepesh has changed. Consuela is in the hospital, poised to succumb to her cancer. As he prepares to abandon the young woman he is speaking to so that he can attend to Consuela, he exclaims: "I have to go. She wants me there. She wants me to sleep in the bed with her there. She has not eaten all day. She has to eat. She has to be fed."[60] A woke Kepesh is mired in the details of her disease and suffering. He is now powerless, enmeshed, and unfree—but full of empathy.[61]

## Secrecy, Stigma, Bliss, Catastrophe

In his early book-length works (*Goodbye, Columbus and Five Short Stories*, 1959; *Letting Go*, 1962; *When She Was Good*, 1967; *Portnoy's Complaint*, 1969; and *Our Gang*, 1971), Roth depicted romantic relations between men and women who were, at most, a few years apart. Yet starting with *The Breast* (1972) the author hammered away at the old man/young woman theme for thirty-seven years, right on down to his penultimate novel, *The Humbling* (2009). Why are these types of relationships so much more common in his fiction than ones in which the lovers are roughly the same age?[62]

Given Lisa Halliday's comments above, we might speculate, boldly, as follows: Philip Roth wrote about these relations in fiction because Philip Roth experienced these relationships in nonfiction. Their peculiar dynamics intrigued him, both personally and professionally. Maybe he, too, once asked himself, as did an aging Kepesh, "How much longer can there possibly be girls?"[63] It's just a hunch. "Reverse biography" raises a question. Let the biographers dredge deeper, should they see fit.[64]

For my part, I'm more interested in the patterns, rules, and outcomes that govern the author's depictions of age-dissimilar romance. I draw your attention to four of them. The first iron law of these affairs is that absolutely no one should know about them. Consider this harangue delivered to "Philip" in *Deception*. "You wanted secrecy," charges one of his young lovers, "and our relationship was *distorted* by secrecy, by your almost paranoid efforts to keep the whole thing hidden. For the sake of your wife."[65]

Roth's other male characters also appear hell-bent on keeping their spouses in the dark. Whatever relation exists between E. I. Lonoff and Amy Bellette in *The Ghost Writer*, it is imperative that Hope Lonoff not get wind of it (which, of course, she eventually does). Mickey Sabbath tried (in vain) to keep the minutes of his sex chat with Kathy away not only from his wife but from the deans and human resources professionals at Athena College.

Unmarried persons also demand discretion. In *The Humbling*, Pegeen Stapleford, age forty, has her reasons for not wanting her parents to know about her dalliance with Simon Axler.[66] Maybe it's because Axler is sixty-five years old. Maybe it's because Pegeen's folks finally achieved peace with the idea that she was a lesbian.[67] Or maybe it's because Axler knows Pegeen's parents well. So much so, that he was present at Pegeen's birth!

Pegeen does finally divulge the truth. It is hard to know precisely why she suddenly leaves Axler. One surmises, however, that her parents' harsh disapproval has something to do with it all. A cruel corollary of the rule that an age-dissimilar romance must be kept secret is that it is nearly impossible to do so.[68]

This brings us to the second pattern that courses through these tales of intergenerational eroticism: the stigmatization of the lovers. Roth is an author who is fascinated by transgression and sanctimony. Whereas sanctimony outrages him, transgression is an endless source of intrigue. Roth explored the taboo of older men coupling with younger women from countless angles in countless novels. Nothing indicates he was particularly troubled by such unions. He does, however, seem exasperated by the rage that this association induces in wives, monogamous married men who "silently judge . . . or openly preach," women's studies professors, upstanding members of the community, and other scolds.[69]

Professor Delphine Roux of *The Human Stain* is a scold. Aside from letting Roth mock feminists and PC culture, this character helps him draw out one of his favorite moral equations: *sexual sanctimony masks sexual hypocrisy*. Delphine's inner monologues reveal a lot about this woman who led the prosecution of Coleman Silk's racial insensitivity. We learn that she's a bit of a racist.[70] We learn that she despises her feminist colleagues.[71] We also learn that she has a massive crush on Coleman Silk.[72] So, naturally, she sets out to destroy him. It is not a coincidence that *The Human Stain's* narrative is set during the "enormous piety binge" of the Clinton/Lewinsky scandal.[73] "If you haven't lived through 1998, you don't know what sanctimony is," writes Zuckerman.[74]

The scolds cannot see what Roth's fiction implores his readers to observe. Namely, that these romances *can* be serious, even dignified, affairs. Coleman Silk, Nathan Zuckerman, and David Kepesh (after his fall) are enamored of their soul mates. The longing is real. The conversations are genuine. Some of the women, like Faunia and Maria Zuckerman, value and "own" these relationships for reasons that seem believable. Roth is not naive enough to assume that women always enjoy these unions.

We could point to Diana Rutherford in *The Anatomy Lesson*, who has been mistreated by a long line of older men, including a deranged Nathan Zuckerman.[75] In general, however, Roth flags no moral concerns about romances between consenting adults, no matter what their age difference might be. He rarely asks if these relationships signal something sinister in the senior partner and deficient in the junior. Even when his women characters mature and reflect back on their older lovers (e.g., Amy Bellette in *Exit Ghost* and the unnamed former student in *Deception*), they harbor no resentment or complain that their innocence was manipulated.

We have spoken of the secrecy and stigma as recurring patterns. This brings us to our third and fourth features: bliss and catastrophe. The very thought of a relation with a younger woman is a comfort to an aging fellow. E. I. Lonoff in *The Ghost Writer*, age fifty-six, shares this lyrical reverie of what a new life with a younger woman might entail: "She would be thirty-five and she would make life beautiful for me. She would make life comfortable and beautiful and new. She would drive me in the afternoon to San Gimignano, to the Uffizi, to Siena. In Siena we would visit the cathedral and drink coffee in the square. At the breakfast table she would wear long feminine nightgowns under her pretty robe. They would be things I had bought for her in a shop by the Ponte Vecchio. I would work in a cool stone room with French windows. There would be flowers in a vase."[76]

A little later the fussy novelist drives Amy Bellette *and* his wife, inadvertently, out of his life. In *The Counterlife*, Henry Zuckerman's fragile heart fails him in pursuit of his "office blow job" with Wendy.[77] Sabbath has his academic career and marriage ruined because of the hullabaloo surrounding his leaked sex transcript. Pamela Solomon in *I Married a Communist* abandons the insufferable Ira Ringold. David Kepesh is razed down to his studs because of Consuela's departure. Faunia and Coleman are murdered. When Pegeen Stapleford dumps Simon Axler, he goes up to the attic, places the barrel of a gun into his mouth, and urges himself "to pretend that he was committing suicide in a play."[78]

The patterns of secrecy, stigma, and bliss we have been tracking also transpire in *Exit Ghost* (2007). Then someone perishes. Nathan Zuckerman, now aged seventy-one, falls for a married, thirty-year-old woman named Jamie Logan. Suffering from prostate cancer, Zuckerman recognizes "a yearning whose might I would have hoped had all but withered away."[79] He experiences the "bitter helplessness of a taunted old man dying to be whole again."[80] Even though the relation is likely never consummated, calamity is not far behind. By story's end we are informed that Zuckerman is "Gone for good."[81]

In *Asymmetry*, Alice groaned that her relationship with Ezra was not "normal." For Roth, that's *not* the drawback of age-dissimilar romances; his heroes rage against "normal." What the author seems to concede is that while such relationships can provide sexual thrills, genuine conversation, and emotional intimacy, they are simply unsustainable.[82]

# Misogyny and Autobiography

But *Portnoy's Complaint* was so hysterically funny, I howled all through it.
Philip to a T—doing *exactly* what he did to me, the morbid wacko sex fiend
and nonstop dick diddler with his obscene mouth. How many guys I knew
like that, all focused on their whangs and blaming Mom.

—ALICE DENHAM, *Sleeping with Bad Boys: A Juicy Tell-All
of Literary New York in the Fifties and Sixties*

Throughout his tumultuous career Philip Roth was repeatedly
asked about the relation between his life and his art. Were the
parents he lampooned in *Portnoy's Complaint* anything like his
own mom and dad? Did this or that randy male protagonist bear any
similarity to him? Remember that seductress portrayed in such and such
a novel, was she reminiscent of any woman he might have personally
known?

Pitched in a tone of unrelieved testiness, his answer to all of these queries
was always "no." In italics.[1] Roth was downright perturbed when his readers
spotted him lumbering like an erect Sasquatch through the forest of his own
fiction. In interview after interview, the famous author denied any causal
link between things he personally experienced and things he enshrined on
the page. He repeatedly cautioned us: do not assume that the figures and
ideas in his novels bear any relation to him, to individuals he personally
knew, or to ideas he may ever have held.

Here is Roth in 2014 making this point—and sounding far more didactic and cocksure than a thinker of his sophistication ought to be: "Whoever looks for the writer's thinking in the words and thoughts of his characters is looking in the wrong direction."[2] In 1981 he bristled at an interviewer who suggested his work may be "autobiography barely disguised."[3] Roth shot back that his goal was not to "reveal myself, exhibit myself, or even express myself" but to "invent myself . . . invent my worlds."[4]

To use a term very much of this #MeToo moment, Philip Roth was "gaslighting" his audience. Denying a neon-light-blinking truth, he commanded his readership to erect a mental Wall of Separation between his life and art. He urged them to fence off anything they might know about his biography, from anything they might read in his novels. Every now and then, however, the author would inadvertently breach his own barrier. We'll return to that below.

For now, I solemnly affirm that I consider these disavowals preposterous (and deeply frustrating). My affirmation is neither bold, nor original—more than a few critics before me have had the audacity to cross the master, and make this point.[5] But just so that there are no misunderstandings, permit me to review why Roth's denials are so absurd, and bewildering.

Philip Milton Roth wrote about fellows who greatly resembled Philip Milton Roth.[6] These "fictional" secular Jewish lads grew up in his very Newark neighborhood. They went to the same Weequahic high school that Roth ('50) graduated from. They matriculated at institutions of higher education sort of like Newark College of Rutgers and/or Bucknell, just like Philip did![7] They too served in the United States Army and were discharged because they suffered from chronic ailments whose provenance was unclear. The University of Chicago is where they then went to study and teach literature. In that same city, these Roth-like men met and cohabited with a troubled woman about whom we shall hear more in a moment. Eventually, they underwent intense psychoanalytic therapy.[8] And that just takes us to the mid-1960s!

Philip Roth not only wrote about guys like him, but women who knew guys like him. These lovers and wives were dragooned into his storyworlds. His early feminist critics, for their part, were incensed by these portrayals. They were, undoubtedly, well aware of a cardinal rule of pre-#MeToo literary analysis: never confuse an author with his characters. Nevertheless, they *did* "confuse" this author with his characters. It is our task to figure out if they were justified in doing so.

## Philip Roth: Misogynist?

To get our bearings, let's start by understanding how feminist writers engaged with Roth prior to the #MeToo era. The author had been accused of being a misogynist at least since the 1969 *Portnoy's Complaint* and its "CUNT CRAZY" central protagonist.[9] It didn't stop there. From *My Life as a Man* (1974), to *Sabbath's Theater* (1995), to *The Dying Animal* (2001), to his obituaries in 2018, the great author's alleged animus toward women was a subject of boundless and bitter contention. Shortly after his death, Lisa Halliday, a novelist and former lover of Roth, sighed in exasperation, "Every complaint that anyone has ever made tends to be, well, he's a misogynist."[10]

Two complaints, actually. If you analyze the vast commentary about Roth and women, you'll notice that two separate concerns often become fused. The first is that Philip Roth himself is a misogynist. The second is that his fiction is misogynistic. These assertions needn't always be coupled. Roth is certainly correct: fiction is not (necessarily) autobiography. When you write fiction, you are not always writing about yourself. You can—and likely, should—avail yourself of every opportunity to lie, dissimulate, and make stuff up. This means that an author who hates women has a creative license to mask that prejudice in his or her prose. Similarly, a nonmisogynistic novelist can indulge his or her dark side and compose sexist stories that elicit nightmares in readers. That's fiction!

In an interview I conducted with the novelist Cynthia Ozick, she articulated this principle with panache: "I am a nice Jewish girl. And I behave politely, and very nicely. I'm simply, you know, not evil. But when I write I am capable of becoming evil. I can fall into the satanic, the cruel, the violent. I can fall into the deepest heresy. I love heresy. I love magic. I love superstition. I love the gods-filled hymns of paganism. . . . In my outward role as a nice Jewish girl, I despise all these things and deride them as abominations."[11] Ms. Ozick's intervention helpfully reminds critics that, in theory, we must disentangle the person writing the prose from the prose that the person writes.

Many, however, refused to extend that critical courtesy to Philip Roth. His feminist detractors weren't just claiming that his stories were overpopulated by sexist men. They weren't just pointing out that an abundance of shrill, deranged, and broken ladies littered his storyworlds. No, they went further and drew the aforementioned link. Philip Roth *himself* hated women, they maintained, and *that* accounted for his misogynistic body of work.

Mary Allen, in a 1976 study, observed that Roth deployed his considerable talents in the service of his "enormous rage and disappointment with womankind."[12] "The women [in his fiction] are monstrous," Vivian Gornick argued, "because for Philip Roth women are monstrous."[13] A 2006 essay entitled "Philip Roth Hates Women" makes very similar points to a 2018 obituary with an almost identical title ("Philip Roth Hated Jewish Women"). In the first, Julia Keller, who is otherwise in awe of Roth's talent, complains that he has "a large and terrible flaw: his women have no souls."[14] In the second, Tamar Fox laments: "He hated me. Hated Jewish women. Wanted to fuck us, but primarily wanted to fuck us over."[15]

Roth, however, had defenders—many of whom would consider themselves feminists of one type or another. They generally left aside the question of what kind of guy Philip Roth was and focused solely on the fiction. The fiction, they concluded, was *not* misogynistic. We'll deal with that question in the next chapter. For now, I think it is important to understand why these writers absolved him of the charge of misogyny.

For some, his writing was descriptive, not prescriptive. He was using his art, they contended, to show us what people are really like, not to make the world a better place. "He wanted to know humanity, and to reflect it," insisted Lisa Halliday, "not to change it, or to make it into a moral project."[16] If he put misogyny into his fiction, that's because misogyny is part of our lives. For Maggie McKinley, following the lead of Chimamanda Ngozi Adichie and Zadie Smith, the "beautiful, ugly, heartbreaking, complicated, irresolvable center of Philip Roth's work" is that "people are not perfect."[17]

Some went further, suggesting that Roth in his prose was a kind of a feminist himself, a sister in struggle. Velichka Ivanova contends that in Roth's novels, "masculinity is problematic rather than assumed and natural."[18] Some readers even found Roth empowering. Meghan Daum "appreciated the honesty" of Roth's men behaving badly.[19] Through them, she understood that "any woman who sits across from a man in a bar is on some level sitting across from an ape."[20] "In granting me access to the interior lives of men," Daum observes, "he effectively handed their power to me."[21] In these more positive evaluations, Roth sounded the depths of a roiling testosterone ocean, hauling to the surface squalid, slithery truths about men and their creepy ways. All the better to know what terror down there lurks.

Looking over the secondary literature, I'd estimate that Roth's feminist detractors outnumbered his feminist supporters by a ratio of 8–2 or 7–3.[22] Still, the fact that Roth consistently finds defenders among feminist critics is, I think, significant. I doubt we'd see the same ratio among African American literary scholars who read chapter 1 of the present book.

This points to one key difference in the treatment of race and gender in Roth's writing. My assumption is that Philip Roth did not personally know many African American people. For a non-Black writer who wants to tell stories about Black people, it doesn't matter, to use the old racist adage, if "some of my best friends are Black." What matters is that this writer speaks and *listens* to lots of Black people, best friends or not. This is the starting point.

That Roth did not do this is evident from his stories; his Black characters are usually waiters, maids, or tap dancers. We learn more about their bodies than their thoughts. They have little to say, lurk in the margins, and are almost always one-dimensional. This author, by contrast, knew *many* (white) women. These women, especially those with whom he was romantically involved, surfaced prominently in his stories.

In terms of the #MeToo issues we've been tracking, this is where things get complicated.

## Maggie, Meta-, and Misogyny

Margaret Martinson Williams (or Maggie, as she was called) married Philip Roth in 1959.[23] They separated in 1962.[24] Maggie died in a car crash in 1968.[25] I've only seen one picture of her. I've never read a biography of her much longer than an epitaph. Almost everything I know about this woman I know because versions of her kept appearing in Philip Roth's novels.

In the 1974 *My Life as a Man*, there are *two* incarnations of Maggie, and both die awful, piteous deaths. The first "Maggie" is the character Maureen Tarnopol, married to Peter Tarnopol. Once a promising novelist, Peter recounts to us his woeful "True Story." A major portion of his tale centers on Maureen: how miserable she made him, how difficult it was for him to write amid her lunacy, how she poisoned his life for more than a decade.

In Peter's telling—and it's crucial to stress that *Peter* is telling this story—Maureen is jealous, manipulative, combustive, and demented. She fakes her own pregnancy.[26] Thereafter she fakes her own abortion.[27] She performs these ruses in an effort to have Peter marry her.[28] Peter does eventually agree to that but soon leaves her. Thereafter, he lives in penury because Maureen and her lawyer garnish his meager wages (though throughout that period he cohabits with a wealthy—and psychologically unwell—widow named Susan Seabury McCall).[29]

Peter and Maureen's disastrous union wends from fight to fight until Peter tries to murder her. The violence of this lengthy scene is unlike anything encountered in Roth's writing before or after. If I believed in trigger warnings, I'd issue one here:

> I stood up and went to the fireplace and picked up the black wrought-iron poker that Susan had bought for me in the Village. "And now," I announced, "I am going to kill you, as promised." No word from the floor, just a whimper. "I'm afraid they are going to have to publish your fiction posthumously, because I am about to beat your crazy, lying head in with this poker. I want to see your brains, Maureen. I want to see those brains of yours with my own eyes. I want to step in them with my shoes—and then I'll pass them along to Science. God only knows what they'll find. Get ready, Maureen, you're about to die horribly."
>
> I could make out now the barely audible words she was whimpering: "Kill me," she was saying. . . . "kill me kill me—" as oblivious as I was in the first few moments to the fact that she had begun to shit into her underwear. The smell had spread around us before I saw the turds swelling the seat of her panties. "Die me," she babbled deliriously— "die me good, die me long—"[30]

Peter tried, but failed, to kill Maureen. Peter rejoices, however, when six months later she dies in a car crash: "Called to her eternal rest, the miserable bitch."[31] Then again, the story ends with his "eyes leaking" and "teeth chattering."[32]

If one ever wanted to argue that leading male writers of the twentieth century formed something of a Boys' Club, one need look no further than the way Roth's chum, Milan Kundera, read *My Life as a Man*. The great Czech novelist was also triggered by the scene of Maureen's beating. *But the trigger was provided by Maureen's depravity, not Peter's.* "I know her by heart through my nightmares," whinged Kundera; "from the time I was eighteen I have feared one day becoming her victim, and all my life I have constantly been defending myself against her dreaded attacks."[33]

For the most part, however, critics were taken aback by the depictions of Maureen in *My Life as a Man*. "Misogyny," wrote Vivian Gornick, "leaks like a slow, inky poison all over its pages, obscuring artistic coherence, disintegrating moral intelligence."[34] Barbara Quart observed that this "desperate" "tedious" novel "give[s] the sense of drowning in obsessive self-justification and self-pity."[35]

*My Life as a Man* is an experimental novel, and this is relevant to our attempt to understand these links between autobiography and misogyny in Roth. The entire book is like a vast weapons testing ground where Roth detonated all sorts of new narrative ordinance.[36] One of which was to show us the imperfect short stories that Peter wrote under duress. We actually get to read those tales at the *beginning* of *My Life as a Man*. The stories have their moments, but for the most part they are uneven, unfocused, and poorly paced. They read like drafts, texts that could use a lot more editing and shaping.[37]

Meta-master Roth is keen to make a point about the artistic process. He wants to show us that the dismal circumstances of Peter's life impelled him to write dismal fictions. In an existence so full of tumult it is difficult for Peter to summon the psychic acuity to create great art. I salute Roth for his writerly courage. He begins *My Life as a Man* with subpar writing. Most novelists want to open with their best stuff, the stuff that will hook their readers, mesmerize the critics, reduce other writers to alcoholism, etc. Roth doesn't do that. He doesn't do that because of his fealty to metafiction. He wants us to grasp that we are reading stories Peter wrote while in a state of psychic freefall. All of which is to say, Roth took some real artistic risks.[38]

One of the stories Peter wrote, and we read, is based on Maureen. "Courting Disaster (Or, Serious in the Fifties)" is about a writer named Nathan (who resembles Peter) who marries a woman named Lydia (who resembles Maureen). Lydia was the victim of sexual assault by her father when she was twelve.[39] In her first marriage, Lydia endured a physical and psychological battering. Scarcely capable of holding down a job, she is given to fits of emotional volatility. Her institutionalization in a mental hospital occurred when she was found consuming for breakfast "a bowl full of kitty litter, covered with urine and a sliced candle."[40] Lydia commits suicide by slitting her wrists with a can opener.[41] Nathan eventually seduces her daughter, and when she is sixteen, they run off to Italy.[42]

So, yes, Roth *really* took risks in *My Life as a Man*. One of which was swamping the novel with insane, unlikable, and victimized women, all of whom were based on women he knew personally. Another risk was sketching protagonists, like Peter and Nathan, who so resembled Philip Roth.

### Revenge (Porn)? "The Motive Dictating Everything"

*My Life as a Man* dizzyingly and exhaustingly asked a question about the relation between life and art. Peter, as we noted, endured terrible experiences with Maureen. This led him to "imagine" Nathan's terrible experiences with Lydia. This pattern raises an obvious query: what compelled *Philip Roth* to "imagine" Peter and Maureen and Nathan and Lydia? Could it be that Philip Roth is bleeding *his* personal experiences onto Peter's pages, just as Peter bled his onto Nathan's?

Scholars have long suspected this was the case. Ira Nadel refers to *My Life as a Man* as "a painful look at [his] first marriage" to Margaret Martinson Williams.[43] But this was not the first or last time Roth wrote about Maggie. The scholar Julie Husband maintains that the (less dark) Martha Reganhart, in the 1962 *Letting Go,* was modeled on Williams as well.[44] The biographer Claudia Roth Pierpont—the unparalleled master of prying sexual secrets out of Philip Roth—argues that the abused Lucy Nelson in *When She Was Good* (1967) was also based on the enigmatic Maggie.[45] She refers to that novel as "an obsessive work, deeply personal if strictly disciplined, about the destruction of the soul of the woman he felt had nearly destroyed him."[46]

In the 1988 *The Facts: A Novelist's Autobiography,* Maggie is resurrected. Sort of. Her name is changed to Josie Jensen (why? At this point she had been deceased for twenty years). Her ex-husband, "Philip Roth," recounts her fake pregnancy and fake abortion—territory he had marched his readers through in *My Life as a Man.*[47]

Though in *The Facts* Roth finally started to achieve some critical distance. The portrait of a psychotic Maureen Tarnopol in *My Life as a Man,* he now concedes, was an act of (failed) revenge on Maggie.[48] He even admits that she played a role in his growth as an artist. At first, his rage and anger toward her were "the motive dictating everything."[49] Roth believes, however, that he finally grew up and figured out a way to use his hatred for her to better inspire his art. This remarkable concession, I caution you, is made at the end of *The Facts: A Novelist's Autobiography;* what's true and not true in this text is hard to discern (see chapter 7). So take it for what it is when Nathan

Zuckerman (!) explains to Philip Roth (!) that Josie (i.e., Maggie) is the person who made him who he is. "Everything you are today," Zuckerman taunts Roth, "you owe to an alcoholic shiksa."[50]

Just when it seemed that our author had achieved "closure," Maureen is exhumed yet again in the 1993 *Operation Shylock: A Confession*. Gazing at a hellion named Wanda Jane "Jinx" Possesski, Philip Roth marvels at her "racial resemblance to the square-headed northern good looks of my long-dead enemy."[51] Convinced that she is Maureen reincarnate (or "the fucked-up shiksa," as he now calls her), he blurts out: "Can't you even return from *death* without screaming about the morality of your position versus the immorality of mine?"[52]

In sum, his volcanic rage toward this woman spewed a lava trail of sulfurous fiction. Consider that nine versions of her have been identified by scholars in eight of his novels from 1962 to 1993.[53] Appropriately enough, Roth's last published comment about Maggie was, "I don't owe her shit."[54]

But his treatment of his first wife was no one-off, or youthful indiscretion. The author repeatedly inserted other romantic partners into his novels. Ann Mudge, described by Ira Nadel as a "New York socialite and Roth's companion from roughly 1964 to 1969," is assumed to be "the prototype of 'The Pilgrim' (Sarah Maulsby) in *Portnoy's Complaint* and Susan McCall in *My Life as a Man*."[55] She appears as May Aldridge in *The Facts*, and perhaps as a wife to the unnamed protagonist in *Everyman*.[56]

In 1968 Roth eased away from Mudge, as he met another woman twelve years younger than he. Her name is Barbara Sproul. She bears resemblances to the saintly and soon-to-be-ignominiously-dumped Claire Ovington, whom we meet in *The Breast* and the *Professor of Desire*.[57]

Let's never forget that Gayle Milman, a "quick-witted, intelligent, and vivacious" Jewish woman, was the clay from which Dina Dornbusch emerged in *My Life as a Man*.[58] Then there is the person upon whom Maria Zuckerman is based in *The Counterlife*. Claudia Roth Pierpoint will not name her but speaks of Roth's "secret affair" with a person who was "English, an Oxford graduate, and initially called to interview him for the BBC."[59]

There are many more. Janet Hobhouse, the novelist who wrote about Roth in *The Furies*, likely makes a cameo in *Deception*.[60] Drenka Balich, the sexual decathlete from *Sabbath's Theater*, naturally "was initially inspired by a married Connecticut neighbor with whom he had begun an affair in the late 70s."[61] Most of these important revelations were brought to us by Philip Roth's confidante and literary biographer, Claudia Roth Pierpoint.

In light of her diligent labor extracting this material, I am baffled as to why she warns us that "there is no older or more familiar trap in reading Roth's work . . . than to mistake a book's voice for the author's autobiographical confession."[62] This may be a trap with other writers, but as her own book indicates, *not with this one*. A few sentences after issuing this warning, she then points out that Roth "did have a torrid affair . . . with a forty-year-old former lesbian," just like Simon Axler had in *The Humbling!*[63]

It is widely thought that the author was settling scores in the 1998 *I Married a Communist*, published when he was sixty-five years old. That novel featured the character of Eve Frame, a mock-up of Roth's ex-wife, the actress Claire Bloom. The portrayal of her as a manipulative, hysterical, self-hating Jewish woman is a nasty piece of work. Many agree this sketch was meant as a revenge killing for Bloom's own unflattering rendering of Roth in *Leaving a Doll's House*.[64]

For those keeping tally—and gasping—at how many women from Roth's life ended up downstream, floating in his literary lagoons (nine so far and a tenth en route below), we should recall that there are likely many more we don't know about. These nine instances lead me to agree, in one particular way, with charges of misogyny leveled at Roth. I am not saying that Roth the Man was a misogynist (though he might have been; a biographer can explore that possibility). Nor that his fiction, in and of itself, is misogynistic (see the next chapter). Rather, I contend that the act of transposing the anger he feels toward a woman/women he *personally* knows into fiction created for public consumption is misogynistic. His art is functioning as a form of retribution.

"Revenge porn" provides an intriguing analogy. Defined as "the intentional embarrassment of identifiable individuals through the posting of nude images online," revenge porn retains a few intriguing similarities to the way Roth exposed Maggie and Claire Bloom.[65] In both, a male takes the most intimate moments of a relationship with a woman and uses a platform, be it literary or digital, to broadcast them to a larger public. In both, the goal is to humiliate, intimidate, and avenge a perceived slight. Obviously writing a novel is a more aesthetically challenging feat than shooting a poorly lighted video surreptitiously. Yet from the point of view of the victimized woman whose confidence and consent are violated, the discomfort will be similar.

And let it never be said that Roth was unaware of the pain that this kind of fictional exposure could induce. In *The Counterlife* various characters express their outrage upon discovering that confidences they shared with Nathan Zuckerman were slated to appear in his next novel.[66] "He was a

Zulu . . . a pure cannibal, murdering people, eating people," cries his brother Henry Zuckerman upon reading the manuscript in which a few of his dalliances with women are exposed.[67] As we shall see, Roth was frank in confessing that "exploiting personal intimacy and betraying confidences" was his professional obligation.[68] This may be true, but it does not clear him of the charge of misogyny.

### Roth-like Men

As we reflect on the interplay between Roth's art, life, and the misogyny of which he is accused, I call your attention to a letter I found in the Library of Congress, dated April 13, 1959. It reads: "Our client, Miss Maxine Groffsky, informs us that you have written a work of fiction in which she is not only recognizably portrayed as are members of her family but, in addition, she claims you have traduced and maligned her."[69] The reference is to the character Brenda Patimkin in the 1959 novella "Goodbye, Columbus."

This example can be crane-dumped atop an existing landfill of evidence proving that autobiographical details pervade Roth's fiction. Scholars have amassed this heap of data almost inadvertently. We are, after all, not biographers (see the introduction to this volume). But, on the backstroke, we keep learning more about this looping interface between Roth's art and his life.

When Alan Cooper was studying Roth's relationship to Judaism, he realized that "whole episodes and some key plots of the sixties' and seventies' novels were indeed drawn from Roth's young adult life, that major characters were fictionalizations of friends, relatives, lovers, and his first wife."[70] When Jeffrey Berman conducted his research on psychoanalysis in Roth's novels, he concluded, "It is now clear that Roth's fiction is more autobiographical than anyone has suggested."[71] Neither was scavenging for biographical treasures. Nor was I when I watched PBS's *Philip Roth: Unmasked:* I did not expect the author to casually drop that the unnamed protagonist in *Everyman* was "drawn from certain aspects of my brother's experience."[72] The point is, the more Roth you read, the more Roth you know, so to speak.

All of this means we must push back, *hard,* against this author's repeated denials that autobiography surfaced in his fiction. We should ignore Roth (and Zuckerman), who howled about dim readers and dumb critics.[73] Rather, we should give ear to Alvin Pepler, a weird fellow we encounter in *Zuckerman Unbound:* "Fiction is not autobiography, yet all fiction, I am convinced, is in some sense rooted in autobiography, though the connection to actual events may be tenuous indeed, even non-existent. We are, after all, the total of our experiences, and experience includes not only what we in fact do but what we privately imagine. An author cannot write about what he does not know."[74]

And this wasn't the only time the author recognized this possibility. Consider this fascinating rumination on his craftwork made in 1984: "Making fake biography, false history, concocting a half-imaginary existence out of the actual drama of my life *is* my life. . . . *You don't necessarily, as a writer, have to abandon your biography completely to engage in an act of impersonation. It may be more intriguing when you don't. You distort it, caricature it, parody it, you torture and subvert it, you exploit it*—all to give the biography that dimension that will excite your verbal life."[75]

Aha! Here, Roth acknowledged *some* autobiographical influence on his writing. The fiction, apparently, wasn't totally sealed off from his experiences as a man.[76] Valuable as this concession may be, I think much more than "impersonation" transpires in Roth's stories. There's a good deal of fairly straightforward, albeit brilliantly transfigured, autobiography in his writing—nothing wrong with that. That's fiction too! It's the *transfiguring* wherein his unique artistry lies. We Roth scholars need to understand the transfiguring.

His early feminist critics who linked the fiction with the man weren't off the mark. His unique voice granted his audience access to raw male modalities—lust, impotence, oedipal rage, and so forth. These thrills, as with all thrills, had a downside. The turbulent Roth-like men who stomped through his novels had intense, messy dealings with women—women who resembled women whom Philip Roth knew outside of the novels. These women in his life resurface in his prose. And it is here that the charge of misogyny becomes hard to avoid.

That's because these women were not so much invented by an author indulging an artist's license to be woman-hating, or "evil," as Cynthia Ozick put it. Rather, they appear to have been catapulted upon the page directly out of his mental tumult. In other words, Roth did not "invent," "distort," "caricature," "parody," "torture," and "subvert" his own feelings about these women *enough*. When it came to his rage toward certain women, he didn't transfigure strenuously.

My recommendation is that from here on in, we flip the paradigm. We should always assume that Roth's fiction provides plausible clues to his life *unless proven otherwise*. Naturally there will be lots of "proven otherwise." Yet I do not see how we can any longer discount glaringly obvious facts: Philip Roth's fiction was inextricably linked to his experiences.

This means we need to effectuate a mental shift. We must abandon our reluctance to correlate Art with Life—thanks to the #MeToo moment, that's suddenly doable. The intellectual challenge is to analyze how Roth's life was transfigured into fiction. The process involved the treatment of raw autobiographical sludge into potable literary products. Zuckerman had his own metaphor. He described it as "intertwin[ing] the facts *with* the imagination."[77] Our job is to reveal the rules governing this operation. What facts did he intertwine? What facts wouldn't he intertwine, and why? How much distance from an event did he need before he intertwined it with art?

Alongside the "racial biography" proposed earlier, maybe someone should take a crack at a gendered biography as well. This study would look at the women in Roth's life (including his mother) and ask how they surfaced in his art. In dribs and drabs, we've already gained some insight into both these matters. Many are those who took it upon themselves to write about Roth.

To read former *Playboy* playmate Alice Denham's account of her evenings with him in the early 1960s is to read about Roth as a raging sex-fiend, a phallus waiting to discharge.[78] To read his ex-wife's, Claire Bloom, in *Leaving a Doll's House* is to encounter an egotistical, misogynistic monster.[79] To read Alan Lelchuk's *Ziff: A Life?* is to glimpse a Mephistophelian ladies' man.[80] To read Lisa Halliday's *Asymmetry* is to meet a needy, but ultimately likable, sexed-up old geezer.[81] To read Janet Hobhouse's *The Furies* is to observe an intriguing but aloof and fanatically secretive lover.[82]

To read Claudia Roth Pierpont's *Roth Unbound* is to be wowed by how often the women in his life were reprocessed into prose. In her sections on Roth's tortured marriage to Maggie, she asks: "What does it mean for a writer to put someone he considers a psychopath at the center of a novel?"[83] To me, it means that Roth's demurrals about the Wall of Separation between his life and his art are, I repeat, preposterous. It means we need a critical, distanced, biography that delves into his relationship with her and other women. It means we need a critical, distanced biography of Maggie—a woman who Roth repeatedly dragged into his turbulent, self-referential storyworlds. Last, it might mean that our writer was spot-on when he told Pierpont, "There are two things to fear in life: death and biography."[84]

# · 4 ·

# Before We Conclude That Roth's
# Fiction Is Misogynistic

Misogyny, a hatred of women, provides my work with neither a structure,
a meaning, a motive, a message, a conviction, a perspective, or a guiding
principle . . . as though I have spewed venom on women for half a century.
But only a madman would go to the trouble of writing 31 books in order to
affirm his hatred.

> —PHILIP ROTH, "My Life as a Writer: Interview
> with Daniel Sandstrom"

I feel the presence of Philip Roth in a Philip Roth novel more than I
feel the presence of any other novelist in any novel that I've ever read.
Flaubert may have proclaimed *"Madame Bovary c'est moi,"* but when I
read about Emma and her travails, I don't ask myself: *"Is she Gustave?"*[1] As I
peruse Toni Morrison's *Beloved,* I don't assume she's hovering off to the side
somewhere while Baby Suggs gathers the community and preaches from "a
huge flat-sided rock."[2] Even with autofictional works, I don't sense the specter of the flesh-and-blood author so intensely. I enjoyed Chris Kraus's *I Love
Dick.*[3] The text didn't, however, make me think that much about its central
protagonist, the "39-year-old experimental filmmaker" Chris Kraus.[4]

When I read most Philip Roth novels, it's different. There he is. Hanging
around. I can't stop noticing him. Atop the thin ledge of my book cover he
prances, pretending to be a tightrope walker. Sometimes he sits down and
cracks out a fishing pole. Legs dangling, he stares plaintively ahead in a
dead-on spoof of the act of staring plaintively ahead. Looking at us, with
"those fucking orbs" of his.[5] He's there, in and around the fiction.

Philip Roth is in and around his fiction. That's his choice. That's his charm. That's his aesthetic. But when he dragoons women he knew into the fiction as well, this leaves him vulnerable to the charge of misogyny. In the previous chapter, I argued that there *was* something venomous—to use his term—about how he vengefully ferried his romantic partners into his prose. It is in this *nexus* between his life and his art where a charge of misogyny seems most warranted. I call this Roth, "Nexus Roth." He's the Roth who transforms, refines, alchemizes, or caramelizes his personal experiences and then processes them into stories.[6]

This even includes his personal experiences of being called a misogynist! How "meta-" is that? In *The Anatomy Lesson,* a strung-out Nathan Zuckerman laments the fact that he is considered one of the "top misogynists in the arts."[7] He recalls with dismay a magazine cover which shrieked: "WHY DOES THIS MAN HATE WOMEN?"[8] "Those girls," Zuckerman sighs, "meant business."[9] Maybe Roth sighed as well, since this is the title of an actual 1976 piece in the *Village Voice.*[10]

He's at it again in *Deception.* "Philip" and a lover gleefully conduct a mock trial: "You are charged with sexism, misogyny, woman abuse, slander of women, denigration of women, defamation of women, and ruthless seduction. . . . You are one with the mass of men who have caused women great suffering and extreme humiliation. . . . Why did you portray Mrs. Portnoy as a hysteric? Why did you portray Lucy Nelson as a psychopath? Why did you portray Maureen Tarnopol as a liar and a cheat? Does this not defame and denigrate women? Why do you depict women as shrews, if not to malign them?"[11] Life experience has been recycled into text.

In this chapter, I want to think about an oft-made accusation. Namely, that Roth's *fiction* is misogynistic. In order to do this, I find it useful to think of three Roths. First, there is Real Roth. He lived in a clapboard farmhouse, breathed air, and loved baseball. Only a biographer can reveal whether Real Roth was a misogynist. Next, there is Nexus Roth, the guy who loops his life into his fiction (and back again?). That two-dimensional fellow, I have concluded, can be labeled a misogynist.

Then there's the actual, 8,500 fictional pages he composed. Just the words on the page. I refer to this as Page Roth. In what follows, I am going to concentrate mostly on Page Roth—the writings themselves. By doing so, we will see that it is hard to conclude that this Roth writes misogynistic fiction.

Naturally, we need to articulate a clear definition of "misogynistic fiction." Easier said than done. We know what misogyny is. But what misogyny is *in fiction*—that's much harder to pinpoint. Blame it on literature; its bag of tricks is bursting with narrative voicings, authorial peek-a-boo, perspectival multiplicity, indeterminacy, and so much else. Unanimous verdicts are hard to reach. The best writers turn their audiences into hung juries.

To set the conversation in motion, I propose three imperfect criteria. We might think of misogynistic fiction as characterized by (1) a paucity of female characters, voices, perspectives, etc., (2) a preponderance of female characters with negative characteristics, and (3) asymmetries in how men and women are depicted by an author. With that said, let's try and see if Page Roth's fiction is misogynistic.

## The "Women-Curious" Phase: 1960–1967

We'll begin with the proposition that there are few women characters in Roth's writing. That is demonstrably false. Though, as we shall see in a moment, Roth in his salad days did exhibit that tendency for a while.[12]

What is true, I believe, is that there is a moderate-to-substantial difference in how much effort, energy, and imagination the author invested in portraits of both genders. One critic accused him of "avoidance of the psychological penetration of his female compatriots."[13] Another suggests that when it comes to women, "Roth doesn't bother to get beneath their skins with the same reckless elan with which he tunnels past the obfuscating epidermis of his male characters."[14] I think these observations are often valid, but they need to be tweaked in light of the broader analysis we are going to undertake.

There are, indeed, far more male protagonists, and male characters, and uniquely male-centered dilemmas (e.g., impotence, prostate cancer, etc.) across his body of work. This doesn't necessarily mean Roth ignored or neglected female characters. It also doesn't mean that he didn't try to train the full arsenal of his literary intellect on their depiction. In fact, he tried from an early age. Insofar as this effort is completely overlooked or unknown, it might be helpful to consider it here.

I'd like to draw your attention to his writings between 1960 and 1967, or what I call the "Women-Curious" phase. During that interval Real Roth had a rough go of it. His marriage to Maggie came undone in 1962. "I was in hell," he told PBS; "I couldn't write."[15] Maybe. But he actually published a fair amount, before and *after* 1962. In this span, representations of women abound. We need to factor this material into any consideration of Page Roth's supposed misogyny.

This "Women-Curious" phase is sandwiched in between the sexist outrages of the 1969 *Portnoy's Complaint,* and the tedium of Roth's male-dominated early works. Prior to 1960, the writer's stories weren't so much demeaning to women as they were completely uninterested in them (which is demeaning in a different way).[16] His Bucknell juvenilia of 1952 through 1954 are almost bereft of female characters (an elderly Roth would refer to those pieces as "awful little things").[17] The next tales, from 1954 to 1959, usually feature all-male casts.[18] This includes six pieces in the 1959 collection *Goodbye, Columbus.* All but one have extremely minor roles for women, or no roles at all. The exception is the novella "Goodbye, Columbus," and its whip-smart heroine, Brenda Patimkin. Her fierce energy catapults Roth into the 1960s and into more textured female portraiture.

Now we get to the intriguing interval between 1960 and 1967.[19] Roth publishes two novels and two short stories which mark a radical departure from what came before and what came after. What's different? For one thing, gendered perspective; for the first time in his career the thought processes of women appear in Roth's prose. To use a technical term, the author probes the "interiority" of female characters.

*Letting Go,* of 1962, features delicate and detailed representations of two complex and thoughtful women, Libby Herz and Martha Reganhart. The 1967 *When She Was Good* takes a deep dive into the unraveling mind of Lucy Nelson, plausibly construed as a victim of Middle American patriarchy. The portrayals of the heroines have been canvassed by many scholars, and I have little of substance to add.[20] My interest lies in two obscure short stories from the same era. Both are focalized solely through the consciousness of women. Both remain almost completely unstudied by Roth scholars.

"The Good Girl" appeared in the May 1960 issue of *Cosmopolitan* magazine. The tale is recounted through the spry mind of Laurie Bowen, an underclassman at Cornell University.[21] This eighteen-year-old Elizabeth Taylor look-alike is under almost constant sexual siege from "[the] desperate advances of her young men friends."[22] One clever swain, a graduate student, regaled her with the observation that she had "the eyes of a Modigliani nude."[23] But Laurie fends off every one of these suitors by recourse to a graceful stiff-arm technique.[24] Doing anything otherwise, she believes, would consign her to the emotional misery experienced by her promiscuous female acquaintances. In her reflections on other women, she correlates momentary sexual pleasure with long-term psychic pain.[25]

The story opens up with Laurie returning home from a date, a belly-dancing performance no less, with one Richard Renner of Brown University.[26] Predation ensues. In the lobby of her parents' apartment, an inebriated Renner propositions Laurie and refuses to take no for an answer: "his fingers . . . had spread wider and wider, and were now at the very highest point of what Laurie could allow herself to think of as her waist."[27] The self-possessed young woman repulses what, in the present era, would be considered a sexual assault. Flustered though she may be, Laurie parses the episode with a blithe world-weariness that balances apprehension with a sense of humor (perhaps this is where Roth's gendered limitations are most evident; most women would not find much humor in this situation).

Richard, for his part, is undeterred. Forcing his way on to the elevator, he "corralled her in a corner. He kept her pinned with elbows and knees."[28] Laurie's subsequent inner dialogue is certainly not in the #MeToo spirit. She concedes that she fancies her tormentor: "she really wouldn't mind kissing him. She was—to use a word she found at once vague and childish—attracted to him."[29] Laurie eventually does dispatch Richard, only to alight into her parents' apartment at the height of a drunken party.

Dodging middle-aged revelers, Laurie immediately retreats to the bathroom. There she sullenly reflects on her evening and on the sexually adventurous (and hence emotionally scarred) woman she is not.[30] Then, standing in front of the mirror, Laurie does something unexpected: "she closed her eyes, humming, and like the [belly] dancer reached her hands up to her breasts. She began to move her hips in a slow circle."[31]

Laurie is changing. But why? Was it artless Richard's predatory advance? Was it her encounter with party guest Cynthia "Crazylegs" Lasser, Cornell '36, who drunkenly accuses Laurie of both prudery and promiscuity (and who endorses the latter)?[32] Was it the sight of a desired, but already half-consumed, postparty apple, that set her off?[33] It's not entirely clear why her soul undergoes this transformation, yet by story's end, the emotional temperature of the tale rises considerably. With her "glistening Modigliani eyes," she advances toward her room.[34] Laurie enters the "dark privacy of her bed, where oriental music rose like a fever in her brain."[35] This "good girl," Roth leads us to believe, is about to do something bad.

Leaving aside the pervy voyeurism of it all (the accompanying *Cosmopolitan* illustration shows Laurie in bra and panties being tugged to perdition by the woozy Ms. Lasser), I note the following. First, twenty-seven-year-old Philip Roth is trying to imagine how a woman might conceptualize a handsy, sexually aggressive fellow—*like him!* Yes, I know, Real Roth has infiltrated our discussion of Page Roth. But I couldn't help myself. I think of Alice Denham's memoir of her dates with Roth in this period.[36] This helps me visualize the Real Roth in Renner (or should we say the Renner in Real Roth?).

But back to Page Roth. The fact that Laurie appears poised to pleasure herself is significant. A properly misogynistic climax to the story might have depicted the aroused young women hankering for date-rapist Richard. Too, the tale seems prescient. In 1960 America's sexual revolution is looming; one could easily see "good girl" Laurie morphing into a "free love" Flower Child and wandering about Haight-Ashbury without any shoes.

If Roth possessed something like a feminist consciousness, it is not apparent in this story. But trying to represent a young woman's conscious-ness was his objective in "The Good Girl." He may have missed the mark, but it's not as if he was uncurious about women or made no effort to under-stand their perspective.

## Women = Men

Philip Roth's female friends steadfastly denied that a hatred of women informed his work. Claudia Roth Pierpoint protests: "He writes about women the same way he writes about men. . . . He has all kinds of female characters in his work, and none of them are more bad or good than the men. They're looked at exactly the same way."[37] Reflecting on charges made against Roth's writing, she concluded, "I don't believe for a moment that he's a misogynist in his work, no."[38] Pierpoint oversells the argument, but the "Women-Curious" phase does render her assertion more plausible. Laurie is, in fact, *exactly* like Roth's archetypal male protagonists: she undergoes sudden, radical *change* (see my next chapter).

This brings us to a somewhat better story, "The Psychoanalytic Special" of 1964. The piece tries to reveal the mind-set of a serial adulteress. Thirty-one-year-old Ella Wittig commutes to Manhattan weekly in order to see her psychologist.[39] She is trying to stanch the pain of a recent affair gone awry.[40] Ella specifically chooses a male therapist, Dr. Spielvogel (yes, that Dr. Spielvogel!).[41] With her female psychoanalyst, Ella complains, "she was continually having to defend herself against the charge of promiscuity."[42] As in "The Good Girl," women are depicted as policing one another's confor-mity to sexual standards.

In light of the #MeToo moment, a few points are of relevance. Crucially, there is no "slut-shaming" in "The Psychoanalytic Special." Ella has had a variety of sexual encounters—three husbands, three lovers, six one-night stands (a seventh by the conclusion, and an eighth possibly en route).[43] Yet Page Roth does not play her passions for facile laughs. "The charge of promiscuity," we are told, "was *inapplicable* in her case."[44] This woman is deeply invested in her paramours, to the detriment of her husband and young daughter. Her goal is to find the man who will be her "eternal husband."[45] Ella is as serious about her lover(s) as Emma Bovary and Anna Karenina are about Rodolphe and Vronsky, respectively (and like Anna, she has an affinity for trains).

Ella may be indeed serious, but Roth is acutely aware of how paradoxical her quest is. She invariably gets bored of whomever her present partner might be. Then she finds someone new. Then the pattern repeats. Reflecting amid the rubble of her February-to-June affair, she exclaims, "What had happened with Perry must never happen to her again."[46] Locked in misery, *she* must find the key and let herself out. "Yes, she craved freedom—but only so as to be taken again. And this time for good."[47]

That this heroine resembles a male Roth hero is a point that should not be underestimated (that she resembles Roth himself is a thesis one might devise after reading Benjamin Taylor's memoir of his friend, "an ardent lover and a sexual anarch").[48] Like Laurie above, Ella is in flux. She construes her adulterous affairs as a portal to transformation (e.g., "Desperately she wanted to be changed" to become "a new woman").[49] Further, Ella's thought process is similar to that of later Roth heroes. In chapter 6, we'll survey his proclivity for portraying men in a state of frenzied mental overdrive. Ella is cut from the same cloth. Her inner dialogues are brimming with confusion, vulnerability, and insight.[50] In a charming aside, Ella observes: "it did not dull the pain any to be energetically aware of every detail."[51]

Ella is a peculiar and passionate woman. We should note that twenty years later Page Roth explored this personality type again. "His Mistress's Voice," published in the 1986 *Partisan Review*, is also rarely studied. Our unnamed woman narrator speaks in the first person. She rehearses her frustrations with her mother, her lover the district attorney, and another lover (who resembles Philip Roth). Her narrative is long and convoluted, interrupted by paroxysms of rage. The final page clarifies matters somewhat. There, the woman intimates she is about to commit suicide. Is this because the Philip-like lover (?) wrote her a note in which he told her to "Take a 747. Go away"?[52]

In any case, all the works above suggest we tweak or reassess charges of misogyny. Each is about a woman. Each tale treats the heroine in ways that later heroes are treated. Each grants us access to the interiority of a complicated person. Whether Roth actually understands these women is a different issue. As is the question of whether these pieces rise to the level of sublime literature.

## Misogynistic Counterfactuals

As we saw in chapter 3, the accusation was often made that Roth's fiction abounds in women who are unwell and unlikable. This claim, in and of itself, is factually correct.

This isn't, however, proof positive of Page Roth's misogyny. That's because there are all sorts of other women who populate his storyworlds. Kind women. Industrious women. Thoughtful women. Not every Rothian female is as deranged as Lydia Ketterer of *My Life as a Man,* or as world-wrecking as Pegeen Stapleford of *The Humbling.* Roth's detractors have assailed him for this portraiture. In fairness to him, we need to look at numerous counterfactuals.

Let's start with his many Jewish mothers. This might seem like an awfully strange subset of data to invoke when defending this author from charges of misogyny. The younger Roth garnered feminist outrage for his savage sketches of Jewish matriarchs.[53] One thinks of his depiction of Mrs. Patimkin in the 1959 "Goodbye Columbus."[54] Even that cold suburbanite is a breath of fresh air compared to the mother lampooned in *Portnoy's Complaint.* Roth's relentless mock-up of Sophie Portnoy ("She sews, she knits, she darns—she irons better even than the *schvartze.* . . . she alone is good") was so corrosive that a critic placed him among "vengeful little boys who blame their powerlessness on their *Yiddishe mommes* and other women who faintly resemble them."[55]

Maybe Roth was stung by the criticism. I strongly suspect he was. For after *Portnoy's Complaint* he suddenly stopped fracking this rich, comic Jewish Mother Earth. No longer would we encounter exclamations such as: "BECAUSE WE CAN'T TAKE ANYMORE! BECAUSE YOU FUCKING JEWISH MOTHERS ARE JUST TOO FUCKING MUCH TO BEAR!"[56]

Instead, post-*Portnoy's,* he started ladling out Jewish matriarchs so virtuous that they appear to have leaped off of the pages of the book of Proverbs, freshly polished silverware in hand. Steadfastly devoted to their children and families, they cling to their Jewish faith, serenely but tenaciously. Their decency, loyalty, and common sense inoculates them from being likened to a witch or a "big smothering bird beating frantic wings about my face and mouth *so that I cannot even get my breath,*" as was Sophie Portnoy.[57]

In *The Anatomy Lesson* a touching portrait is drawn of Selma Zuckerman. Nathan's mother is described as "a quiet, simple woman, dutiful and inoffensive."[58] While recovering from a stroke, her neurologist asked her to write her name on a piece of paper. She jotted the word "'Holocaust,' perfectly spelled"—an inscription that unnerves her son.[59] Like many of Roth's post-*Portnoy* moms, Selma might not be boisterous in her public commitments to her religion, but she is nevertheless a Jew through and through.[60]

In *The Plot Against America* we encounter a similar type. Her name is Bess Finkel Roth, which just happens to be the name of Philip Roth's actual mother. "Her job," writes our narrator named Philip Roth, "was to hold our world together as calmly and as sensibly as she could; that was what gave her life fullness and that was all she was trying to do."[61] Mama Roth is full of emotional intelligence—which she needs because her son and sister are Nazi sympathizers, and her nephew and husband almost kill one another in a living room brawl.[62]

Mothers aside, we find in Roth's work what we might call "wise lovers." These are smart women who ultimately make intelligent decisions—like the decision to flee Page Roth's male protagonists. Karen Oakes in *My Life as a Man* is a nineteen-year-old undergraduate who is emotionally stable enough to withdraw from Professor Peter Tarnopol's master class in male neediness and entitlement.[63] Diana Rutherford in *The Anatomy Lesson* is a brazen twenty-year-old coed who picks up Nathan Zuckerman on the street.[64] She enters, then exits, his rotation of four lovers. Impulsive as she may be, it is young Diana who talks some sense into her raving, drug-addled paramour. Touchingly, she urges a demented Zuckerman to stand down in his epic feud with an esteemed literary critic.[65]

What a fine young woman Marcia Steinberg is! In his final novel, *Nemesis,* Philip Roth depicted yet another sensible, faithful lover of his protagonist. The protagonist in question is Bucky Cantor, who succumbs to polio. Bucky needs "this intelligent girl to tell him everything, really, about life beyond the playground."[66] Marcia displays the unpretentious fealty to God and Judaism which characterizes many of Page Roth's women. She engages in spirited theological disputation with Bucky, whose contraction of the crippling virus turns him into a religion-loathing, proto–New Atheist.[67] Afflicted by a terrible disease, Bucky urges this kind woman to leave him, to "marry a man who isn't maimed, who's strong, who's fit, who's got all that a prospective father needs."[68] But virtuous, loyal Marcia won't let go. So Bucky essentially shunts her out of his life.

Roth never tried harder to celebrate a woman's intellect and personality than he did with the character of Maria Zuckerman in *The Counterlife*. Depending on how you read this postmodern text, Maria may or may not be Nathan Zuckerman's wife. She may or may not be pregnant with his child. But in no reading of this experimental novel is she ever a sexual swashbuckler like Mary Jane Reed (*Portnoy's Complaint*), Sharon Shatzky (*My Life as a Man*), or Birgitta Svanström (*The Professor of Desire*). Again and again, Zuckerman coos over her "enrapturing brains," her emotional depth and intellectual subtlety.[69] Maria and Nathan spend long afternoons together not intensely exploring carnality, but just talking ("This endless talk that never reaches a climax").[70]

I've speculated that misogynistic fiction could be defined as literature with few women, or literature with a whole bunch of unlikable ones. Even if those were valid criteria, neither applies to Page Roth; his stories are densely populated with females, many of whom are exemplary souls. After all, Anne Morrow, in *The Plot Against America*, saves the Republic![71] I am not convinced, therefore, that Page Roth's surfeit of vixens and shrews confirm a charge of misogyny.[72]

## Subtler Asymmetries

While the examples above suggest that we reevaluate charges of misogyny leveled against Page Roth, other indications confirm the accusation. As I look across his nearly sixty years of fiction, I notice a subtle asymmetry of male and female representation in his work.

In a Roth tale, men can be anything from boxers to puppeteers, introverts to extroverts, athletes to polio victims, aspiring writers to soldiers, sociopaths to pillars of the community, and so forth. Women, by contrast, inhabit a much narrower spectrum of identities. An astonishingly high percentage of Roth's ladies, be they likable or not, play one of two primary roles: they are either lovers or mothers. Outside of the "Women-Curious" phase, it's rare to come across a significant woman in his stories who isn't (1) romantically involved with the male protagonist, or (2) the person who gave birth to him.

This tends to constrict the types of things that his female characters can do. One thing women can't easily do is to simply be friends with a male.

Platonic friendship between the genders is of no interest to this writer; relations between men and women are either based on genetic affinity or sentiments of love and/or lust. Sometimes Roth's worldview seems radical. But sometimes it seems marooned in the 1940s and 1950s.

Another thing women can't do in a Roth tale, as Julia Keller notes, "is interact with each other."[73] To buttress her point, I might observe that actual dialogue between two women is seldom seen in his stories. On occasion, mothers might talk to their daughters (almost invariably about men).[74] Here and there, sisters might chitchat (ditto). A college-bound woman might cry her eyes out to a friend about her father's secret dalliance with a younger woman.[75] Lesbian lovers in *The Humbling* might speak, or scream, at one another. None of that, however, happens too frequently across sixty years of Page Roth.

Even in "His Mistress's Voice," discussed earlier, the narrator spends the balance of her monologue speculating about her male lovers. She exclaims: "I can't talk to women. I can't cry with women. I can't fight with women. I can't get past some superficial barrier that's not even important. . . . I like women because they *are* women, but they don't matter to me at all. It has to be a man for me."[76] This does lend credence to one critic's observation that "Roth does not imagine the possibilities for female alliances they themselves likely would have imagined."[77]

Roth's writing, then, usually flunks the popular "Bechdel Test"—a useful tool for thinking about misogynistic art. This handy metric emerged from a 1986 graphic novel entitled *Dykes to Watch Out For* by Alison Bechdel in which two women identify the criteria which motivates them to see, or not see, a movie.[78] In particular, they will avoid films where women rarely talk to one another, and/or only talk to one another about men. These cartoon women would probably never reach for a Roth novel. He had a superb ear for dialogue. Yet he seemed uninterested in training it on discussions between women and women.

## The Progress of Page Roth?

The Real Roth: we hardly know him. And we're unlikely to ever know him, as long as the only persons who write about him are close friends, ex-lovers in good standing, and hand-selected biographers. There is so much about this author's engagement with women that is unknown to us. Who is going to tell that story?

Nexus Roth, by contrast, is somewhat knowable. We know that he abduction-vanned former girlfriends and wives into that odd safe house that was his fiction. The depictions of these women were often insensitive, even cruel. I have no hesitancy or regret deeming Nexus Roth "guilty" of misogynistic art. True, Real Roth warned that he was "'ruthless' in exploiting personal intimacy."[79] "Anybody who enters a writer's life," cautioned Roth, "intimately knows that we play for keeps."[80] This is the novelist's equivalent of "she was asking for it." The issuing of the warning, however, does not make him any less guilty of the crime.

Which brings us to Page Roth. By quarantining him away from Real and Nexus Roth, we were able to gain a little more clarity. This exercise let us better concentrate on long-term patterns, all the while getting omnipresent Philip Roth out of our interpretive hair. Do these patterns absolve Page Roth of the charge of misogyny? Not entirely, though they recommend prudence, more research, and better definitions.

The periodization alluded to above offers some new perspectives. The "Women-Curious" phase of 1960–67 is followed by something different: the "Women-Odious" phase. Between 1969 and 1977, Roth outraged all and sundry with over-the-top novels and stories.[81] During (and long after) this period, feminist critics expressed their alarm. As early as 1969 Marya Mannes complained that, for male writers like Roth, a "woman gets the short end of the stick even if she gets the long end of the antihero."[82] "Feminist readers," observed Hermione Lee with understatement, "often have a difficult time with Philip Roth's books."[83]

Roth responded with denials and heat. But it is also true that in the aftermath of these scrums, subtle shifts in his portraiture became evident. Certain types of characterizations mostly dropped out of his prose. Is it a coincidence that he never savaged a Jewish mother again after *Portnoy's Complaint*? From the late 1970s forward, his depictions of women change substantively. Starting with *The Ghost Writer* (1979) there is a tendency in Page Roth's writing to present female characters who are more layered, complex, and aware of sexism. Maybe Real Roth was affected by the criticism. Maybe he was just returning to ways of writing about women that interested him in the early 1960s. Maybe both, or maybe, as some suggest, he simply grew up.[84]

*The Ghost Writer*, for instance, gives us an unlikely scene stealer, in the person of plucky Hope Lonoff. Her closing rant against her husband is sort of like Beyoncé's "Irreplaceable," cross-pollinated with Nancy Sinatra's "These Boots Are Made for Walkin." Hope has had it up to here with her dull, self-absorbed, and likely philandering partner. Earlier, we quoted Megan Garber's crackling takedown of male artistic "genius."[85] Through the character of Hope, Roth demonstrates no small degree of self-awareness; he understands what it's like for a woman to be subjected to a genius.

A novel like *Indignation* also shows hints of what might be termed a feminist consciousness. The text exhibits a razor-sharp understanding of the sexual hypocrisies of 1950s America. The ridicule heaped on Olivia Hutton by the men of Winesburg College for being a "slut" and a "cunt" leads her to an apparent second nervous breakdown.[86] Roth is highly sensitive to the double standard, painting her as a victim of the era's sanctimony. That she appears genuine and kind throughout makes us wonder about our protagonist. One exits *Indignation* thinking Marcus Messner, otherwise a brave iconoclast, was conformist and cowardly in his treatment of this woman. When we factor in the persistent allusion to the incestuous sexual abuse suffered by Olivia ("You never know the truth of what goes on in people's houses. When the child goes wrong, look first to the family"), then it appears Roth sketched a layered portrait of a woman devastated by misogyny and incest.[87]

This doesn't mean that his work, post-1979, never upset feminist readers. Every now and then the author could unleash a novel like *Sabbath's Theater, The Dying Animal,* or *The Humbling.* The latter text so incensed one of Katie Roiphe's female friends that she stopped reading the book and tossed it into a garbage can.[88] As for *Sabbath's Theater,* it, too, outraged many. But since feminism is not one thing, equipped with one voice, and singing one tune, we shouldn't be surprised that not every feminist shared that opinion. As one commentator put it: "Both Mickey [Sabbath] and his creator, Roth, manage to simultaneously charm and disgust us. Sabbath might be off-putting, but he is armed with humor and charisma beyond his filth."[89]

Roth had, and has, legions of feminist critics. He also had, and has, equally thoughtful feminist defenders.[90] The latter are, undeniably, fewer in number than the former. Yet they aren't rare, and their ranks somehow replenish every decade. This provides yet another reason to be cautious about labeling his fiction misogynistic. I think of Helen Meyer's anguished assessment of Roth's work in the aftermath of his death.[91] "I couldn't put him on a patriarchal pedestal," observes Meyers, "but neither would I leave him behind in the misogynist mud."[92]

# PART II

Roth Unsexed

## • 5 •

# You Must Change Your Life!

He put his hands over his eyes. "The change, the change," he said. "I don't even know when it began. Me, Lou Epstein, with a rash. I don't even feel anymore like Lou Epstein. All of a sudden, pffft! and things are changed."
—PHILIP ROTH, "Epstein"

The counselors and campers were, of course, startled to learn that everything in camp had suddenly changed—that everything in *life* had changed.
—PHILIP ROTH, *Nemesis*

Everyone knows that Philip Roth trained his spotlight on Priapic Bad Boys and their indecent japery. Everybody knows that he chronicled male lust. Everybody knows that eroticism and fornicatory urge were his staple themes. What everyone knows, to a certain extent, is true. Fewer know, however, that he was equally, if not *more*, preoccupied with a completely different, unsexed, and ultimately weightier, dilemma. Philip Roth was obsessed by the ways in which men and women—but mostly men—*change*.

"My hero," he once observed, "has to be in a state of vivid transformation or radical displacement."[1] This is one of the few instances where I actually concur with the master's interpretation of his own work. He did indeed dramatize people who were vividly and radically shifting from one state of being to another. Even the community of Roth scholars tends to underestimate how central and enduring the theme of change is to his life's work.

From the stories in the 1959 *Goodbye, Columbus* collection to his final product, *Nemesis* (2010), he depicted transformations that were comic or tragic, gradual or sudden, emotional or physical, explicable or inexplicable. Throughout a half century of writing, Roth probed, to borrow a pretty phrase from *The Human Stain*, "the mystery of being alive and in flux."[2] He hurled his heroes, as Nathan Zuckerman put it, "into the mutability" again and again.[3]

To suddenly feel "the terrible desire to be somebody else" (as does a character in *Deception*) is as normal for a Roth character as breathing.[4] All of which is to say that Roth pursued the change motif across decades and with great thoughtfulness. More thoughtfulness, I think, than the manner in which he pursued the blue material that made him in/famous in literary skin flicks such as *Portnoy's Complaint* or *Sabbath's Theater*.

In what follows I want to look at the many changelings Roth dreamt up in his novels and short stories. The data at our disposal is overwhelming in its volume and complexity. To impose some order on this carnival of human flux, I will situate his characters' transformations across a spectrum whose poles might be labeled "Normal" and "Paranormal." We'll start our inquiry on the clear-skied "Normal" side of the continuum. Here we'll encounter heroes who set out to make themselves anew. Nothing unusual about that. They succeed or fail for perfectly plausible reasons. Everything, more or less, makes sense. The hero's trajectory looks and feels like routine "character development."

Then we will embark on a journey toward the "Paranormal." As we tack toward that stormy horizon, things start to make a little less sense. The people in his stories undergo dramatic transformations, even though they did not seek them. There is some uncertainty, even mystery, as to why and how someone's being has shifted. Finally, we venture to the outer limit and watch Roth explore occult concepts with strange names like "metempsychosis." The changes now defy the laws of gravity, not to mention the laws of the modernist novel. In terms of content *and* form, we are in the Twilight Zone.

Once we get there, the dimensions of a lesser-known, less carnal, but much more integral Philip Roth will come into sharp relief—as will a few biographical unknowns.

## Self-Reinvention

One type of change we encounter in Roth's writing centers around an act of the will, what scholars refer to as "agency." Here, a person *tries* to become different. Transformation as aspiration. Or, as Nathan Zuckerman's father in

*The Counterlife* always maintained: "anyone could change *anything* in himself through the diligent exercise of his will."[5]

This theme of "self-reinvention" figures often in anglophone literature. One thinks of novels like George Eliot's *Silas Marner,* Thomas Hardy's *The Mayor of Casterbridge,* or F. Scott Fitzgerald's *The Great Gatsby.*[6] In these masterpieces the agent's desired outcome is more or less achieved (though complications obviously arise). James Gatz did, after all, become Jay Gatsby of West Egg—"a son of God," in Fitzgerald's words.[7] In a Roth novel, by contrast, characters who try to change often fail, and quite spectacularly at that![8]

Let's begin with a little-known 1964 story by Roth entitled "An Actor's Life for Me." It's a disheveled tale about Walter Appel, a failed playwright who years back "had been a hot-shot in the theater department, at a liberal arts college in Pennsylvania."[9] Cognizant of his limitations, Walter "put on a tie and jacket, and with the decision firmly made to change his life, he went off to look for work that he could do."[10] His newfound employment in "the business end of the theater" takes Walter to London and to various adulterous complications.[11]

By story's end, Walter has descended into madness. He is consumed by the fear that his wife, Juliet, spends her evenings gazing out her window at a man who sits naked in his living room across the way. The decision to "change his life" thus paid little in the way of healthy psychic dividends.

Halfway through *The Anatomy Lesson* we learn that the novelist Nathan Zuckerman wants to dramatically alter his existence. We'll delve deeper into how he arrived at that crossroads momentarily. For now, we simply note that he no longer wishes to be a novelist. The beleaguered author confesses to feeling "like some enormous tube of linguistic paste" being squeezed for words, thoughts, ideas, and allusions.[12] "Enough of my writing," sighs Zuckerman, "the whole God damn thing has been a colossal mistake."[13] What Nathan now wants to do, incongruously, is to become a physician.

With this objective in mind, the forty-year-old plans what he calls "a second life," "a new existence."[14] What better way to achieve that identity than to enroll in medical school at the University of Chicago, where he once studied literature in the 1950s? En route to the Windy City (and without any official letter of acceptance in hand, I would stress), he then fabricates a *third* existence for himself. Nathan tells anyone who will listen—and those who won't—that he is the publisher of *Lickety Split,* a pornographic magazine.[15]

In *The Anatomy Lesson* a character goes in pursuit of dramatic self-reinvention. But "his plan to change his life" does not end well.[16] By the final page, Nathan is neither an ob-gyn nor an anesthesiologist, as he had intended.[17] Instead, he is a patient in the very Chicago hospital where he once dreamed of conducting rounds. His jaw is wired shut as he recovers from injuries sustained after his female chauffeur manhandled the publisher of *Lickety Split* in a cemetery.[18] During his lengthy convalescence he glumly patrols the corridors of his ward gawking at other people's misery and pondering their suffering. There is warrant for the reading that a humbled, silenced Zuckerman is finally experiencing actual empathy for others. The impossibly self-absorbed Nathan has changed. Not in the way he had anticipated, though.

There are other Roth works in which characters try, and fail, to alter who they are. *When She Was Good* introduces us to Whitey Nelson. The man is an alcoholic layabout and a serial abuser of his wife. Again and again, Whitey tries to get on the straight-and-narrow path only to end up in prison or to be run out of town by Lucy, his irate daughter. Whitey's father-in-law, Willard, spends fifteen years observing the failures of his goof-off son-in-law. Willard muses to himself: "*There is nothing the man* [Whitey] *can do. He is afflicted with himself.*"[19] Whitey Nelson, like Nathan Zuckerman, did not succeed in making himself anew.

The central protagonist of *The Human Stain,* by contrast, does effect the change he seeks. In chapter 1, we met Coleman Brutus Silk, for whom "the thrill of leading a double life" impelled him to pass as a white Jew.[20] Unlike all of the change projects mentioned above, his endeavor was "successful." From the 1940s to 1998, his act of reinvention worked brilliantly. Then again, Coleman's impersonation of a Jew was so spot-on that it drove Les Farley, the local anti-Semite, to murder him.[21]

## Metamorphosis (Explicable)

Coleman Silk is a fairly unusual Roth hero. That's because, unlike the other characters mentioned above, he meticulously plans and executes his own "vivid transformation." By contrast, the majority of fluxing men in this author's tales exhibit no such mastery of self, no such triumph of agency. Far from methodically captaining their metamorphosis, they are blindsided by the changes that befall them. They lurch or explode into new selves, and they have no idea why. Readers, however, *do* understand why. Or at least, we understand *better* than the stunned hero whose existence has been turned upside down.

An example can be found in "Epstein," an entertainingly scummy short story Roth published at the beginning of his career.[22] As our epigraph indicates, the fifty-nine-year-old Epstein is acutely aware that something unprecedented is afoot. Might this realization have been fostered by the "venereal rash" that has appeared on his penis?[23] That scarlet stigma was bestowed upon him, in all likelihood, via his adulterous dalliance with Ida Kaufman, the widow down the block.

We are never explicitly told why the respectable, married proprietor of a small business (Epstein Paper Bag) decided to pursue this side hustle.[24] Epstein himself is at a loss for an explanation. "The change, the change," he cries out, "I don't even know when it began."[25] Yet Roth provides us with a surfeit of clues. I can't do a better job of describing what might have compelled Epstein to upend his miserable existence than Judith Jones and Guinevera Nance did back in 1981 as they inventoried his woes: "His son Herbie . . . is dead of polio; his rosy-complexioned baby Sheila has grown into a pimply, fat socialist who curses him for being a capitalist; and his once beautiful and sexually adventurous wife, Goldie, has become an unappetizing cooking and cleaning machine with pendulous breasts, who smells like Bab-O."[26] I would add that Epstein may have been enticed by a chance viewing of his nephew having sex in his living room ("Epstein tingled").[27] All of these factors summate to push the aging man into new and uncharted territory.

In "Epstein" we encounter a hero who is conscious of the changes that overtake him. He is nevertheless flummoxed as to *why* he is changing. From the vantage point of the reader, however, the tumult in his soul makes some sense. The dreariness of his domestic situation explains, somewhat, his bold risk. Roth seeds the story with details that make Epstein's sudden urge to have a tryst with Ida Kaufman *plausible.* Notice the cognitive discrepancy between the protagonist and the reader: we know something that Epstein may not.

A similar imbalance between audience and character is seen in "Eli the Fanatic."[28] When we first meet him, Eli Peck is a secular Jewish attorney representing the well-off Jews of his hometown, Woodenton. His clients object to the presence of a local yeshiva full of Holocaust survivors that has just set up camp. In the WASP-y enclave of Woodenton, reason the secular Jews, it's important to fit in. Initially, Eli champions the interests of his assimilated coreligionists. When all is said and done, however, Eli does not fit in; he is marching down Main Street in the black vestments of an ultra-orthodox Jew.[29]

It's a curious transformation. Eli, like Epstein, doesn't seem to entirely grasp what is transpiring. "Eli," we read, "had the strange notion that he was two people."[30] But Roth permits his audience to draw some reasonable inferences about his metamorphosis. Maybe Eli has just lost his mind. After all, we are told he had a previous mental breakdown in which he "sat in the bottom of the closet and chewed on . . . bedroom slippers."[31] It thus makes sense that he refers to himself as "Eli, the Flipper."[32] Then again, maybe he feels genuine sadness for the traumatized survivors up on that hill. Or maybe he does an about-face because his secular clients are so devoid of empathy for those bedraggled refugees. Eli might not be aware of why he changes, but from our point of view his change is comprehensible.

*The Anatomy Lesson* also places the reader on a higher plane of awareness than the character. As we saw earlier, Nathan Zuckerman tried to remake himself as a doctor and a pornographer. Yet prior to that act of reinvention, Zuckerman was afflicted by a change he certainly did not seek. For eighteen months he has been felled by "a causeless, nameless, untreatable, phantom disease."[33] The writer is wracked by debilitating pain whose medical source neither he, nor his bevy of doctors, chiropodists, and quacks can identify. Incapable of writing, Nathan struggles to make it through each day. In an effort to alleviate his suffering, he abuses Percodan, pot, and vodka. Amid his addiction and ailing, he is sexually serviced by a rotating "harem of Florence Nightingales"—four women who attend to him regularly.[34]

Yet the more we read of *The Anatomy Lesson,* the less mysterious Zuckerman's condition is to us. The famous writer harbors considerable guilt about his best-selling book *Carnovsky.* Many of his grinning fans believe it is a vicious parody of his own family and Judaism (the resemblances to the reception of *Portnoy's Complaint* are not subtle). His brother Henry won't even speak to him anymore, all on account of that book. His father's "fatal coronary" was also caused by the outrageous portrayals found in the hit novel.[35] As for his mother, she has just passed away. On top of his new orphan status, Nathan's latest publication has been ripped to shreds in a scathing review by one of his literary idols. Surely, thinks the reader, the misery that afflicts Zuckerman bears some causal relation to the collapse of his family and his career.[36]

Simon Axler, in *The Humbling,* also can't account for a sudden reversal, in this case the disappearance of his artistic skill. The star of the stage wakes up one day, transformed: "He'd lost his magic. . . . His talent was dead."[37] For the reader, admittedly, it is somewhat more difficult to pinpoint the cause of Axler's reversal, though Roth reminds us that in the arts a fall from grace is inevitable. Axler's agent, Jerry Oppenheim, consoles him: "That happens to practically everyone sooner or later. There's no ironclad security in any art. People run into an obstacle for reasons no one knows. . . . The obstacle disappears and you go on."[38]

Axler, unfortunately, never does surmount the obstacle. Instead, in a chapter entitled "The Transformation," he strikes up an affair with a woman named Pegeen. She, naturally, is in the midst of her own soul shift.[39] Her previous erotic attachments were solely to women, but now she explores this romance with Axler.[40] Turns out that Pegeen's former female lover, Priscilla, is herself transitioning to male gender status.[41] *The Humbling* is filled with flux.[42]

In all of these stories, characters are changed *against* their will. The case of Axler notwithstanding, Roth is keen to show us the psychological factors which lead these men to a crack-up. Epstein, Eli, Zuckerman of *The Anatomy Lesson,* suffer from "preexisting conditions" that thrust them into adultery, religious orthodoxy, and physical misery, respectively. If we think of these changelings as patients, then Dr. Roth offers the reader a fairly clear diagnosis of how and why they came to this state of being.[43]

## Metamorphosis (Inexplicable)

From the early 1970s onward Philip Roth's style itself starts to undergo its own fascinating shift. He continues to tell some stories in the realist tradition, but elsewhere his tales veer into surrealism, metafiction, and autofiction. The turning point appeared to have occurred in the early 1970s.[44] True, after the 1974 *My Life as a Man,* some of his narratives remain strictly within the boundaries of the normal. But many others now cantilever into the bizarre. A long-standing interest in psychological themes is, by the 1970s, matched by a new curiosity about the parapsychological.[45]

As all of this is transpiring, Roth increasingly decouples transformation from *plausibility;* not only do his characters seem baffled by what is happening to them, *but we are as well.* Even the novels, in and of themselves, leave us stumped; they do things that novels do not generally do. To invoke our metaphor from above, the reader is no longer a physician diagnosing the character's afflictions alongside Dr. Roth. Now the reader is hospitalized, a clueless patient as well.

*The Breast* (1972) features a character being changed in ways that are not humanly possible. This uneven novella introduces us to thirty-eight-year-old

David Kepesh, associate professor of comparative literature at Stony Brook University.[46] With little forewarning, the scholar undergoes an "endocrino-pathic catastrophe."[47] In the wee hours of February 18, 1971, he is transformed into a 155-pound breast, six feet in length and sporting a five-inch nipple.[48]

The transformation leaves him flummoxed, but certainly not speechless. Kepesh is acutely aware of his change and spends the entirety of his narra-tion trying to make sense of his fifteen-month ordeal.[49] Yet while he might possess self-awareness, he lacks accurate self-knowledge. The professor does not know why, or even *if*, the metamorphosis is actually occurring. In the words of one Roth scholar: "the line between actuality and mental confusion wavers."[50]

Just when we are getting acclimated to the possibility that Kepesh has, indeed, transmogrified into a humongous mammary gland, he alerts us to other ways of accounting for his ordeal. He might be imagining or dreaming the whole thing. He might be experiencing a psychological breakdown. Or, he might simply be delivering an undergraduate lecture.[51] The work teases the reader with all of these explanations but never provides us with an answer.

The paranormal turn in Roth's work doesn't apply only to the contents of the stories but to their *form* as well. From the 1970s forward, peculiar hap-penings occur within the *structure* of Roth's novels. One such example is *The Counterlife*—a work that is an orgy of change, in both its content and its form.[52]

The novel opens up with the tragicomic saga of Henry Zuckerman. The disenchanted dentist is having an affair with Wendy, his twenty-two-year-old hygienist. The dilemma is that Henry suffers from a heart condition which compromises his ability to engage in sexual congress. Faced with the specter of a dangerous operation which will restore his potency, Henry goes for it! He then dies on the operating table.[53]

And then come the inexplicable changes that the reader cannot grasp. In chapter 2, Henry is now alive. He survived his bypass surgery. His post-operative depression is so extreme that Henry's wife urges her despondent spouse to take a vacation to Israel in order to "begin your new life."[54] For this secular dentist, a "new life" entails a shift in identity. He confides to his brother Nathan: "I began to realize that of all that I am, I am nothing, I have never been *anything,* the way that I am this Jew. I didn't know this, had no idea of it, all of my life I was swimming *against* it."[55] Living with a group of militant settlers up in the Judaean hills and toting a firearm, Henry has become a fanatic. Nathan journeys to the Holy Land in the hope of talking him down from the ledge. The siblings quarrel inconclusively.[56]

And then come more inexplicable changes. In chapter 4, we learn that it is *Nathan* who is contemplating an operation to restore his sexual potency. He knows the risks. But it's an operation that he's hell-bent on having because he is in love with his upstairs neighbor, Maria. Nathan goes under the knife and dies, as Henry once did.[57]

After Nathan's funeral, Henry ransacks his brother's writing studio. Only to learn that the whole Wendy episode (which we read about in chapter 1 and thought was "real") was just "Draft #2" of Nathan's forthcoming manuscript, as was the business of Henry becoming a militant settler in Israel.[58] Also, Maria has an extended conversation with Nathan Zuckerman's ghost.[59] I'll forgo a discussion of the part where an incensed Maria informs Nathan (who is now alive again) that she is "leaving the book."[60]

*The Counterlife* is a work where we are "doomed to befuddlement."[61] Roth subjects his characters, his novel, *and* readers to transformations that are incomprehensible. But this leaves one more changeling who has yet to be subjected to all this transition and confusion: Philip Roth himself.

## "Met Him What?" Metempsychosis

The 1993 *Operation Shylock: A Confession* marks the moment of Peak Freakiness in Philip Roth's long career of writing fiction. But is *Operation Shylock* even fiction? The novel's central protagonist purports to be the real Philip Roth. This is not the first time we've met Philip Roth in Philip Roth's literature. The Newark native stars in four other novels and one short story.[62]

Scholars refer to this technique as "autofiction."[63] It can be defined in various ways, but for our purposes an autofictive work is one in which someone who appears to be the real-life author surfaces in the storyworld. *Operation Shylock* goes above and beyond the call of autofictional duty: it indulges the conceit that just one Philip Roth is not enough.

For in this "confession" it has come to Philip Roth's attention that *another* Philip Roth is on the prowl in Israel.[64] This impersonator (?) looks almost exactly like Philip Roth.[65] He dresses identically to Philip Roth. He has the same handwriting—and even pubic hair—as Philip Roth.[66] He retains many of Philip Roth's childhood memories. He also shares Philip Roth's penchant for pissing off fellow Members of the Tribe: his controversial activism centers around convincing Ashkenazi Israeli Jews to return to their European "homelands."[67]

All of this doubling transpires in a book that professes to be an account of what happened when Roth consented in 1988 "to undertake an intelligence-gathering operation for Israel's foreign intelligence service, the Mossad."[68] On the final page of the book, however, a "Note to the Reader" casts doubt upon that outrageous boast.[69] It informs us that what we have just read is "a work of fiction."[70]

Sprawling and scattershot, Operation Shylock is something of a hot mess. Michiko Kakutani in the New York Times complained about "the author's tiresome games with mirrors."[71] I concur with this assessment, as well as John Updike's verdict—a verdict which (according to Claire Bloom) may have quite literally driven Philip Roth mad—that Roth's "narrowing, mag-nifying fascination with himself has penetrated to a quantum level of inde-terminacy."[72] In terms of the themes we've been tracking above, however, Operation Shylock is uniquely instructive. This is because it features every model of human change that Roth ever dreamt up, plus a possibility we have not previously seen.

The new development occurs when Roth ruminates upon something called "metempsychosis." The New Catholic Encyclopedia describes it thusly: "A doctrine asserting not only the preexistence of the human soul before union with matter but also, after death, a return to life on earth in a different body, perhaps through several successive reincarnations."[73] The concept first surfaces in the writing of ancient Greek thinkers. Here is a "metem-psychotic" passage from Ovid's Metamorphosis:[74] "Our souls are deathless, and ever, when they have left their former seat, do they live in new abodes and dwell in the bodies that have received them. . . . All things are changing; nothing dies. The spirit wanders, comes now here, now there, and occupies whatever frame it pleases. From beasts it passes into human bodies, and from our bodies into beasts, but never perishes."[75]

Even in antiquity, this doctrine of transmigrating souls "only had a lim-ited audience."[76] A modern would have to read ancient Greek or Latin, or maybe dabble in the occult, to even know it existed. The question arises as to how Roth became familiar with such an obscure and esoteric idea. On the basis of a study I conducted on Roth's sources, my guess is he encoun-tered it in modern, not ancient, literature.[77]

In The Remembrance of Things Past, Marcel Proust invokes metempsy-chosis on his very first page. But in French. The problem is that if you read the English translation—and I don't believe Roth's French was up to speed—you'd never know that the term "metempsychosis" was used (it's translated completely differently).[78] For these reasons, I'd wager that non-Francophone Roth first pondered metempsychosis when he encountered it in James Joyce's *Ulysses*. There, Molly seeks Leopold's definition of metempsychosis. "Met him what?" he responds.[79] Upon closer introspection, Leopold recognizes the concept and explains with a frown: "It's Greek: from the Greek. That means, the transmigration of souls. . . . Some people believe, he said, that we go on living in another body after death, that we lived before. They call it reincarnation. That we all lived before on the earth thousands of years ago or some other planet. They say we have forgotten it. Some say they remember their past lives."[80]

Warming to his theme, Leopold Bloom continues: "That we live after death. Our souls. Metempsychosis . . . is what the ancient Greeks called it. They used to believe you could be changed into an animal or a tree, for instance. What they called nymphs, for example."[81]

Joyce was cleaving closely to textbook definitions of the term.[82] *Operation Shylock,* by contrast, is all over the map. At points the term is used to describe simple self-reinvention. This is apparent as Philip Roth opines: "Maybe this stuff everybody is watching has inspired half the human population with the yearning for a massive transfer of souls . . . the longings for metempsychosis."[83] I don't want to be a pedant or a stickler, but definitions are definitions: how can one *yearn* and *long* for metempsychosis? It only happens after you die.

In another reflection, Roth continues to play fast and loose with the definition of metempsychosis: "I understood that people are trying to transform themselves all the time: the universal urge to be otherwise. So as not to look as they look, sound as they sound, be treated as they are treated, suffer in the ways they suffer, etc., etc., they change hairdos, tailors, spouses, accents, friends, they change their addresses, their noses, their wallpaper, even their forms of government, all to be more like themselves or less like themselves, or more like or less like that exemplary prototype whose image is theirs to emulate or to repudiate obsessively for life."[84] Here again, metempsychosis is described not as an event that happens after you expire *but during the course of your life.* And here again, Roth's usage contravenes the classic sense. His concept of soul change appears to be something that people aspire toward—they *try* to transform themselves. This is different from textbook metempsychosis.

These confusions continue throughout *Operation Shylock.* The character Jinx Possesski is described as "endlessly reborn."[85] That is indeed a metempsychotic thing to do. But as Roth reflects on her rebirthing history, he calls it "metamorphosis": "She spins a tale of lifelong servitude and serial transformations: from the unloved Catholic child of bigoted ignoramuses into the mindless promiscuous hippie waif. . . . What *metamorphosis* next for Wanda Jane 'Jinx' Possesski." [86] Metamorphosis is similar to metempsychosis in some ways. But it's different in that it does not presume souls escaping the vessel of a freshly expired body.

But just when we are despairing that Roth hopelessly jumbled metempsychosis, he graces us with a perfect example. Gazing at Jinx Possesski lying "absolutely mummified" on his bed, the "real" Philip Roth experiences the displeasure of recognition.[87] This woman, he concludes, is a reincarnation of his first wife, Margaret Martinson Williams. Remember her? The woman that Roth kept smuggling spitefully into his prose (see chapter 3).[88] The soul of Maggie has migrated into the body of Jinx Possesski. Bingo! That's metempsychosis![89]

## You Will Be Changed!

Let biographers and critics recognize that as much, if not more, of Philip Roth's intellectual energy was devoted to fluxing than to fucking. Ever since the publication of *Portnoy's Complaint,* Roth was tarred as a purveyor of smut. The accusation might very well have been warranted, but far fewer noticed his deeper preoccupation with change and, as we shall see in the next chapter, how the human self is *built* for change. One who did notice was Maria Zuckerman. In *The Counterlife,* she lambasted Nathan Zuckerman: "I recognize that radical change is the law of life and that if everything quietens down on one front, it invariably gets noisy on another; I recognize that to be born, to live, and to die is to change form, but you overdo it."[90]

If Roth overdid sex in his writing, then he overdid change tenfold (though no one was offended by the excesses of the latter). The subject consumed him from the very beginning of his career to his final fictional words. A half century after a perplexed Epstein morphed into an adulterer, Roth served up yet another example of what I labeled above "Metamorphosis (Explicable)." This occurs in *Nemesis,* his farewell novel about a gifted twenty-three-year-old Newark athlete named Bucky Cantor. Endowed with the physique of a Greek statue, this "compact muscleman" suddenly succumbs to the polio virus.[91] Roth ends the work—and his career—with a sequoia-tinged reminiscence: the virile Bucky launching a javelin like Hercules. How different he was before the disease ravaged his tendons and bones.[92]

Roth's studies of fluxing souls, minds, and bodies were mostly devoted to individual men. Though not all of his changelings are men or even individuals for that matter. As regards women, we could point to the willful self-reinvention of Faunia Farley in *The Human Stain*. Like her paramour, Coleman Silk, she morphs into what she is not: illiterate and dumb. Merry Levov, in *American Pastoral,* offers us another of those hard-to-grasp, almost creepy, Rothian imaginings of transformation. She shifts from daddy's little girl, to a domestic terrorist, to a homeless practitioner of the Jain faith—though the reasons for this character's development are not entirely clear.[93] As we saw in chapter 4, the prototype for feminine change first appeared in the 1964 "The Psychoanalytic Special." Ella, the adulteress, "desperately . . . wanted to be changed" to become a "new woman"—but that never came to fruition.[94]

This brings us to *collective* metempsychosis/metamorphosis, which we encounter in *The Plot Against America*. There, the United States of 1939–45 that we know (and love) is suddenly reborn as something eerily different. In that counter-USA, an isolationist president with Nazi sympathies governs a white Christian nation. Pogroms against Jews are totally possible in this America turned upside down.[95] More group reversals are seen in *The Counterlife*. There, Zionism is referred to as "a manifesto for human transformation" in which Jews could "go ahead and un-Jew themselves in their own little homeland."[96] Zionism, then, becomes a vehicle for the metamorphosis of the entire Jewish people.[97]

If I am correct about the centrality and *primacy* of the change motif in Roth's thought, then a few questions come to mind for Roth's biographers.[98] First, I wonder what intellectual influences may have nourished this fixation. Throughout his writing the author cites well-known fictions of flux such as Jonathan Swift's *Gulliver's Travels,* Nikolai Gogol's *The Nose,* Robert Louis Stevenson's *Dr. Jekyll and Mr. Hyde,* and Franz Kafka's *The Metamorphosis*. But could an interest this deep and long lasting have been inspired *solely* by fiction?

Were there nonliterary taproots of Roth's preoccupation? Did he study existentialist philosophy in college, ruminating over Jean-Paul Sartre's declaration that "Man is nothing else but what he makes of himself"?[99] Did he travel to India, like some sort of second coming of John Coltrane and the Beatles, and become infatuated with the doctrine of *samsara*, or "the transmigration of souls"? Did he suffer from a mental condition that made him acutely engaged with the problematic of how transformation afflicts human beings? Reverse biography compels us to ask if an obsession with labile personalities in Roth's fiction corresponded to his nonfictional state of mind.

Or maybe he simply fell under the spell of Rainer Marie Rilke's famous aside, "You must change your life" (Du mußt dein Leben ändern).[100] This is a verse which he cited again and again in his prose.[101] "You must change your life," is, in the opinion of Debra Shostak, "the dictum that has ruled the choices and agonies of Roth's characters."[102]

Above, however, I called attention to another dictum that has ruled the choices and agonies of Roth's characters. These protagonists are often transformed *against* their will. For every Coleman Silk who charted his own idiosyncratic course, there's a bevy of bewildered Simon Axlers; heady gents who wake up one day disassembled by renovations performed upon their souls. How often does it happen in a Roth tale that "everything good [is] undone in a moment!"[103] So while Roth intoned the credo, "You must change your life!," his art silently screamed: "Your life will be changed, my friend. Your life will be changed, whether you like it (or understand it) or not!"

## · 6 ·

# Go Flux Your Self!

*Philip Roth as Self-Help Guru*

The self, then, as a performed character, is not an organic thing that has a specific location, whose fundamental fate is to be born, to mature, and to die; it is a dramatic effect arising diffusely from a scene that is presented.
—ERVING GOFFMAN, *The Presentation of Self in Everyday Life*

W e don't usually think of Philip Roth as a life coach who dispenses advice to his readership, and with good reason. But as I am going to demonstrate, he clearly had opinions concerning the best way for you to think about, and even *be,* your self. So why not hear this inadvertent self-help guru out?

Making sense of this author's lifelong interest in the self—and how it changes—is quite a challenge. Part of the problem is the sheer number of self/change narratives in his work (see chapter 5). The other difficulty is that Philip Roth's answers to questions like "What is the self?" and "What is the ideal self?" emerge from his strenuous research into a completely different problematic—namely, "What is Philip Roth's self?" He thus tended to use his own persona as the raw data set from which to infer universal laws about us all. This rather sketchy methodological design yielded some odd results. To wit, the ideal self which Roth envisions tends to resemble his own.

In what follows, I will spend very little time reflecting on Philip Roth's self. That chore can be left to his biographers. I, for my part, will try to clarify Roth's basic, and counterintuitive, theory of the self. First, I'll suggest a few unexpected sources for these bold ideas. Then, I'd like to imagine our author as if he were some sort of personal philosophical trainer, sharing wisdom and tough love with all and sundry. If you're not averse to extracting life lessons from fiction (or metafiction, no less!), then Roth offers counsel as to how to be your self. Or, more precisely, how *not* to be, your self.

## The Looking Glass Self

In order to get our bearings, we must first familiarize ourselves with an obscure passage in one of Roth's most obscure works. Weighing in at 630 pages, the 1962 *Letting Go* is Roth's longest fictional product. It is also among his most disappointing. This aimless, endless novel sandblasts readers' faces with interminable dialogues between marginally interesting people who can't stand one another. This tedious tome, I concede, does display a few redeeming virtues, one of which being a nifty-as-heck meditation on the self.

*Letting Go* introduces us to Paul Herz. He's a melancholy sort who, as his name indicates, is experiencing a great deal of pain. Paul has been disowned by his Jewish parents for marrying a Catholic woman.[1] As quirky and likable as his wife, Libby, might be (she converts to Judaism for him), Paul doesn't love her in the least. Professionally, he's on the skids as well. As an adjunct writing instructor in his English department, his tenured colleagues condescend to him with aplomb.[2] It goes without saying that penniless Paul makes little headway writing his first novel.

These accumulated agonies accompany him to New York, where he visits his ailing father and careers toward a nervous breakdown.[3] In terms of theories of the self, this is where things get interesting. Through an internal monologue we learn that the flailing Paul wants "to divest himself of himself."[4] The anguished writer wants to "peel[] back layer after layer [of himself], until what gleamed through was some primary substance. Peeling, peeling, until what was locked up inside was out in the open."[5]

Paul reasons that there must be a *genuine* self underneath his ostensibly damaged persona. His project consists of digging beneath the artificial overgrowth. He wants to drill down and access what he calls "His Paulness. His Herzness."[6] The man wants to find his true self, to figure out who he really is at his core.

The classic Roth hero, as we shall see below, is not only a thinker, but an *over*thinker. True to type, Paul mindfully wrestles with his dilemma. His thoughts eventually carry him to a crucial realization: *he has no primary substance, no essence, no core.* Paul knows he can leave his wife. He knows he can just walk away from his department. He knows he can shunt his nagging parents out of his life. But were all of this "self-divestment" to occur, it dawns on Paul, *there would be nothing left to Paul.*[7] Whereas Paul initially wanted to cast off those around him and all the psychic turmoil they create, he realizes such an exorcism is futile.

"[A]ll he had rid himself of was all there was," sighs our narrator.[8] Paul concludes that the relations he has with his wife, annoying colleagues, and parents—acrimonious and unfulfilling as they may be—make him who he is: "He *was* Libby, *was* his job, *was* his mother and father."[9] The lesson learned is that his Paulness is constituted by his relations with others.

Heady stuff, but not necessarily original stuff. *Letting Go's* reflections on selfhood sound like a riff on a theory known as the "Looking Glass Self." The approach was the brainchild of the American sociologist Charles Horton Cooley (1864–1929). This sociological pioneer was a member of the Chicago school, and an early forerunner of the hugely influential theory of Symbolic Interaction which we will encounter momentarily.[10]

As sociologists are wont to do, Cooley was keen to challenge individualistic conceptions of self formation. These conceptions, sociologists contend, disregard the defining role that society and socialization play in making a person who she or he is. Cooley, the founder of the American Sociological Association, wanted to demonstrate that our selves were forged in dynamic encounter with other selves.[11] Or, as one commentator put it, "Actors can define their identities only within the framework of social community."[12] The metaphor of the "Looking Glass" is invoked because "the judgement of others constitutes a social mirror in which the actor sees himself or herself reflected in the perceptions and evaluations of others, and so experiences a sense of selfhood."[13]

In Cooley's hypothesis, the self is an interactive vessel. It is permeable, porous, and fluid. Most importantly, a self's nature is contingent upon its engagements with others. You do not, Cooley and his colleagues insisted, create your self. You have no essential core. You have no Paulness (assuming your name is Paul) that preexists your encounters with others. Rather, your self is a crowd-sourced deliverable. You owe who you are, to who *we* are. So when Paul Herz grimly concludes after unloading his parents, wife, and career that "All he had rid himself of was all there was," he is echoing sociology's challenge to overly individualistic theories of personality formation.[14]

I suspect, but cannot prove, that Roth was familiar with Cooley's thesis. Were I a biographer, I'd consult my subject's college and graduate transcripts to see if he studied sociology or social psychology in the 1950s. I'd wager that Roth probably came across the Looking Glass Self hypothesis either as an undergraduate at Bucknell (1951–54), or as a master's student and short-lived Ph.D. candidate at the University of Chicago (1955–56).[15] That would be an awfully logical place to learn about the Chicago school.

For our purposes, however, we have brought to light submerged assumptions upon which Roth's conception of selfhood will rest. The self, for him, is not constituted by unchanging, timeless, or unmovable matter. Rather, selfhood is constituted by, and contingent upon, our interaction with others.[16] This suggests a fluidity to our identities, as opposed to a fixedness. The self—and that includes your self—can be anything. It's an open, not a closed system; more free jazz than classical; more freestyle than breaststroke. To circle back to an insight made in the previous chapter, a self fluxes. More precisely: the self is *built* for flux.[17]

## The Impersonating Self

After *Letting Go* (1962), Roth succumbed less frequently to sociological fever and the sweet delirium of provocation it induces. Instead, he engaged in self-analysis, as it were. From *Portnoy's Complaint* forward, the author grew rich and famous by publishing stories about selves that, to varying degrees, resembled his own.[18] And then, suddenly, the sociological madness returned.

In *The Counterlife*, Roth doesn't necessarily stop fictionalizing himself. After all, Nathan Zuckerman, the narrator for much of the book, is the most Rothian of Roth's doppelgangers (maybe even more so than the character "Philip Roth" he features in a few novels). But in this metafictional tale, Roth has sociology on the brain. As he did a quarter century before in *Letting Go,* the author plucked the seed of a theory off the pages of a sociology textbook and mated it with fiction.

Nathan of *The Counterlife* echoes Paul of *Letting Go* when he wonders aloud if an "irreducible self" actually exists.[19] Like Paul, he is challenging the premise that within us there dwells some unsounded depth where our true essence is sheltered. In an aside well known to Roth specialists, Zuckerman informs us: "The treacherous imagination is everyone's maker—we are all the invention of each other, everybody a conjuration conjuring up everyone else. We are all each other's authors."[20] With this mantra, Roth has once again gone the Full Cooley; the self, he insists, is externally and socially determined.

But this is just the beginning of *The Counterlife*'s sociological take on personality. In a rambling disquisition, Zuckerman avers that a self does not have qualities, but an *ability*. We should not, he insists, conceive of selves as possessing the characteristics of kindness, cowardice, empathy, etc. Rather, all selves have the capacity to *pretend* to have those attributes. Zuckerman expounds on this counterintuitive principle thusly: "If there even *is* a natural being, an irreducible self, it is rather small, I think, and may even be the root of all impersonation—the natural being may be the skill itself, the innate capacity to impersonate. I'm talking about recognizing that one is acutely a performer, rather than swallowing whole the guise of naturalness and pretending that it isn't a performance but you."[21]

Notice how Zuckerman yokes Paul Herz's insight about the self having no essence (or "natural being") to this riff on "the innate capacity to impersonate." It is precisely because the self has no "natural being" that it must put on a false front as another self. "In the absence of a self," Zuckerman instructs, "one impersonates selves, and after a while impersonates best the self that best gets one through."[22] Ramming the point home, Zuckerman exults, "It's *all* impersonation."[23]

I would note in passing that the author had flirted with this idea for decades. In *The Professor of Desire* (1977), David Kepesh very self-consciously reflects on the *next* impersonation that he is about to pull off. Notice how the nomenclature seen above resurfaces in this quote: "At twenty I must stop impersonating others and Become Myself, or at least begin to impersonate the self I believe I ought now to be. He—the next me—turns out to be a sober, solitary, rather refined young man devoted to European literature and languages."[24]

Roth's championing of the human capacity to impersonate forces us to ask, what is a self? The answer: nothing. No thing, really, other than an inveterate purveyor of deadly serious shams and spoofs. "Look, I'm all for authenticity," lectures Zuckerman, "but it can't begin to hold a candle to the human gift for playacting. That may be the only authentic thing we *ever* do."[25] The self for Roth is an entity that strategically and automatically morphs into other selves.

With this, Roth veers suspiciously close to the thought of the sociologist Erving Goffman (1922–1982), his "dramaturgical approach," and the school known as "Symbolic Interaction."[26] So close, in fact, that it seems highly likely that Roth was familiar with his work. Whereas Cooley was not well known outside of academe, Goffman was a scholar of international stature.

His provocative publications had broad import and were discussed in the types of magazines of opinion that our author would likely have read.[27]

The Canadian Jewish sociologist—an oddball by all accounts—was endowed with a dry, mordant, I would even say cruel, wit.[28] In *Stigma: Notes on the Management of Spoiled Identity* Goffman speaks of "tortured performances." One example being "when an individual, confined to a wheelchair, manages to take to the dance floor with a girl in some kind of mimicry of dancing."[29] His research was peppered with cutting asides such as that one, as well as literary allusions.[30]

Roth and Goffman both inclined toward a rather jaundiced view of human nature.[31] The sociologist was assailed for presenting the self as "alienated" and acting in "bad faith."[32] In one particularly memorable assault, he was said to be "utterly incapable of seeing beyond the mean human possibilities embodied in his sadly limited view of the world."[33] Roth's critics have leveled strikingly similar allegations at him ever since the publication of *Portnoy's Complaint*.[34]

The very title of Goffman's most famous work, *The Presentation of Self in Everyday Life* (1959), should suggest what the iconoclastic social theorist was after. Goffman devoted much attention to the metaphor of humans as skilled actors, striving to convey messages to their "audiences" via carefully crafted social stagings. Here is one of his well-known asides: "Sometimes the individual will act in a thoroughly calculating manner, expressing himself in a given way solely in order to give the kind of impression to others that is likely to evoke from them a specific response he is concerned to obtain."[35]

Drawing upon the Chicago school's suspicion about the self having an essence, Goffman held that a person can be likened to a performer, albeit one that is a "dramatic effect" arising from encounters with others.[36] The heavy, and heavily qualified, use of theater metaphors accounts for why Goffman's approach is often referred to as the "dramaturgical" method.[37]

Notice how Zuckerman popularizes, and valorizes, many of the assumptions we've mentioned above in the following rant: "I, for one, have no self, and . . . I am unwilling or unable to perpetrate upon myself the joke of a self. It certainly does strike me as a joke about *my* self. What I have instead is a variety of impersonations I can do, and not only of myself—a troupe of players that I have internalized, a permanent company of actors that I can call upon when a self is required, an ever-evolving stock of pieces and parts that forms my repertoire. But I certainly have no self independent of my imposturing, artistic efforts to have one. Nor would I want one. I am a theater and nothing more than a theater."[38] These sentiments seem awfully congenial to Goffmanian dramaturgy. That we perform, dissimulate, manage impressions of others, play roles, collaborate with other "actors"—this is the crux of Goffman's interactionist approach.[39]

Goffman's subjects are—note this—rarely as aware of their status as actors as Nathan is in *The Counterlife*.[40] In other words, Roth's characters are brimming with self-awareness and staggering levels of reflexivity (see below). The people whom Goffman studied, by contrast, tended to "perform" their "scenes" rather unconsciously.[41] Further, it's not clear from the passage cited above, if Zuckerman believes that this "imposturing" self is unique to him (i.e., "I, for one . . ."), or resides in *all* of us—which is how Goffman would have seen it. Earlier Zuckerman alleged that the quality was universal.

But those are just quibbles compared to the jaw-dropping contradiction we encounter on the final page of *The Counterlife*. Suddenly, *and in opposition to every single thing he previously told us about the self and his self,* our narrator insists that in his marrow, *he is a Jew.* Zuckerman describes himself thusly: "A Jew without Jews, without Judaism, without Zionism, without Jewishness, without a temple or an army or even a pistol, a Jew clearly without a home, just the object itself, like a glass or an apple."[42]

Come again? Zuckerman, an avowed anti-essentialist, is now claiming to be just a Member of the Tribe, like an apple is just an apple? Has Zuckerman abandoned the idea of human existence being constant impersonation? Has he found that his supple, shifting, flickering self is, after all, irreducibly dark and Jewish? Has he dismissed his acting troupe? Shuttered his theater?

This unexpected, essentialist twist is explained by Zuckerman as the fault of British anti-Semitism. He has absorbed so much raw Jew-hatred in London that his self has been altered. "England's made a Jew of me in only eight weeks," sighs Nathan.[43] Zuckerman's self has been remade by (anti-Semitic) others and restored to its pristine Jewish state. Or something like that.[44]

It's a stunning soul shift for Zuckerman and quite a philosophical flip-flop for Roth. This endorsement of an authentic Jewish self makes no sense in the context of the dramaturgical theory he espoused earlier in *The Counterlife*. Then again, this reversal occurs in an experimental novel which "tends to turn lives and realities inside out."[45] Either Roth made a mistake, or he made a point. I think it was a case of the latter. The point being that in the course of a lifetime, dramatic, unforeseen, polarizing reversals afflict us all.

## The Kinetic Self

We tend to imagine the self as this closed-off thing, sequestered behind moats and towering walls of psychic guardedness. The Chicago school and Symbolic Interaction breached that barrier with sociological grappling hooks and trebuchets. They maintained that the self loops interactively with the social environment outside its brainy fortress. The self, they maintained, is osmotic; it is pervaded by others.

Roth shared this tendency to focus on how each of us is shaped by the external world. Yet he was not a sociologist. As a novelist, it was natural that he fixated on the self in all of its fascinating *interiority* as well. Much of his writing gazes in on what takes place deep within a person's mind. As is appropriate for a practitioner of the literary arts, Roth dares to penetrate this restricted space.

Fiction's paramount skill, its superpower if you will, is how it licenses itself to achieve the impossible: to tell us what a human being is actually thinking. Fiction purports to do what only God purports to do: to access the hearts and minds of women and men. When Silicon Valley creates an app that flashes your innermost thoughts on a screen positioned near your apprehensive head, then the market for novels and short stories will become even more depressed than it already is (see the conclusion).

Upon first glance, Roth's penchant for disclosing psychic interiority is not unusual. Fictionalists have been revealing what people are "really" thinking since the invention of the soliloquy, the interior monologue, and the third-person narrative voice. The Rothian wrinkle is to cast light on a particular type of human psyche, which I refer to as the "Kinetic Self." I associate a variety of attributes with the Kinetic Self, the most common being frenzied intellectual motion. Such a self exists in a state of relentless mental chop and churn. S/he thinks, and then s/he overthinks. And then s/he thinks some more.

*The Breast* offers us a textbook example of a cognitively hyperactive soul. Voiced in the first person, the novella reveals Professor David Kepesh's ramblings on his unwelcome metamorphosis into a mammary gland. As Bernard Rodgers Jr. once said of this book's narrator, "He is pure self-consciousness and can do nothing *but* think about his condition and its possible causes."[46] And think he does! So much so that his thought collapses in on itself; the man (?) has no idea what or where he is. But he will ceaselessly tax his cognitive powers to figure it all out across eighty-nine breathless pages. Thus the reader encounters countless serpentine musings like this: "I was afraid that the further I went the further I would go—that I would reach a point of frenzy from which I would pass over into a state of being that no longer had anything to do with who or what I once had been. It wasn't even that I would no longer be myself—I would no longer be anyone."[47]

Zadie Smith once referred to Roth heroes as "motormouths."[48] It might be equally apt to view them as "motorminds." Look at the cerebral torque of Nathan Zuckerman in *The Counterlife* as he contemplates undergoing the operation that will either restore his sexual function or end his life. Nathan's manic "reasoning" is as follows: "Caught up entirely in what has come to feel like a purely mythic endeavor, a defiant, dreamlike quest for the self-emancipating act, possessed by an intractable idea of how my existence is to be fulfilled, I now must move beyond the words to the concrete violence of surgery."[49] While Roth's protagonists might make idiotic decisions, let it never be said that they do so thoughtlessly.

It's not only perfervid cognitive movement that makes the Kinetic Self so uniquely Rothian. What's unique to Roth is not that he shows us how a self thinks, *but how a self thinks about its self.* This act, sometimes referred to as "recursivity" or "self-reflexivity," is performed by countless of his protagonists.[50]

Witness the recursive inner voice of Lucy Nelson in *When She Was Good:* "Herself! But what would that be like? What was she even like?—that real Lucy, who had never had a chance to be—Singing, smiling, wondering to herself—who would she be? what ever would she be like?"[51] Similar self-scrutinizing impulses are found in Paul Herz, whom we encountered earlier. He dreams of returning to his "old *old* self again."[52] "He remembered a self of his," continues the narrator, "that was more substantial than the one he was saddled with now; he remembered being *in* the saddle. He remembered being happier."[53] The final sentence of *My Life as a Man*—which, I confess, has never totally made sense to me—also exemplifies this self-reflexive strain: "Oh, my God, I thought—now you. You being you! And *me!* This me who is me being me and none other!"[54]

The Kinetic Self doesn't only think about itself; it poses questions to its self. In the 1959 story "The Conversion of the Jews," our thirteen-year-old protagonist, Ozzie Freedman, is escaping from his rabbi, whom he has just called a "bastard."[55] While he takes refuge on the roof of his Hebrew School, the narrator describes the following conversation: "A question shot through his brain. 'Can this be *me?*'... 'Is it me? Is it me ME ME ME ME! It has to be me—but is it!'"[56]

This seemingly banal operation of self-questioning has significant implications. For starters, it means that the Kinetic Self is divided. The self can ask questions about itself, which means it can disagree with its self.[57] The self does not tow the company line. The self is not a "yes" man or woman. Instead, it is endowed with a talent for self-scrutiny, self-criticism, and even self-mockery. One thinks of Neil Klugman in "Goodbye, Columbus" having a dialogue with himself (and God) as his girlfriend is being fitted for a diaphragm.[58] Neil wonders aloud, "Can I call the self-conscious words I spoke prayer?"[59] In that conversation, God is referred to as a "clown" and Neil as a "*schmuck.*"[60]

In *Indignation* we learn that the Kinetic Self can carry nearly all of the aforementioned skills and talents into the Everlasting. Our narrator, Marcus Messner, has apparently just been murdered in the Korean War. A little thing like being dead, however, is not going to prevent him from posing questions, reflecting on his own being, and even thinking about his own thoughts. Reader, please enjoy one of the most remarkable passages in all of Roth's fiction:

> And even dead, as I am and have been for I don't know how long, I try to reconstruct the mores that reigned over that campus . . . alive as I am here (if "here" or "I" means anything) as memory alone (if "memory," strictly speaking, is the all-embracing medium in which I am being sustained as "myself"), I continue to puzzle over Olivia's actions. Is that what eternity is for, to muck over a lifetime's minutiae? Who could have imagined that one would have forever to remember each moment of life down to its tiniest component? . . . You are not just shackled to your life while living it, you continue to be stuck with it after you're gone. . . . And would death have been any less terrifying if I'd understood that it wasn't an endless nothing but consisted instead of memory cogitating for eons on itself?[61]

Kinetic Selves suffer from ontological hypochondria. What I mean is that they are always thinking about the state of their being. These selves are in roiling conversations with their own selves, their back-and-forth crackles with maniacal, often negative, energy. To the honor roll of Kinetic Selves above we could add Alexander Portnoy, Peter Tarnopol, Mickey Sabbath, and, of course, autofictional "Philip Roth."

I am unambiguously of the opinion that Roth felt a kinship with Kinetic Selves. He knew them from personal experience, so to speak. As far as the author was concerned, such a self was a better self. My verdict is based not only on how often he wrote about kinetic individuals, but how infrequently (and negatively) he portrayed their counterparts. Static selves are people with minds that are at ease. These simpletons don't ask themselves hard questions. They don't suffer pangs of conscience. Within their minds there is no chop and churn, no ontological hypochondria, there is no back-and-forth.

One example is Roy Bassart of *When She Was Good*. This young mid-westerner's deepest thoughts center on how to scope out a better angle by which to ogle cheerleaders at football practice.[62] Flossy Koerner in *My Life as a Man* is intellectual stasis personified. She seems to have never figured out that her best friend, Maureen Tarnopol, was insane, as was her husband Peter, or that they each hated one another.[63] If Nathan Zuckerman's or David Kepesh's manic minds are powered by nuclear fuel, then Roy's and Flossie's are run by a horse-drawn carriage.

In *Operation Shylock* Roth imagines the stream of consciousness of Ivan the Terrible, the infamous butcher of the death camps. What we learn from his rant is that the man really liked massacring Jews, no questions asked (and lots of exclamation marks):

> To wield a whip and a pistol and a sword and a club, to be young and healthy and strong and drunk and powerful, *boundlessly* powerful, like a god! Nearly a million of them, a *million,* and on every one a Jewish face in which he could read the terror. Of him. *Of him!* Of a peasant boy of twenty-two! In the history of this entire world, had the opportunity ever been given to anyone anywhere to kill so many people all by himself, one by one? What a job! A sensational blowout every day! One continuous party! Blood! Vodka! Women! Death! Power! And the screams! Those unending screams! And all of it *work,* good, hard work and yet wild, wild, untainted joy—the joy most people only get to dream of, nothing short of ecstasy![64]

It may just be a coincidence that Roy, Flossie, and Ivan are gentiles. In Roth's writing, for the most part, static selves are not Jews. But it's not as if there is some sort of Jewish Kinetic genetic inheritance. Here and there, we find static Jews. At a *shiva* for Henry Zuckerman depicted in *The Counterlife,* Nathan comes across some relatives who are allergic to change. He runs into Dr. Barry Shuskin, a devotee of "cryonics." This man wants to be frozen after his death and "put on hold, hopefully for a couple of hundred years. Until science has solved the problem of thawing out."[65] At some point in the future Barry will be removed from his stainless steel container and resurrected. The changelessness of it all irks Zuckerman. He chuckles at a man "who would lie there like a lamb chop till the twenty-second century and then wake up, defrosted, to a billion more years of being himself."[66]

Later in the novel, Henry Zuckerman, in an assault on Nathan's worldview, defends the Barry Shuskins of the world, or at least those who might emigrate to Israel: "Here people don't jerk around like your fucking heroes worrying twenty-four hours a day about what's going on inside their heads and whether they should see their psychiatrists."[67] Still, in the main, Roth's Jewish "fucking heroes" are shown to have self-reflexive, tensile, garrulous inner selves. As a character in *Operation Shylock* pointed out, "inside every Jew there is a *mob* of Jews."[68] The possession of an unsettled mind, running in a thousand different directions, seems to be a Jewish predilection!

## Sloganizing the Self

Taken as a whole, Philip Roth's decades of reflections on the self are neither precise, nor exacting, nor internally consistent. Though maybe it's all to the good. After all, how many of us want the fiction we imbibe to be precise, exacting, and internally consistent? While there is, admittedly, something scattershot, even anarchic, about the way the author engaged the dilemma of selfhood, his ideas, in and of themselves, are spectacular. That the self has no essence; that the self is a fiction; that the self chronically and ingeniously cloaks its own empty shell—these are all grand, unruly, counterintuitive, absurd, and fascinating intuitions.

It would be hard to parse all of Roth's provocations under one pithy slogan, but maybe, "*Don't be your self!*" gets at the gist of the matter.[69] Roth also rages against the converse mantra, namely, "*Just be your self!*" What unites these taglines, and nearly all that we encountered above, is the author's boredom with the self *as is*. He rejects the unreconstructed self; the self as you find it; the self before it questions itself into oblivion; the self before it is upended and gobsmacked by some cataclysmic change, willed or unwilled. Your self as presently configured, he intimates, likely won't suffice. Sorry.

This impatience with smug self-satisfaction accounts for why so many of his heroes strive to transcend the "given" self. A Roth protagonist abandons the "comfort zone," refuses "to settle." It thus makes sense that his Kinetic heroes are ontologically restless. By that I mean to say they are constantly questioning the state of their very being.[70] His heroes actively seek to reflect on themselves and change themselves. In this manner, they are different from the great mass of humanity.[71]

This aversion to complacency also helps explain why the theme of human transformation, studied in the previous chapter, was infinitely alluring to this writer. His interest in metamorphosis is organically tied to his demand that we rise above our ho-hum selves. In other words, for Roth a "change" narrative is simultaneously a perfect "self" narrative. That's because the better self is one that gets over its self, changes, and becomes something new.[72] As Hermione Lee phrased it, the Rothian hero is "attempting to break through some prevention or blockage" and emerge "into a free, full sense of self."[73]

I feel compelled to point out that becoming a perfect self by becoming something new is not synonymous with becoming something content. As we saw in the previous chapter, Roth's changelings are not necessarily better off as a result of their ordeal. Quite the contrary, the transformations they experience often wreck their lives. One grim reward for all of their existential transience, as we shall see in *The Facts* (chapter 7), is self-knowledge, that most emotionally disquieting of personal attainments.

There is another prize for becoming something new. Even though your new predicament might be personally catastrophic, you have been elevated to a loftier status. This sentiment is articulated by David Kepesh in *The Breast,* as he ponders his new being as a gigantic, fleshy organ: "After all . . . who is the greater artist, he who imagines the marvelous transformation, or he who marvelously transforms himself? Why David Kepesh? Why me, of all people, endowed with such powers? Simple. Why Kafka? Why Gogol? Why Swift? Why anyone? Great art happens to people like anything else. And this is my great work of art!"[74]

I think Roth is saying here that the self that changes or is changed deserves aesthetic scrutiny. Of particular interest to Roth is that anguished soul who is aware of this change as it is happening. This is why our author writes about such selves in novel after novel.

So, *Don't be your self!* Once you aren't your self, you are worthy of being rendered into fiction by a writer like Philip Roth. Once you aren't your self, you have become fiction. Once you aren't your self, you are a work of art.[75]

# · 7 ·

# Fiction Is Truth! (Right?)

There's the not-so, that reveals the so—that's fiction.
    —PHILIP ROTH, *Exit Ghost*

The truth, to me, is what novels are for.
    —PHILIP ROTH, "His Mistress's Voice"

In the riven Land of the Arts, Philip Roth was a crypto Fictional Supremacist. He consistently depicted literature as stronger, braver, and more nuanced-er than nearly all other modes of aesthetic expression. His prejudice was never chanted aloud in jackboots, or sloganized with a torch held aloft. But read him carefully across the length of his career and you'll notice a clear pattern: the author consistently derides other art forms (and their practitioners) while ascribing virtual superpowers to fiction-making.

Let's start with theater. David Kepesh in *The Professor of Desire* describes acting as "the most pointless, ephemeral, and pathetically self-aggrandizing of pursuits."[1] It's no surprise that the thespians Roth depicted in his novels appear to be not mentally well. These include the shrieking, self-hating Jewess Eve Frame (*I Married a Communist*); the high-strung "Chekhovian actress" Eva Kalinova (*The Prague Orgy*);[2] Mickey Sabbath's insane first wife, Nikki;[3] the sinister college Shakespearean Bertram Flusser, who slathers his enemy's dorm room in semen (*Indignation*);[4] and the suicidal Simon Axler in (*The Humbling*). "Actors," opined Philip Roth's grandmother, "are not serious human beings."[5]

Poets are unhinged. At least that's the impression we'd get from the oversexed Ralph Baumgarten (*The Professor of Desire*), and Coleman Silk's oppositional-defiant son, Mark, a "narrative poet" (*The Human Stain*).[6] Photographers fare equally badly. Roy Bassart (base art?) in *When She Was Good* is a snap-taking simpleton; all his mental apertures seem shuttered. One of the few visual artists we meet in Roth's fiction is, naturally, a teenager who loves to sketch "beautiful likenesses" of American Nazi politicians.[7] Dance is a de-individuating endeavor. When Nathan Zuckerman, in *The Ghost Writer*, watches his ballerina girlfriend perform, he can't even spot Betsy in the crowd ("I spent most of the evening just trying to find her").[8]

Music, however, evades Philip Roth's chauvinism. He often references particular songs and classical compositions in his storyworlds. These melodies and harmonies can cure writer's block. They can mend broken hearts, too. David Kepesh in *The Dying Animal* works through his romantic misfortune by banging out Brahms, Schumann, and Chopin on his piano (and masturbating).[9]

Musicians, for their part, induce feelings of transcendence. In *The Human Stain*, the pianist Yefim Bronfman mauls his instrument as he plays Prokofiev.[10] Before the performance, Zuckerman was reflecting darkly on "the stupendous defamation that is death sweeping us all away."[11] During the performance, Zuck lightens up. While listening to the dynamic Bronfman ("Mr. Fortissimo!"), he exclaims: "Nobody is dying, *nobody*—not if Bronfman has anything to say about it!"[12]

But as much as Roth appreciated music, his obsessive passion was narrative prose. He once described literature, with a wink, as "the only refuge of the godly," and "the domain of the truly virtuous."[13] His esteem for this art form is reflected not only in how much fiction he wrote, but in how much he wrote *about* fiction. I think of the 2001 book *Shop Talk: A Writer and His Colleagues and Their Work*—that high-minded, and deadly dull, collection of interviews he conducted with celebrated authors such as Milan Kundera.[14] Then there is Roth's conspicuous ancestor worship. Like all good Prose Patriots, he venerated his wordy forebears. In his own fiction, Roth made more than 1,700 references to 246 novelists, short story writers, and poets![15]

His bias also expresses itself in what one scholar called his "metafictional preoccupation with the creative process."[16] The author kept crafting fictions about men enmeshed in fiction. From the 1962 *Letting Go*, to the 2007 *Exit Ghost*, Roth published twenty-five novels. Of those, nineteen feature narrators/central protagonists who are either writers or professors of literature.[17] It was in these novels about novelists writing novels that Roth would develop, in fits and starts, the most extreme claim he ever made on behalf of his art. By creating fiction, he boldly argued, we can discover truth. The paradox is lush. Fiction is supposed to be the realm of "make believe," is it not?

I want to break down three distinct claims in Roth's work: (1) writing fiction generates truth/(s) about your self; (2) writing fiction generates truth/(s) about others; and (3) writing fiction generates unseen truth/(s) about the world at large. These assertions ascribe science-like, godlike superpowers to the novelist's craft. As with all supremacists, Roth had difficulty mounting a credible defense of his prejudice. Still, his project is so delightfully brazen and intellectually buccaneering that it deserves our careful scrutiny.

## 1. Self-Fiction Generates Self-Knowledge

### My True Story

If you want to learn the truth about your self, says Philip Roth, then embrace fiction. He doesn't mean that you should simply read literature. Rather, the author wants you *to be an author too.* Generate fiction about your self, he intimates, and self-knowledge may follow.

*Generate fiction, self-knowledge follows.* A character experimented with this equation in the 1974 *My Life as a Man.* He failed. The book begins with two short stories about a writer named Nathan Zuckerman. When the second tale concludes, we come to a section break announcing a separate novel entitled *My True Story.*[18] Its author is one Peter Tarnopol, who recounts his accumulated woes in the first person. We now better understand that the two stories at the beginning were written by this Peter.[19] So within the covers of *My Life as a Man* we encounter two fictions (the ones about Nathan Zuckerman) that were created by Peter, followed by Peter's "autobiographical" true story.

It soon hits us that there are whopping similarities between Peter's life and that of Nathan, his subject in those two stories. Both come from loving/smothering Jewish families. Both are fictionalists. Both teach creative writing. Both have affairs with sexually adventurous young ladies. Both marry unstable, suicidal women whom neither actually loves. Both become widowers at an early age.

There is, however, one salient difference between fictional Nathan and Peter, the "real" author who created him. The second short story, "Courting

Disaster (Or, Serious in the Fifties)," reveals that Nathan engaged in a sexual relationship with his teenage stepdaughter, Monica.[20] He and "Moonie" eventually ran off to Italy after her mother's suicide.[21] Peter, who invented Nathan's taboo narrative, never mentions incest in his own "True Story." There isn't even an underage girl around to parallel the statutory rape depicted in "Courting Disaster."

For now, let's simply note the pattern established in *My Life as a Man*. Peter Tarnopol, a writer in distress, crafts make-believe tales about a character named Nathan who resembles him [i.e., Peter] greatly. In light of our equation above (i.e., *Generate fiction, self-knowledge follows*), it is important to point out that even though two fictions were generated (by Peter), *no self-knowledge was achieved*. Nothing indicates that Peter learned anything about himself as a result of writing gloomy stories about his alter ego Nathan.

Peter is a mess from the beginning of his "True Story" to the last sentence. The tale concludes with his wife, whom he previously tried to murder, perishing in a car crash. "Eyes leaking, teeth chattering," and his dead nemesis very much on his mind, Peter glances at his new "helpless" girlfriend, Susan.[22] The end.

Fourteen years later, however, Roth would explicitly suggest that fiction-making could deliver insight into the self.

### The Front Man

*The Facts: A Novelist's Autobiography* is a wild, uneven read. It kicks off with Philip Roth's epistle to his fictional creation, Nathan Zuckerman. Philip wants Nathan to offer him a frank assessment of the autobiography we are about to digest.[23] "Tell me whether you think I should publish it," asks the famous writer.[24]

The ensuing 160 pages of this memoir are meandering and dull. To use a musical metaphor, the book seems to "drop time." Its cadence slows to a crawl. Roth, I believe, may have done this on purpose. If I am correct, he performed an act of literary daredevilry; he aspired to *intentionally* induce boredom in his readers. All the better to heighten the thrills and sharpen the contrasts in the text's remarkable final chapter.

What a finale that is! In those rumbling, thirty-odd pages, Nathan accepts Philip's invitation to tell him if his memoir is any good.[25] Roth requested candor. Candor is what Zuckerman delivers as he demolishes *The Facts* and its author. In page after punishing page, Zuckerman lambastes the autobiography of the man who made him. Nathan urges his Creator not to publish what we have just read.[26] Even his wife, Maria Zuckerman, gets in on the fun (and the evisceration). She jokes to Nathan that "there must come a point where even *he* [i.e., Roth] is bored with his own life's story."[27]

Amid all of this mayhem, a few arch arguments are made about how we get to know ourselves. What Zuckerman wants to impress upon the dim-witted Philip is that he is going about his self-discovery project all wrong. The best way to procure self-knowledge, Zuckerman instructs, is not through "factual" autobiography. Instead, this is accomplished through creating fictions of the self—a mode that licenses us to make believe, to play, and to lie.

Roth, Zuckerman charges, can't tell the truth about himself by speaking *as* Philip Roth. Rather, he requires a nonexistent surrogate like Zuckerman as his "medium for genuine self-confrontation."[28] "You either don't know or cannot talk about it [i.e., your life]," taunts Zuckerman, "without me as your front man."[29] Philip Roth can only gain self-knowledge by impersonating Nathan Zuckerman. To wit, by creating a fiction to inhabit.

Autobiography is not commonly assumed to be fiction. It purports to be *non*fiction about the self. But for Roth, autobiography is "the most manipulative of all literary forms."[30] In *The Facts* he implies that this entire genre is fake precisely because of its obsession with factuality. When an artist doesn't deploy his or her imagination, then everything becomes untrue. You want the truth about your self, asks Roth? Then whip up a fiction.[31]

Only a fiction about you can deliver the accurate revelations that autobiography promises. Or, as he put it in *Operation Shylock,* fiction "provides the storyteller with the lie through which to expose his unspeakable truth."[32] Perhaps this is why, in a mischievous aside in *The Facts,* Zuckerman proposes that "the fable" *Portnoy's Complaint* is actually closer to the true autobiography of Philip Roth![33] Whether that is just canny misdirection is best left to a professional biographer. But for now we have established our first principle: fiction-making is a pathway to self-knowledge.

## 2. Fiction about Others Creates Knowledge about Others

### The Ghost Writer: *Getting People Wrong*

*The Facts,* we just saw, taught us to generate fictions about ourselves in order to know our selves. But what about others? Can fiction help us figure out a person who is not us?

Perhaps the reader is starting to notice that unknowability—of ourselves and others—is a major preoccupation for Roth.[34] This dilemma inspired him to pen the following reflection, one of the most well-known and spectacular he ever composed:

> And yet what are we to do about this terribly significant business of *other people,* which gets bled of the significance we think it has and takes on instead a significance that is ludicrous, so ill-equipped are we all to envision one another's interior workings and invisible aims? Is everyone to go off and lock the door and sit secluded like the lonely writers do, in a soundproof cell, summoning people out of words and then proposing that these word people are closer to the real thing than the real people that we mangle with our ignorance every day? The fact remains that getting people right is not what living is all about anyway. It's getting them wrong that is living, getting them wrong and wrong and wrong and then, on careful reconsideration, getting them wrong again. That's how we know we're alive: we're wrong.[35]

To confront the problem of "getting them wrong," Roth posited another equation: *Generate fictions about others, knowledge about them will follow.* The thesis was test-run in *The Ghost Writer.* The experiment, like the one in *My Life as a Man* described above, was a failure.

The narrative action in *The Ghost Writer* commences on a December afternoon in 1956.[36] Nathan Zuckerman recounts a visit he made at age twenty-three to the home of his literary idol, E. I. Lonoff.[37] Once there, he spots a beguiling young woman named Amy Bellette sitting, or practically preening, in the living room.[38]

Nathan wants to know her—sexually of course, because that's the type of guy Nathan used to be. Yet he also wants to know her story. Who is Amy and what is her relation to the aging, married Lonoff? He tries to unpuzzle this in the third chapter of *The Ghost Writer,* a truly strange and brilliant experiment conducted by Roth.[39]

In chapter 3, the narrative voice in *The Ghost Writer* suddenly shifts from first to third person. Nathan is no longer telling the story, as far as we can surmise. We are hearing a different story about the same people we met in the first two chapters. The bizarre section recounts that Amy Bellette is—or believes she is—Anne Frank. The story goes that as a teenager and amid the chaos of the aftermath of World War II, Anne escaped from Europe and washed ashore in the United States. Anne Frank, in this account, is alive (though not necessarily psychologically well). She is reading published versions of her now-famous diary. She lives in a world where everyone believes she was murdered by the Nazi killing machine. She is even attending, incognito, the Broadway production of *The Diary of Anne Frank*.[40]

But when chapter 4 rolls around, all of that appears to have been some sort of fantasy, a dream, or maybe an alien text that invaded our novel. Nathan is back to being our narrator. He refers to that whole Anne Frank business we just read as "the fiction I had evolved about her and the Lonoffs."[41] After breakfast, Nathan musters the courage to query Amy about her resemblance to Anne. She flatly denies it ("I'm afraid I'm not she").[42] A quarter century later in *Exit Ghost* (2007), Amy reappears and we unlock the mystery. Yes, she was a Holocaust survivor as Nathan suspected. But, no, she is not Anne Frank. Her ordeal took place in Norway, not Amsterdam.[43]

In parentheses, permit me to note that I found a draft of *The Ghost Writer* in the archives of the Library of Congress in which Amy Bellette *was* Anne Frank. Roth never published that version. Maybe that's all for the good, because in one scene he has Anne Frank—Anne Frank the most beloved martyr in modern Judaism!—exclaim to Nathan in a motel room, "Fuck me, damn it!"[44] To which Nathan exclaims, "Oh, the Jews—!"[45]

In *The Ghost Writer*, Nathan Zuckerman tried to enkindle a fiction about a mysterious, unknowable other. When all is said and done, the novelist concedes that his story did not yield the truth about her. She was not Anne Frank as Nathan had imagined. Fiction, therefore, has its limitations. But as Roth matured, he would become emboldened in his quest to demonstrate the potency of his preferred art form.

## American Pastoral: *The Story within the* What?

*The Ghost Writer* asked whether a concentrated act of literary imagination can foster insights into an unknowable other. The answer was "no." Philip Roth revisited the problematic two decades later—and this time a more provocative possibility was allowed to roam free.

Whenever I meet a person who has read *American Pastoral*, I ask them what they make of "the story within the story." To which my interlocutor almost always responds, "The story within the *what?*" Even when I assign this novel to my closest-reading undergraduates, there is a tendency for them to overlook what is unusual about *American Pastoral*.

What is unusual is that another fiction bursts out within its already fictional pages, as if a tree grew out of the canopy of another tree at a hard right angle. With the exception of scholars/Roth-obsessives, few readers actually notice this narrative swerve. Which is weird because our narrator, Nathan Zuckerman, *explicitly* tells us a few chapters into the tale that, from here on in, he is completely making the rest of the story up. This can get confusing, so first let me explain Roth's deft metafictional feint. Then I'll expound on the broader implications of his clever ruse.

For the first eighty-six pages of *American Pastoral,* the novelist Nathan Zuckerman recounts his writerly struggle to make sense of Seymour "Swede" Levov. When Nathan was a kid he idolized this person, a star high-school athlete, five years his senior. The Swede graduated in 1945 and then went on to become a Marine drill instructor.[46] The sheer manliness of the guy, along with his blond hair, blue eyes, and "Viking mask," made him an object of admiration and fascination in Nathan's wartime Jewish Newark.[47]

Some forty years later, in 1985, Nathan stumbles across the Swede and his family at a Mets game.[48] The men exchange pleasantries and then go their separate ways. A decade after that, out of the blue, Swede sends the famous novelist a cryptic letter. He invites Nathan out to dinner, ostensibly to discuss a tribute that he, Swede, is trying to compose about his recently deceased father.[49] Flattered that his one-time idol deigns to speak with him, Nathan accepts the invitation.

He will regret having done so. The dinner is a complete disaster. Swede prattles on and on about the minutiae of the leather glove trade which he inherited from his dad. He talks endlessly about his sons. He rounds out the night with some vinegary observations about the depravity of black adolescents in Newark. On the bright side, he appears to be in good health.[50]

Nathan complains that the dashing seventy-year-old "is not mentally sound."[51] "The man within the man was scarcely perceptible to me," sighs the novelist.[52] He continues: "I could not make sense of him. I couldn't imagine him at all."[53] Zuckerman exits his dinner thinking "this guy is the embodiment of nothing."[54]

Months later, Nathan meets Jerry Levov, Swede's brother, at their high-school reunion.[55] Jerry reveals that the Swede has just died from prostate cancer. And then there are more disclosures. Jerry explains that the wife-and-kids set that Nathan saw at the Mets game was actually Swede's second family. His first marriage, to a former Miss New Jersey beauty queen, ended in divorce.[56] The breakup was exacerbated by their daughter, Merry. The mercurial teenager got caught up in 1960s radicalism and planted a bomb that murdered an innocent bystander.[57] Needless to say, Nathan gleaned none of that at the baseball game or the Italian restaurant.

All of the events described above take us to page 86 of *American Pastoral*. On page 87, Nathan initiates the aforementioned narrative swerve. It is here where the second story, the fiction within the fiction, emerges. At this point in the text, Zuckerman is stymied. He can't figure out who Swede is. As for these new, shocking revelations made by Jerry, Zuckerman is flabbergasted. Who could have imagined that Swede, a seemingly bland jock, had such a rich backstory involving a beauty queen and a terrorist daughter, no less? And now he's dead.

Nathan is a novelist by trade. He is built to narrativize. But how, he wonders aloud, will he tell Swede's story? He has no facts, other than (1) his memories of the Swede from a half century ago, (2) their brief meeting at the Mets game in 1985, (3) the disastrous dinner in 1995, (4) Jerry Levov's rant including that bombshell about Merry, and (5) some press clippings about the bombing itself.[58] How can he transform those facts into fiction?

It is here that Nathan makes his bold metafictional move. Bereft of any data, he consciously decides to conjure up a fiction about Swede. There is no ambiguity about this—Zuckerman essentially stares into the camera, packs his pipe, and tells his audience that he's about to wing it. "Anything more I wanted to know," he declares, "I'd have to make up."[59] Zuckerman informs his readers that he is about to imagine Swede's story. "I pulled away from myself," he says, "I dreamed a realistic chronicle."[60]

The inspiration to pursue this course of action descends upon Nathan as he is dancing with an old flame at his reunion. He sways to the song "Dream" with his old flame Joy Helpern.[61] Please note that music inspires the act of prose creativity that is about to follow.

And what an act it is! Nathan's imagining begins—but why?—with incest. To fire up his creative smithy, he envisions a scene in which the thirty-six-year-old Swede kisses his eleven- year-old daughter Merry on her "stammering mouth with the passion that she had been asking him for all month long, while knowing only obscurely what she was asking for."[62] And we're off! What follows is a 340-page gallop in which Nathan Zuckerman dreams up Swede Levov's most intimate thoughts and life experiences.

He imagines Swede's courtship and marriage to Dawn; Merry's childhood and rebellious adolescence; Merry's bombing and its aftermath; the collapse of Swede's marriage, and the return of Merry the fugitive. It is all highly detailed, *and absolutely none of it has any basis in "fact."*[63] Every single sentence is conjecture, contrivance—Nathan's imagination run amuck.

Earlier I confessed that I badger readers of this novel, asking them whether they noticed that whole business about Nathan making up Swede's story from scratch starting on page 87. They respond with blank stares. They forget the novel within the novel after the "Dream" sequence imagined by Nathan. I think I know why they forget. They forget *because Zuckerman makes them forget.* The entirety of the remaining text occurs with little obvious clue, prompt, or reminder or farewell or "peace out." There is no further signal from our narrator that what we are reading is a total fabrication.

After page 86, the literary scaffolding of *American Pastoral* simply disappears. Gone is the *Shop Talk* talk about how a writer crafts a story about a mysterious fellow like Swede. Gone are the windy asides on how an author grapples with opaque subject matter. Gone, in fact, is the author; we no longer hear about Zuckerman and his story, his challenges, his own bout with prostate cancer, his place in the narrative. Zuckerman created a frame within a frame on page 86, *but he never exits that frame.*

On page 423 the story finally ends (in fact it ends two different ways— something else that readers consistently fail to notice). Its last sentence reads: "What on earth is less reprehensible than the life of the Levovs?"[64] But where is Nathan? His entire metaliterary project inspired by Joy Helpern and a song named "Dream" has vanished from the storyworld. Roth never reminds us that Zuckerman is imagining this all. This is why readers tend to forget.[65]

Literary critics, however, cannot forget. It's our job to wonder why a meticulous craftsman like Philip Roth would construct a story this way. Why didn't Nathan Zuckerman pull out, or step aside, from his fantasy? Why does he let his make-believe narrative of Swede with all of its bizarre details (e.g., a hallucinatory dialogue between Swede and Angela Davis) stand as the truth of the story? Why no admission of defeat (and fiction) as occurred in *The Ghost Writer* when Zuckerman conceded he botched Amy Bellette's bio?

My answer: Zuckerman (and Roth) wish to argue that this completely fabricated version of Swede is, for all intents and purposes, *true*—at the very least *a* truth. Roth wasn't ready to go there in 1979, with *The Ghost Writer*. But by the 1990s, as we are about to see, he was prepared to make extreme claims about the word-and-thought-defying power of fiction.

### 3. Fiction and Truth

*Seeing the Shit*

"The serious writer," avers a memorable Roth character, "introduces into the world something that wasn't there even at the start."[66] This is precisely what we just saw Nathan Zuckerman, a serious writer, do in *American Pastoral*. He introduced into the world a completely *imagined* story about Swede Levov.

In *The Human Stain*, Nathan does it again. He *imagines* postcoital conversations between Coleman Silk and Faunia Farley.[67] He *imagines* what these lovers think about one another. He even *imagines* assorted white supremacist inner monologues by Les Farley.[68] Few readers shelve *The Human Stain* doubting that Farley murdered the couple, though Zuckerman tells us he's imagining that too.[69]

Might I add that Zuckerman does all of this imagining, *even though he has concrete facts at his disposal?* Larry Schwartz has made the astute observation that Zuckerman ignores other sources that might have helped him tell Coleman's story.[70] One of which is, literally, Coleman's story—a book he wrote about his ordeal at Athena College called *Spooks*. Zuckerman never consults the manuscript which Coleman gave him. Why? Because he'd rather dream it all up on his own.

In *Operation Shylock*, the character "Philip Roth," another serious writer, *imagines* the dying days of his impersonator Moishe Pipik and his paramour Jinx. It's a surreal episode, involving the Manson family, a prosthetic penis, and necrophilia, all of it *imagined*.[71] Once again, a novelist explicitly reports to us that he is about to deploy his imagination. Then something is introduced into the world that wasn't there at the start.

What's curious about these novels is that the imagined/introduced results are rarely refuted, doubted, or unimagined. Instead, they are served up to the reader in a manner that indicates they might have actually "happened." The story Nathan fabricated about Swede *is* Swede's story. The same holds for what he wrote about Coleman, Faunia, Pipik, and Jinx. That which was dreamt up assumes the status of that which is real within the storyworld.

Maybe it's just me, but I feel this operation carries significant philosophical freight. What Roth did in *American Pastoral* and elsewhere intrigues me. I wonder if he meant to say that by creating narratives we introduce something into the world that is objectively true, or at least more true than what other discourses might serve up.[72]

This tendency to lionize literature is common in Roth's work. Take, for example, Leo Glucksman, who makes a memorable cameo in I Married a Communist.[73] Leo, whose comment about "serious writers" we encountered above, is a junior scholar of literature at the University of Chicago (his second passion, naturally, is music).[74] This eccentric, "foppishly over dressed boy genius" mentors underclassman Nathan Zuckerman.[75] That Mr. Glucksman wishes to seduce his young charge does not, in my opinion, undermine or invalidate any of his substantive claims.[76]

In 1953, Nathan Zuckerman is writing plays—bad plays—in the service of radical left-wing worldviews. The aspiring playwright thought it might be instructive to share this agitprop with the worldly Glucksman. Asking for feedback in a Roth novel is never a good idea. This is especially true given that Leo is a true believer in "formalist," or "New Critical," aesthetics that abhor the contamination of sacred Art with vulgar Politics.[77] Leo proceeds to tear apart Nathan's work (entitled "The Stooge of Torquemada"), describing it as "crude, primitive, simple-minded, propagandistic crap."[78]

"Stooge" triggers a massive harangue from Glucksman, who reminds Nathan that great art has no mandate to serve "the people." Art, he intones, is sovereign. It obeys no master, be it the masses, or politicians. Art is only interested in art, and for these reasons it is wildly disruptive.[79] Or, in Leo's arch phrase, "literature disturbs the organization."[80]

But Leo's not done. As he leans into his screed, the aesthete ascribes special abilities to those who create fiction: "If you are a writer . . . you see differences, and of course you see that this shit is a little better than that shit, or that that shit is a little better than this shit. Maybe much better. *But you see the shit.* You are not a government clerk. You are not a militant. You are not a believer. You are someone who deals in a very different way with the world and what happens in the world."[81]

What a spectacular rant! Leo's speech is the type of philippic I'd love to inflict on my undergraduates. Pacing the classroom, the floorboards creaking under my agitated tread, I'd thrust my mottled wooden cane in their faces as I growled Professor Glucksman's truth-to-power oratory.

The problem, however, is that Leo's entertaining screed doesn't stand up to rational scrutiny. Why is it that writers "see the shit"? No answer is offered other than great artists couldn't care a whit about cultivating an audience—they only care about producing great art. That's very nice, but it evades the fundamental question. Serious writers can glimpse what is invisible to others. OK. Got it. But what is it about their *medium* that permits them such unique skills of discernment? Is it narrative voice? Free indirect discourse? Parataxis? For all his sound and fury, Leo fails to distinguish between the fiction writer and fiction itself, both of which, he alleges, possess unique powers of observation.

A rationale for fiction's supremacy is also lacking in *The Great American Novel*. There too, literature's capacity to yield a higher truth is passionately proclaimed. Our narrator, a writer aptly named Word Smith, invokes Alexander Solzhenitsyn's speech upon receiving the Nobel Prize. In that address the famed dissident declared: "In battle with the lie art has always been victorious, always wins out. . . . The lie can stand against much in the world—but not against art."[82] Word Smith takes it from there and hails "art for the sake of the record, an art that reclaims what is and was from those whose every word is a falsification and a betrayal of the truth."[83] As in *I Married a Communist, The Great American Novel* offers an assertion, not an argument. Neither novel explains why and how literature succeeds in discovering and defending the truth.

We seem to be at an impasse trying to substantiate Roth's dictum that the creation of fiction yields unique truth about ourselves, others, and the world at large. I wonder, however, if this proposition works better within a postmodern framework rather than the modernist one upheld by Leo Glucksman and Word Smith. What if Roth doesn't necessarily believe that there exists *one* truth about any given matter, but numerous, coexisting truths? Fiction, then, exposes that multiplicity.

To see this relativism in action, one need look no further than the 1986 postmodern masterpiece *The Counterlife*. It is there where Nathan Zuckerman famously exclaims, "Life *is* and"—by which I think he means human existence cannot be reduced to true or false, this or that: "Life *is* and: the accidental and the immutable, the elusive and the graspable, the bizarre and the predictable, the actual and the potential, all the multiplying realities, entangled, overlapping, colliding, conjoined—plus the multiplying illusions! This times this times this times this. . . . Is an intelligent human being likely to be much more than a large-scale manufacturer of misunderstanding?"[84] *The Counterlife* explores the possibility that the self is plural and unruly, as opposed to singular and tame (see chapter 6). A person has no core essence; we are variable and shifting. The novelist's task, then, is to portray all of those "multiplying realities" about ourselves, others, and what lies beyond.

If you believe, as Roth did here, that each person is a repository of selves, a factory of impersonations, then, yes, fiction does seem well equipped to explore all that multiplicity. In *The Counterlife* we meet various Henry Zuck-ermans: Henry the adulterer doing office sex with his hygienist Wendy, *and* Henry the expatriate dentist dreaming of stealing away to Basel with Maria, *and* Henry the fanatical Zionist living in Israel, *and* Henry the well-grounded, resentful brother of Nathan ransacking his studio—all of those are possible iterations of this man. There are numerous Henrys, not just one. Great literature shows us the spectrum of selves that you and I possess.

Leo Glucksman, the high modernist aesthete, insisted that the great writer "sees the shit." The postmodernist might riposte that the exemplary novelist "sees the shits." A novel discloses the many possible flickering truths about me, you, and all creation. Literature forcibly reminds us of the irreducible complexity of Being. Politicians and their slogans can't do that. Activists and their chants can't do that. Autobiography and its self-absorbed mythmaking can't do that. Only fiction, says Roth, can do that.

## A Most Excellent Failure

But can fiction *alone* do that? Cinema, theater, poetry, performance art, opera, comic books—all have the capacity to illuminate multiple truths. As can a cubist painting which captures a bullfighter's snarl from nineteen dif-ferent angles simultaneously. Literature doesn't have a monopoly on mul-tiplicity, or storytelling for that matter. A little less Prose Patriotism would have benefited Philip Roth.

Greater consistency in his embrace of postmodernism would also have served him well. The Nazis—those eternal buzzkills of postmodern ambiv-alence—help us understand why. Was the Holocaust, to employ Zucker-man's explosive conjunction in *The Counterlife,* "and"? Are there lots of valid truths about the murder of more than six million Jews, one of which being there was no murder of more than six million Jews? The Holocaust, as far as Philip Roth is concerned, *happened.* It is not one plausible scenario among "multiplying realities." It is not "and." No work of art can or will ever alter this fact.

Philip Roth can't get his epistemology straight. He oscillates between a modern and postmodern way of conceiving the world. Sometimes he main-tains there is capital *T* Truth. Elsewhere, he explicitly reverses course and insists there are many truths. Does making fiction reveal the former (as Word Smith argues) or the latter (as *The Counterlife*'s riddling Nathan Zuckerman insists)?[85] When we spin a story about ourselves, are we poised to learn who we really are, or do we discover that we are a whole bunch of things? This is a major and unresolved contradiction that lies at the core of Roth's thought.

Also unresolved is the dilemma of *who* deploys the imagination in quest of hidden wisdom. In Roth's more modernist iteration, only top-flight writers, like the Faulkners, the Kafkas, and the Roths, create the fiction that speaks the unspeakable. Postmodern Zuckerman, however, gleefully democratizes the project. He proclaims that we *all* make fiction in our everyday lives. It is thus not clear if the process of fiction-making/truth revealing is reserved for a few elite authors, or everyday folks who "impersonate" en route to the pharmacy.[86]

Trying to argue that fiction generates truth is like trying to prove that up is down. The author did not prove that reality is accessed through make-believe, but he did frame the problem with dash and daring. Ultimately, what fuels his venture is a (quite modernist) optimism about what great Art can accomplish in an existence pervaded by ignorance, insincerity, hypocrisy, deceit, and lies. Roth failed, but it was a most excellent failure. Maybe his exposition will be the forerunner to an eventual breakthrough—the suborbital Project Mercury that paves the way for fiction's bouncy Apollo 11 moonwalk.

I confess to being sympathetic to our author's somewhat scattershot ideas about fiction's remarkable superpowers. It's awfully comforting to think that the skilled play of the imagination discloses truth(s), self-knowledge(s), insight into others, heightened social vision(s), and so forth. It's downright inspiring to believe that we have an interest not merely in reading fiction, but in *creating* it in our own workaday lives. To make the humdrum world more fictional and gain wisdom in the process—one need not be a crypto (Postmodern) Fictional Supremacist to see the allure in that.[87]

All of which leads the reverse biographer to hand off an inquiry to a future biographer. In his own life was Roth as amenable to the idea that reality was a fiction and that fiction was the gateway to reality? Did he consciously make up stories about himself to understand himself? Did he make up stories about others in order to arrive at some sort of truth?

# Philip Roth's Legacy

Art is *controlled,* art is *managed,* art is *always* rigged. That is how it takes hold of the human heart.

—PHILIP ROTH, *Zuckerman Unbound*

The method that was employed in this study may be described as follows: (1) study every piece of fiction Philip Roth ever wrote, (2) identify recurring thematic and intellectual preoccupations (i.e., "obsessional themes") across this body of work, (3) ponder the import of these ideas in and of themselves, and (4) ask if, and how, those fictional compulsions may shed light on the author's nonfictional existence.

The fourth of these directives, which I referred to as "reverse biography" in my introduction, is unusual, controversial even. This approach is unusual because fiction is not fact. Further, a cardinal rule of literary analysis is to never confuse the author of a fictional text with a protagonist therein. For these reasons, scholars of literature are not generally accustomed to, skilled at, or interested in, investigating authors' lives. Reverse biography is also controversial because it violates an effective and time-tested convention of aesthetic inquiry: artists should be granted the sovereignty—the space—to create without having their privacy subject to inquisitions.

I counter that with this *particular* author, employing the *particular* literary genres that he does, and at this *particular* moment in time, "reverse biography" is perfectly justified. Let's start with the author and his genres. Throughout this book we have noted Roth's eagerness to explore the interplay of autobiography and fiction. He likely published more "autofiction" than any other major American author.[1] Elsewhere, he composed a fake autobiography of a nonexistent person, a genre one scholar called "autobiography-as-fiction."[2] He did this in *My Life as a Man*, which I have repeatedly identified as his most pivotal (though not his best) novel. There, Peter Tarnopol tells us that he is about to "*embark upon an autobiographical narrative*" entitled *My True Story*.[3] But whose autobiography was it?

Cynthia Ozick, in a private letter dated April 15, 1974, thought that, by the end of the book, "Roth took over Tarnopol," transforming the latter into the "public phenomenon" known as Philip Roth.[4] He also freighted fictional characters like Alex Portnoy and Nathan Zuckerman with copious attributes, experiences, and acquaintances from his own life. In *My Life as a Man* and many other works, Roth gives us what scholar Debra Shostak in a devious phrase referred to as "fictions of self-exposure."[5]

For all of these reasons I have no moral, intellectual, or professional compunction about looking to Roth's prose as a potential source of accurate biographical data. As we have seen throughout this book, there are simply too many stunning correspondences between the author and his male heroes to abandon this method. The autobiographical quality of his fiction can no longer be gainsaid. When Benjamin Taylor recently revealed that Roth told him that a central incident in the 1962 "Novotny's Pain" came straight out of Roth's experience in the army, I didn't blink.[6]

When I found, in the Library of Congress, the same brochure for Philip Roth's Weequahic high-school reunion as the one cited by Nathan Zuckerman in *American Pastoral,* I just yawned (as I'm sure Roth did the countless times he conducted these Life-to-Art exchanges).[7] Someone should write a book—it will be a long book—about all the autobiographical components that appear in Roth's fiction. To paraphrase Henry Zuckerman in *The Counterlife,* Roth's art/life loops are "staring us right in the face."[8]

Roth insisted cagily, as we saw, that his work was overwhelmingly fictional, peppered with a few irrelevant autobiographical elements. I prefer that we flip the paradigm. Let us *begin* the analysis by looking at his novels as predominantly autobiographical. A few provisos must be noted. The first is that he brought that metamaniacal, self-reflexive energy discussed in chapter 6 to bear on his art/life loops. He crafts "autobiography" with a wink so blinding as to approximate a solar eclipse. Many writers incorporate autobiographical elements in their work. But few spend novel after novel ruminating on the *process* itself. Look for autobiographical elements in Roth's fiction, yes. But recall that he studded that terrain with funhouse mirrors, booby traps, and labyrinths from which there is no egress. Take this conclusion's epigraph and substitute the word "autobiography" for "art," and this will give you a sense of how controlled these (pseudo)revelations are.[9]

Second, we must (better) understand *how* Philip Roth strained his autobiography through a coruscating fictionalizing "transformer." This magical transformer is the intellectual instrument that animates Roth's unique genius. His spectacular talent consisted of taking real life, churning it through this contraption, and processing it into compelling narrative prose. To say there is a sizable autobiographical component to Roth's work is not to deny or minimize his gifts as an artist (which I suspect is why he was so affronted by the charge). The literary challenge for scholars is to break down the methods he used to transpose raw experience in exquisite literature.

The biographical challenge is to figure out *why*, decade after decade, he kept inventing stories about men who so resembled him. I don't think that's an irrelevant dilemma. Loren Glass posed a crucial question to Roth scholars back in 2009. No one, Glass points out, has ever explained "the necessity of Nathan Zuckerman in Roth's career."[10] That's something to reflect upon, is it not? Why did he employ this alter ego as his "front man" in eleven novels (in 1974, from 1979 to 1988, and then again from 1997 to 2007)?[11] With a talent and an imagination as vast and versatile as the one he possessed, why did Roth keep returning to alter egos as a means of telling stories? This is where the usually separate fields of biography and fictional analysis intersect; maybe other scholars will consider developing this line of inquiry.

I hope I have explained the reasons why I think reverse biography is justified as regards Philip Roth. Yet there is another set of justifications for this approach. These have less to do with Roth and more to do with the present cultural moment. Put reductively, art is changing.

A biographical turn is evident in popular culture. How many works of art do we consume nowadays where the artist is explicitly *in* the art itself? Think of Chris Kraus's autofictional classic *I Love Dick*. Larry David's series *Curb Your Enthusiasm* features outraged characters who routinely scream in revulsion, "Larry!" To listen to the rap music of Snoop Dogg is to hear him narrativize his rather compelling life experiences, signing in and off as "D-O-DOUBLE-G." Or consider Kanye West's "Famous" ("if you see 'em in the streets give 'em Kanye's best").[12] These styles range from "autofiction," to metafictional autofiction, to "autobiography-as-fiction," to "fictionalized autobiography."[13] Whatever they're called, these modes of narrative have become the currency of many artistic realms.

These autobiographical forms mesh with today's technological possibilities. In an age of social media, artists are neither advised, nor inclined, to avoid the spotlight; reclusivity is the affectation of a bygone era.[14] When #MeToo theorists brought the artist "back in" as a category of analysis (see my introduction), they were making a move that vibed with the spirit of the age. The link between a creative product and the person who created it is now more readily discoverable than at any moment in history. "With access to infinite information from the internet," writes one legal scholar, "every aspect of a celebrity's life is available to the public."[15]

Nowadays, you often don't have to bring the artist "back in" because, often enough, *s/he is already there* in some form.[16] This means that, for better or for worse, the Wall of Separation is likely to disappear in aesthetic analysis. In the age of social media, reverse biography is destined to become more sophisticated and less controversial.

All of which is to say that reverse biography, problematic as it might be, is appropriate for this moment, for this writer, and for his unique metafictional and autofictional output.

## #MeToo

One of the central cultural dilemmas of our era revolves around how to balance a revelation of odious private deeds against high aesthetic accomplishment. This observation is a variant of Claire Dederer's question, which distills the essence of the #MeToo intervention in the domain of aesthetics: "What do we do with the art of monstrous men?"[17] We ask this question about Paul Gauguin, just as we ask it about R. Kelly, and we are poised to ask this question for a good long time. This concern extends well beyond the arts—as attested by the increasingly tarnished and contested legacies of Thomas Jefferson, Woodrow Wilson, Winston Churchill, Mahatma Gandhi, Martin Luther King Jr., and others.

Applying this question to the novelist Philip Roth is complicated. For starters, we have no overwhelming body of evidence indicating he was actually "monstrous" in real life. Those who knew him and wrote books about him—Lisa Halliday, Ben Taylor, Bernard Avishai, Claudia Roth Pierpoint, James Atlas, Janet Hobhouse—portrayed him as a brilliant, warm, funny person. Naturally, they mention human failings and flaws, but nothing remotely grotesque is intimated. It is remarkable, though, is it not, that six of his associates wrote *books* about him? A seventh is on the way, plus the long-awaited work of the official biographer. In any case, these decent folks would appear to be convincing character witnesses.

As for his alleged monstrousness, that case would have to be made by drawing on a more varied set of resources. In terms of books, we have the testimony of his ex-wife Claire Bloom. Roth was so incensed by her memoir, *Leaving a Doll's House,* that he apparently wrote his own revenge account entitled "Notes for My Biographer."[18] It reminds me of Coleman Silk's *Spooks* (in *The Human Stain*).[19] Both are allegedly brimming with rage, and both never saw the light of day. In the fictional register, a humorously dark portrait of Roth as a master manipulator/hypocrite emerges in Alan Lelchuk's *Ziff* (see the introduction). Still, as measured by books about Roth composed by those who knew him (someone else can calculate the ratio for shorter pieces), the majority inclines to the "nonmonstrous" side of the spectrum.

Interestingly, a case for Roth's monstrousness, or at least some type of nasty churn in his being, was made by Roth himself. We've discussed *The Facts* already—alongside *The Ghost Writer, The Anatomy Lesson,* and *The Counterlife,* I consider it among Roth's finest works. In this text Nathan Zuckerman reads a draft of Philip Roth's "autobiography" and then proceeds to mercilessly razz Roth for daubing his readers with a cloying "nice-guy" depiction of Roth.[20] Zuckerman wagers that this affable self-portrait masks considerable "anger" in Roth, especially at his parents and the "detention house" where they quartered him as a child.[21]

In my "reverse biography," I noticed a variety of "obsessional themes," or ideas to which the author kept returning, apparently unaware that he was doing so. In chapter 1, a reading of Roth's nearly six decades of fiction revealed a disturbing racist undertow in his prose. No relevant biographical information about Roth and race exists that I know of. On the basis of the fiction alone, I'd assume Roth personally harbored that strange mix of tacit prejudice and generalized positive feeling toward blacks which characterized some of his protagonists, and so many white Jews during the civil rights and post–civil rights era. How that all emerged in his prose, especially his writings of the late 1960s and 1970s, is troubling.

The philosopher Sarah Stewart-Kroeker, in a reflection on #MeToo, observes that fans of indicted artists may suddenly feel "shame and betrayal" upon learning of their idols' ethical transgression(s).[22] I'm a critic not a fan. I was never a friend of Roth's. I would never have a written a book about him if I was. But as a person who has derived much pleasure and insight from Roth's work, yes, I feel these emotions. All that I can propose after having identified some very problematic texts in chapter 1 is that a "racial biography" of Roth be undertaken. This undertaking would set his portrayals of African Americans within the context of shifting and tense Black-Jewish relations from midcentury forward.

In chapter 2, I made the rather banal observation that Roth wrote about intergenerational romance because he had experienced it many times in his own life. In chapter 4, I pointed to the period between 1960 and 1967 as demonstrating heretofore unrecognized interest in focalizing female characters. This complexifies assertions that his fiction was misogynistic—a charge which I feel is difficult to either substantiate or repudiate.

In chapters 5 and 6 I encouraged scholars to ask why radical personality change and unstable selves so mesmerized this writer. Why did this artist relentlessly, unceasingly, write about selves that became other selves, and/or selves that lead double or triple or quadruple existences?[23] To me, this is a major biographical enigma. In chapter 7, I called attention to Roth's beliefs in fiction's superpowers.

Even if all the questions I raised in this book are irrelevant for biographers, I think the patterns noted in his fiction were interesting in their own right. Whether these tally up to "monstrousness" does not seem evident to me. I am, to repeat, deeply troubled by how Roth represented race. Precisely as #MeToo analysts suggested, I can never read him the same way.

Let's imagine that an odious revelation about Real Roth (see chapter 4) and his treatment of women does surface on Twitter tomorrow. Could #MeToo critics ever forgive him? It may, admittedly, be too quick to ask these thinkers to advance to the "closure" stage just a few years after the rise of a movement that emerged in response to millennia of terrible behavior among the male creative class.

It is certainly *not* #MeToo's burden to answer this, but morally compelling questions remain: What does genuine contrition for sexual transgression look like? Can an artist, for example, use his art as a means of atonement? There is no easy response to this dilemma. I think those #MeToo theorists who exhibited no desire to censor but instead demanded that misconduct become part of how we interpret the art were on the right track. Meanwhile, how *victims* think about the possibility of forgiving their aggressors, assuming their aggressors have the decency to seek pardon, should guide us in the years ahead.[24]

## The Future

I started this study by wondering about Philip Roth's commercial viability among a readership with cultural sensibilities that may be different from his own. Predicting the legacy of a recently deceased literary superstar is never easy to do. Who knows if one day *Nemesis* will be adapted by high-school educators and become the backlist staple-y *To Kill a Mockingbird* of the COVID-19 era? Then again, who knows if Roth's corpus free-falls into a bottomless obscurity?

Roth, for his part, had prophesied for decades that *all* serious fiction was plunging toward this abyss. In 1993 he fretted that a "decline of reader-ship" had resulted in a dwindling "gulag archipelago of readers."[25] In 2004 he forecast that in "twenty or twenty-five years" people won't read novels at all.[26] "The book," he sighed in 2009, "can't compete with the screen."[27] Literature will soon be consumed by only "a small group of people—maybe more people than now read Latin poetry."[28]

While I have identified unexpected conceptual synergies between #MeToo's approach to aesthetics and that of Philip Roth, this won't alter a basic fact: his reputation alone (e.g., Dead White Male whose alter egos indulge their lustful feelings toward much younger females) may dissuade many women from reading him. This places him in a vulnerable position vis-à-vis the (dwindling) market for serious fiction. As Katy Waldman observed: "It is women who do the lion's share of the book reading, editing, agenting, and buying; this fact may help determine the shape of today's best-seller lists."[29] It does not presently appear likely that those women inhabiting the "gulag," be they inspired by #MeToo or not, have much reason to get beyond the man's "rep."

I believe Philip Roth is a writer of substance and vision whose body of work merits serious contemplation. At the same time, I see very clearly how his fiction can be unappealing to the generation I am teaching today. To this end, I proposed that readers who might legitimately be put off by the sala-cious content in Roth's work explore his "unsexed" fiction. Those materials steer clear of cultural politics. Roth's reflections on the self and how it morphs are of interest to a broad swath of readers. Drawing them to these themes is certainly one way of envisioning a sunnier posterity for Roth. Then again, a lot of his best "change" narratives (e.g., "Epstein," *The Anatomy Lesson, The Counterlife*) are ensconced within works brimming with salacious details.

Though the basic point I made stands: there is a lesser-known Philip Roth who was more intellectually engaged in "vivid transformation" than he was in sex and eroticism. None of this, however, resolves the question of how audiences will grapple with Roth's legacy—a legacy which combines considerable genius with a penchant to maul certain types of sensitivities. The most profound suggestion I can offer is that such an assessment is up to the audience in question.

I wonder, though, if there is import to the fact that when it comes to the Philip Roth of flesh and blood *the case for monstrousness has yet to be made.* The autobiographical texture of his fiction almost goads us into drawing unflattering conclusions about Philip Roth himself. A fascinating biographical question is why Roth kept portraying awful men whom he led us to believe were very similar to Roth. What if we were to discover he was un-Portnoy-like, un-Tarnopol-like, un-Kepesh-like, un-Sabbath-like? If we were to learn that the man was upright and blameless, that his own personality bore no resemblance whatsoever to his fictional predators, we would need to offer apologetic oblations to his spirit, extol his boundless imagination, and concede that, yes, life is sovereign from art.

But the biographical question remains unanswered. In an epoch where the artist can no longer be separated from the art, the answer to that question will be the greatest factor determining his legacy.

# ACKNOWLEDGMENTS

Not being the kind of author who writes books that are warm and friendly, not being the kind of author who tries to please the crowd (or, perhaps, being one who tries but fails?), not being the type of author whose readers buy him drinks or Venmo his dry cleaning upon randomly encountering him in public, it is vitally important that I preserve the friendships I do possess, as well as recognize those people who have helped me with this project. (Do not be concerned: this is, by far, the longest sentence in this book).

In the twenty-six months it took to bring *The Philip Roth We Don't Know* into being, I had the pleasure of working with two outstanding research assistants, Heather Walters and Bethania Michael. The amount of concentration, discussion, and time they put into this venture transformed it into a different text altogether.

They were employed by my Georgetown unit, the Center for Jewish Civilization. Its wonderful administrators, Anna Dubinsky, Brittany Fried, and Jocelyn Flores were the consummate colleagues. Two junior assistants performed small tasks for this book, but major ones for future endeavors. They are Alexander Lin and Ria Pradhan. I commend all of the undergrads in the CJC for being so relentlessly fun to teach.

I appreciate the assistance I received from Georgetown University's library staff, especially Jeff Popovich. Many hours were spent perusing Philip Roth's papers in the Library of Congress. I salute the professionals who made that archive available to the public (before COVID-19 locked it down). Last, it was quite kind of the Bucknell University library staff to send me copies of Roth's early stories.

The team at the University of Virginia Press is composed of people who know how to work with scholars and engage with ideas. Ellen Satrom, Jason Coleman, Emma Donovan, and Emily Grandstaff did so much to bring this adventure to fruition and beyond. Susan Murray performed a really edgy line edit of a quirky text. Eric Brandt, the editor-in-chief, saw possibilities in this book where others did not. He ushered it through all of the cross stations of academic publishing with skill and savvy.

Emi Battaglia has brought her good professional name to the publicity for this book. I am so grateful to my agent and friend Michael Mungiello of Inkwell—ever supportive of his authors and preternaturally aware of every relevant literary issue. I want to thank my friend Professor Shareen Joshi for discussing so many ideas with me during our weekly dog walks.

My two sons are a constant source of joy and fascination. Both are embarking on possible careers in the arts. I've been observing them all these years with awe and trepidation. For art is slimy (see my introduction) in ways good and bad, is it not? My wife, Ippolita, my mother, my sister, Michele, and her husband, Michael, are always in my thoughts. As is my late father, Rubin Berlinerblau, to whom I dedicate this book.

# ABBREVIATIONS

In my introduction, I referred to "longitudinal analysis." Such an analysis required that I answer questions which I posed to myself about Philip Roth by virtue of using his entire fictional corpus as my body of evidence. What comprises that corpus? What follows below are two lists: the first itemizes his twenty-eight novel-length works. The second registers his twenty-five short stories.

The reader should note that all my citations in this book are keyed to Roth's Vintage International editions (the exceptions are *Our Gang* / Random House; *Exit Ghost* / Penguin Press; *Indignation* / Houghton Mifflin; and *Nemesis* / Houghton Mifflin). I find these versions more readable, portable, and inspiring than the cluttered, heavy, frowning Library of America tomes (about which Roth had his own concerns about accuracy).

Please note that I did not include among these fifty-three fictional products, screenplays that Roth composed, such as a television adaptation of *The Prague Orgy*. Nor do I linger on the many excerpts that Roth tended to publish prior to releasing a novel.

Last, some of my abbreviations differ slightly from those used by most Roth scholars (e.g., those used by the journal *Philip Roth Studies*). This was done solely for clarity involving computer software issues.

## Novels

| | |
|-----|-----|
| AL | *The Anatomy Lesson* (1983) |
| AP | *American Pastoral* (1997) |
| BRE | *The Breast* (1972) |
| CLF | *The Counterlife* (1987) |

| | |
|---|---|
| DAN | *The Dying Animal* (2001) |
| DEC | *Deception* (1990) |
| EG | *Exit Ghost* (2007) |
| EVR | *Everyman* (2006) |
| FAC | *The Facts* (1988) |
| GAN | *The Great American Novel* (1973) |
| GW | *The Ghost Writer* (1979) |
| HST | *The Human Stain* (2000) |
| HUMB | *The Humbling* (2009) |
| IMAC | *I Married a Communist* (1998) |
| IND | *Indignation* (2008) |
| LG | *Letting Go* (1962) |
| MLM | *My Life as a Man* (1974) |
| NEM | *Nemesis* (2010) |
| OG | *Our Gang* (1971) |
| OSH | *Operation Shylock* (1993) |
| PAA | *The Plot Against America* (2004) |
| PAT | *Patrimony* (1991) |
| PC | *Portnoy's Complaint* (1969) |
| PO | *The Prague Orgy* (1985) |
| POD | *Professor of Desire* (1977) |
| ST | *Sabbath's Theater* (1995) |
| WSWG | *When She Was Good* (1966) |
| ZU | *Zuckerman Unbound* (1981) |

### Short Stories

| | |
|---|---|
| ALM | "An Actor's Life for Me" (1964) |
| ATF | "Armando and the Fraud" (1953) |
| BT | "The Box of Truths" (1952) |
| CFA | "The Contest for Aaron Gold" (1955) |
| CJ | "The Conversion of the Jews" (1959) |
| DF | "Defender of the Faith" (1959) |

| | |
|---|---|
| DS | "The Day It Snowed" (1954) |
| ELF | "Eli, the Fanatic" (1959) |
| EP | "Epstein" (1959) |
| ETV | "Expect the Vandals" (1958) |
| FDMT | "The Final Delivery of Mr. Thorn" (1954) |
| FEN | "The Fence" (1953) |
| GC | "Goodbye, Columbus" (1959) |
| HMS | "Heard Melodies Are Sweeter" (1958) |
| HMV | "His Mistress's Voice" (1986) |
| LAK | "'I Always Wanted You to Admire My Fasting': Or; Looking at Kafka" (1973) |
| LVE | "The Love Vessel" (1959) |
| MIS | "The Mistaken" (1960) |
| NAPA | "The National Pastime" (1965) |
| NP | "Novotny's Pain" (1962) |
| OTA | "On the Air" (1970) |
| PSLT | "Philosophy, or Something Like That" (1952) |
| PSP | "Psychoanalytic Special" (1963) |
| TGG | "The Good Girl" (1960) |
| YTMS | "You Can't Tell a Man by the Song He Sings" (1959) |

# APPENDIX

TABLE 1. African Americans in the novels and novellas of Philip Roth, 1959–2010

| NOVELS/ NOVELLAS | PASSAGES OF INTEREST | PRESENCE OF A BLACK MINOR CHARACTER, OR ANY REFERENCE TO BLACKS | NEWARK | RACIST BANTER/ SLURS BY WHITES | RACIST BANTER /SLURS BY WHITE JEWS | CARICATURES OF BLACK ENGLISH | OBSERVATIONS ON BLACK BODIES | MENTION OF PROMINENT AFRICAN AMERICAN FIGURES |
|---|---|---|---|---|---|---|---|---|
| "Goodbye, Columbus" (1959) | GC, pp. 7, 14, 21, 31, 34, 35, 36, 47, 48, 59, 74, 90, 91, 92, 94, 120 | X | X | X | X | X | X | Willie Mays |
| Letting Go (1962) | LG, pp. 65, 66, 68, 221, 224, 225, 254, 329, 374, 446, 468, 477, 530, 552, 624 | X | | X | X | X | X | |
| When She Was Good (1966) | WSWG, pp. 30, 118, 243, 244, 247 | X | | X | | | | Nat "King" Cole |
| Portnoy's Complaint (1969) | PC, pp. 7, 10, 12, 13, 52, 75, 82, 106, 130, 156, 161, 170, 172, 209, 216, 273 | X | X | X | X | X | X | Marian Anderson; James Baldwin; W. E. B. Du Bois |
| Our Gang (1971) | OG, pp. 94, 95, 96, 98, 100, 103, 104, 122, 126 | X | | X | | | | Martin Luther King; Curt Flood; Black Panthers |

| | | | | | | Senator Edward Brooke |
|---|---|---|---|---|---|---|
| The Breast (1972) | X | | | | | X |
| Great American Novel (1973) | X | | X | X | X | X Robert (Satchel) Paige |
| My Life as a Man (1974) | X | | X | | X | X Medgar Evers; Langston Hughes; Martin Luther King Jr; Ralph Ellison |
| Professor of Desire (1977) | X | X | X | X | | |
| The Ghost Writer (1979) | X | X | | | | |
| Zuckerman Unbound (1981) | X | X | X | X | X | Wilt Chamberlain; Jimi Hendrix; Martin Luther King Jr; LeRoi Jones |
| The Anatomy Lesson (1983) | X | X | X | X | X | X |

Page references (first column detail):
- The Breast (1972): BRE, pp. 77, 78
- Great American Novel (1973): GAN, pp. 1, 4, 28, 34, 40–42, 91, 114, 132, 148, 149, 151, 152, 158, 170, 227, 228, 229, 268, 296, 297, 298, 306–22, 332, 396
- My Life as a Man (1974): MLM, pp. 64, 105, 191, 269, 272, 273, 309
- Professor of Desire (1977): POD, pp. 231, 235, 236
- The Ghost Writer (1979): GW, p. 89
- Zuckerman Unbound (1981): ZU, pp. 10, 13, 14, 70, 156, 160, 222, 223, 224, 225
- The Anatomy Lesson (1983): AL, pp. 39, 53, 54, 55, 70, 92, 116, 289, 290

(continued)

TABLE 1. (*Continued*)

| NOVELS/NOVELLAS | PASSAGES OF INTEREST | PRESENCE OF A BLACK MINOR CHARACTER, OR ANY REFERENCE TO BLACKS | NEWARK | RACIST BANTER/SLURS BY WHITES | RACIST BANTER/SLURS BY WHITE JEWS | CARICATURES OF BLACK ENGLISH | OBSERVATIONS ON BLACK BODIES | MENTION OF PROMINENT AFRICAN AMERICAN FIGURES |
|---|---|---|---|---|---|---|---|---|
| The Prague Orgy (1985) | None | | | | | | | |
| The Counterlife (1987) | CLF, pp. 10, 19, 78, 124, 125 | X | | | X | | | Muhammad Ali |
| The Facts (1988) | FAC, pp. 32, 33, 108, 111, 128, 146, 147, 148 | X | X | | | | X | Martin Luther King Jr.; Ralph Ellison |
| Deception (1990) | DEC, pp. 26, 83, 83, 84, 85, 86, 87, 109, 177 | X | | X | | | X | Alice Walker |
| Patrimony (1991) | PAT, pp. 47, 85, 108, 109, 110, 125, 126, 127, 185, 202 | X | X | | X | | X | |
| Operation Shylock (1993) | OSH, pp. 164, 254, 395 | X | | | X | | | Jesse Jackson |

| | | | | | | | | |
|---|---|---|---|---|---|---|---|---|
| Sabbath's Theater (1995) | ST, pp. 54, 57, 58, 133, 153, 160, 168, 184, 196, 197, 204, 205, 206, 207, 210, 242, 292, 354, 356, 361, 379, 380, 401, 432, 448 | X | | X | X | X | X | Ray Charles; Freddie Green; Bo Jackson; Lionel Hampton, Jesse Jackson; Michael Jackson Toni Morrison; Fats Waller; Eldridge Cleaver; Joe Louis |
| American Pastoral (1997) | AP, pp. 24, 25, 26, 47, 48, 49, 50, 75, 118, 133, 135, 148, 157, 158, 159, 160, 161, 162, 163, 164, 165, 166, 167, 212, 218, 229, 230, 235, 257, 260, 261, 262, 269, 345 | X | X | | X | X | X | Billy Eckstine; Duke Ellington; Bill Cook; Angela Davis; Illinois Jacquet; Buddy Johnson; LeRoi Jones; Sarah Vaughan; Bobby Seale; Huey Newton |
| I Married a Communist (1998) | IMAC, pp. 23, 33, 46, 47, 48, 49, 553, 91, 92, 93, 94, 95, 119, 126, 145, 146, 147, 316, 317 | X | X | X | X | X | X | Larry Doby; Paul Robeson; Jackie Robinson |
| The Human Stain (2000) | Entire text | X | X | X | X | | X | |
| The Dying Animal (2001) | DAN, 56 | | | | | | | Jimi Hendrix; Charlie Parker; Bessie Smith |

(continued)

TABLE 1. (*Continued*)

| NOVELS/ NOVELLAS | PASSAGES OF INTEREST | PRESENCE OF A BLACK MINOR CHARACTER, OR ANY REFERENCE TO BLACKS | NEWARK | RACIST BANTER/ SLURS BY WHITES | RACIST BANTER /SLURS BY WHITE JEWS | CARICATURES OF BLACK ENGLISH | OBSERVATIONS ON BLACK BODIES | MENTION OF PROMINENT AFRICAN AMERICAN FIGURES |
|---|---|---|---|---|---|---|---|---|
| *The Plot Against America* (2004) | PAA, pp. 23, 32, 72, 73, 93, 99, 104, 106, 149, 229, 232, 247, 260, 261, 282, 366, 374 | X | X | | X | X | X | Booker T. Washington |
| *Everyman* (2006) | EVR, pp. 47, 48, 171, 172, 173, 174, 175, 176, 177, 178, 179, 180 | X | | | | | X | |
| *Exit Ghost* (2007) | EG, pp. 72, 79, 99, 176, 254, 262 | X | | | X | | X | Toni Morrison; Richard Wright; Ralph Ellison |
| *Indignation* (2008) | IND, pp. 40, 41, 42, 147, 199 | X | X | | | | | |
| *The Humbling* (2009) | None | | | | | | | |
| *Nemesis* (2010) | NEM, pp. 82, 247 | X | X | | | | | |

TABLE 2. Age-dissimilar romance in Philip Roth novels, 1972–2009

| YEAR | TITLE | MALE AGE / FEMALE AGE | AGE DIFFERENCE | PASSAGES OF INTEREST |
|---|---|---|---|---|
| 1972 | *The Breast* | David Kepesh 38 / Claire Ovington 25 | 13 years | BRE, pp. 4, 8 |
| 1973 | *The Great American Novel* | Word Smith 52 / Vassar graduate 21 | 31 years | GAN, pp. 26, 30 |
| | | Babe Ruth 32 / Angela Whittling Trust 55* | 23 years | GAN, p. 260 |
| | | Luke Gofannon < 30 / Angela Whittling Trust 60* | 30 years (?) | GAN, pp. 260–62 |
| | | Gil Gamesh < 20 / Angela Whittling Trust 62* | 42 years | GAN, p. 266 |
| | | Ty Cobb (?) / Angela Whittling Trust 62* | Unknown | GAN, p. 259 |
| 1974 | *My Life as a Man* | Father (?) / Lydia Ketterer 12† | Unknown | MLM, p. 34 |
| | | Nathan Zuckerman 26–30 / Monica Ketterer 12–16† | 14 years | MLM, pp. 82, 85 |
| | | Peter Tarnopol 29 / Karen Oakes 20 | 10 years | MLM, pp. 124, 158, 205–9 |
| | | Peter Tarnopol 30 / Nancy Miles ca. 22. | 8 years | MLM, p. 158 |
| | | Father (?) / Maureen 11† | Unknown | MLM, pp. 298–99 |
| 1977 | *Professor of Desire* | David Kepesh 34 / Claire Ovington 24 | 10 years | POD, pp. 149, 151, 228 |
| | | Ralph Baumgarten ca. 35 / Wendy 17 | 18 years | POD, pp. 146–48 |
| 1979 | *The Ghost Writer* | E. I. Lonoff 56 / Amy Bellette 26 or 27 | 30 years | GW, pp. 11, 123, 175 |
| 1983 | *The Anatomy Lesson* | Nathan Zuckerman 40 / Jenny 28 | 12 years | AL, pp. 17, 95 |
| | | Nathan Zuckerman 40 / Diana Rutherford 20 | 20 years | AL pp. 17, 86, 87, 95 |
| | | Chauffeur (?) / Diana 10† | Unknown | AL, p. 90 |
| | | Friend's father (?) / Diana 12–20† | Unknown | AL, p. 89 |
| 1987 | *The Counterlife* | Henry Zuckerman 39 / Wendy Casselman 22 | 17 years | CLF, pp. 10, 33 |
| | | Nathan Zuckerman 44–45 / Maria 27 | 17–18 years | CLF, pp. 67, 72, 184 |

TABLE 2. (*continued*)

| YEAR | TITLE | MALE AGE / FEMALE AGE | AGE DIFFERENCE | PASSAGES OF INTEREST |
|------|-------|----------------------|----------------|----------------------|
| 1988 | *The Facts* | Nathan Zuckerman 45 / Maria Zuckerman 28 | 17 years | *FAC*, p. 186. (Assuming that Maria is 28 years old on the basis of her age in *CLF*) |
|      |        | Josie Jensen's father (?) / Josie Jensen (?)† | Unknown | *FAC*, p. 83 |
| 1990 | *Deception* | Unnamed male lover 45 / Unnamed female lover 25 (?) | 20 years (?) | *DEC*, pp. 56–57 |
|      |        | "Philip" / Unnamed female lover 19 (?) | Unknown | *DEC*, pp. 118–20 |
|      |        | "Philip" 45 (?) / Unnamed female lover 28 (?) | Ca. 17 years | *DEC*, p. 190 (replication of Maria Freshfield in *CLF*) |
| 1991 | *Patrimony* | Herman Roth 86 / Lillian Beloff 70 | 16 years | *PAT*, pp. 9, 10 |
| 1993 | *Operation Shylock* | Moishe Pipik ("Philip Roth") < 60 / Jinx Possesski ca. 40 | 20 years | *OSH*, p. 224 |
| 1995 | *Sabbath's Theater* | Mickey Sabbath 64 / Drenka Balich 52 | 12 years | *ST*, pp. 3, 4, 22, 26, 27, 53, 210–11 |
|      |        | Mickey Sabbath 60 / Christa 20 | 40 years | *ST*, pp. 7, 53, 59 |
|      |        | Mickey Sabbath 60 / Kathy Goolsbee 20 | 40 years | *ST*, pp. 25, 210, 214 |
|      |        | Mickey Sabbath 64 / Madeline 29 | 35 years | *ST*, p. 285 |
|      |        | Barrett < 30 / Drenka Balich 50* | 20 years | *ST*, p. 67 |
|      |        | The Maestro 70+ / Current Mistress 15† | ≤ 55 years | *ST*, pp. 234–35 |
|      |        | Father of Roseanna 56 / Roseanna 13† | 43 years | *ST*, pp. 258–59, 263–72 |
| 1997 | *American Pastoral* | Swede Levov 36 / Merry 11† | 25 years | *AP*, p. 92 |
|      |        | Swede Levov 40+ / Rita Cohen (?) | Unknown | *AP*, pp. 142–43 |

TABLE 2. (*continued*)

| YEAR | TITLE | MALE AGE / FEMALE AGE | AGE DIFFERENCE | PASSAGES OF INTEREST |
|------|-------|----------------------|----------------|----------------------|
| 1998 | *I Married a Communist* | Ira Ringold 36 / Pamela Solomon 24 | 12 years | *IMAC*, pp. 166, 167, 175 |
| 2000 | *The Human Stain* | Coleman 71 / Faunia 34 | 37 years | *HST*, pp. 1, 27 |
|      |       | Stepfather of Faunia (?) / Faunia 5–14† | Unknown | *HST*, p. 28 |
| 2001 | *The Dying Animal* | David Kepesh 62 / Consuela 24 | 38 years | *DAN*, pp. 2, 33–34 |
|      |       | David Kepesh 63 / Carolyn Lyons 45 | 18 years | *DAN*, pp. 47, 70 |
|      |       | Ken Kepesh 42 / Girlfriend 26 | 16 years | *DAN*, pp. 64, 76–77 |
| 2004 | *The Plot Against America* | Rabbi Bengelsdorf 63 / Evelyn Finkel 31 | 32 years | *PAA*, pp. 87–88 |
|      |       | Alvin 23 / Minna 31* | 8 years | *PAA*, p. 288 |
| 2006 | *Everyman* | Everyman 50 / Female model 19 | 31 years | *EVR*, p. 108 |
|      |       | Everman 50 (?) / Merete 24 | 26 years | *EVR*, pp. 95, 96, 110, 118 |
| 2007 | *Exit Ghost* | Nathan Zuckerman 71 / Jamie Logan 30 | 41 years | *EG*, pp. 3, 67 |
| 2009 | *The Humbling* | Simon Axler 65 / Pegeen Stapleford 40 | 25 years | *HUMB*, p. 44 |
|      |       | Simon Axler 65 / Tracy 28 | 37 years | *HUMB*, pp. 108–11, 136 |

*Asterisks indicate a relationship in which the woman is the older partner.

†Daggers indicate child molestation and statutory rape.

# NOTES

## INTRODUCTION

1. Roth, *ST,* 60
2. Roth, *DAN,* 70.
3. For discussions of rape culture, see the essays in Gay, ed., *Not That Bad.* Rape culture is elsewhere described as "a highly contested term that refers to the social, cultural and political processes that condone violence against women but also blame women (and all other victim-survivors) if and when violence is perpetrated against them" (Fileborn and Loney-Howes, *#MeToo and the Politics of Social Change,* 1–2). Another definition describes it as "a cultural environment (a set of beliefs, practices, and attitudes) that enables sexual violence to thrive," with characteristics including "rape myths and victim blaming as well as more subtle and insidious beliefs and practices" (Milena Popova, *Sexual Consent,* 182; see also 4). For a discussion of racist banter, see chapter 1.
4. As we shall see throughout this book, Roth's characters and Roth himself chided political correctness, multiculturalism, and feminism. For some examples, see Roth, *EG,* 185; *DEC,* 107; and countless remarks in *ST.*
5. See chapter 3.
6. "Cancel culture" refers to the tendency of artists accused of sexual transgression to be "banished from public engagement" (E. Goldberg, "Do Works by Men Toppled by #MeToo Belong in the Classroom?"). Elsewhere, cancel culture has been explained in Romano, "Why We Can't Stop Fighting about Cancel Culture." For a discussion of how one canceled writer, Sherman Alexie, is taught in a college class, see Spanke, "Magnificent Things and Terrible Men."
7. Nadel, *A Critical Companion to Philip Roth,* 272–73.
8. For a rundown of how I categorize his novels and short stories, see the list of abbreviations in this volume.

9. Leibovitz, "The Grapes of Roth"; McKinley, "Testosterone and Sympathy," 92.

10. Lopez and Snyder, "Tarana Burke on Why She Created the #MeToo Movement"; Garcia, "The Woman Who Created #MeToo." There were precedents for #MeToo in the form of #BeenRapedNeverReported, which was one of the early examples of "hashtag feminism" (Mendes, Ringrose, and Keller, "#MeToo and the Promise"). For a discussion of some other predecessors to #MeToo, see Gieseler, *The Voices of #MeToo*, 3–4.

11. North, "The #MeToo Movement and Its Evolution"; Gieseler, *The Voices of #MeToo*.

12. Gieseler, *The Voices of #MeToo*, 2.

13. Gieseler, *The Voices of #MeToo*, 2–3; CBS/AP, "More than 12M 'Me Too' Facebook Posts, Comments, Reactions in 24 Hours"; Anderson and Toor, "How Social Media Users Have Discussed Sexual Harassment." The authors report that the hashtag "has been used more than 19 million times on Twitter" between Milano's 2017 tweet and September 30, 2018.

14. Kantor and Twohey, "Harvey Weinstein Paid off Sexual Harassment Accusers"; Traister, "Why the Harvey Weinstein Sexual-Harassment Allegations Didn't Come out until Now"; R. Farrow, "From Aggressive Overtures to Sexual Assault"; Garcia, "The Woman Who Created #MeToo." The movement has been criticized for "initially ignoring the contributions of women of color to the creation of the movement, but even more, for ignoring the unique forms of harassment and the heightened vulnerability that women of color frequently experience in the workplace" (Onwuachi-Willig, "What about #UsToo?," 111). Tarana Burke commented on these issues in "#MeToo Was Started for Black and Brown Women." Leung and Williams, "#MeToo and Intersectionality," 352. On the role that celebrities played in the advent of #MeToo, see Rosewarne, "#MeToo and the Reasons to Be Cautious," 178–80; and Loney-Howes, "The Politics of the Personal," 21–35.

15. Gilbert, "The Movement of #MeToo."

16. E. Goldberg, "Do Works by Men Toppled by #MeToo Belong in the Classroom?" For other definitions, see Gieseler, *The Voices of #MeToo*: "The grassroots activism of #MeToo reiterates the reality and commonality of sexual abuse, harassment, exploitation, and assault for women (and many men) everywhere. The power of a movement like #MeToo is how it spotlights silenced issues of oppression, begins the conversation about these experiences, and transforms the dialogue into a movement" (4).

17. Nussbaum, in "Accountability in an Era of Celebrity," notes that the arts provide "a diffuse workplace" that is "hard to police" (166, 165).

18. As for the conversational intersection itself, sans Philip Roth, see, for example, Dederer, "What Do We Do with the Art of Monstrous Men?" See also Sehgal, "#MeToo Is All Too Real."

19. Vanderhoof, "Me and the Monkey."

20. Waldman, "One Year of #MeToo."

21. Wickenden, "Philip Roth in the #MeToo Era."

22. Daum, "In the Age of #MeToo."

23. Her comments are found in Marchese, "In Conversation." See also Hjalmarson, "Philip Roth and #MeToo." Tamar Fox contextualized Roth's death within the context of the #MeToo movement ("Philip Roth Hated Jewish Women").

24. I take this term from Gieseler, *The Voices of #MeToo.*

25. Kaprièlian, "Philip Roth: Némésis sera mon dernier livre."

26. See chapter 3 for a detailed list of these publications.

27. C. Bloom, *Leaving a Doll's House.*

28. In her memoir, *Leaving a Doll's House,* Claire Bloom details Roth's "profound distrust of the sexual power of women" (146); his tendency to put on "the face of an uncontrollable and malevolent child in a temper tantrum" (158); his adulterous advances made to a much younger woman ("Rachael [Hallawell] had been subjected to sexual advances from Philip . . . perpetrating a virtually incestuous betrayal" [224–25]). Elsewhere, Bloom intimates that Roth's previous marriage to Maggie Martinson Williams was "violent and grotesque" (145). Rounding out this portrait, Bloom calls Roth "spectacularly manipulative" (232).

29. Pierson, "Harvey Weinstein Loses Bid"; Ransom, "Harvey Weinstein Is Found Guilty of Sex Crimes in #MeToo Watershed."

30. Roig-Franzia, "Bill Cosby Convicted on Three Counts of Sexual Assault."

31. Associated Press, "A Timeline of Roman Polanski's 4-Decade Underage Sex Case." As we shall see, Polanski's past misdeeds figure prominently in contemporary #MeToo discussions.

32. In 2014, Allen's adoptive daughter Dylan Farrow wrote an open letter to the *New York Times,* in which she revealed that she was sexually assaulted by him as a child. The piece renewed discussions of the director's misconduct—discussions which had been in play since the early 1990s (D. Farrow, "An Open Letter from Dylan Farrow").

33. In 2018, Junot Díaz was accused by a number of women writers of "mistreatment and misogynistic verbal abuse" (Phillips, "Pulitzer Prize–Winning Author"). After allegations surfaced about Díaz's abuse of women, the poet Mary Karr tweeted her thoughts about male writers implicated in the #MeToo movement. In the tweet, Karr shared her experience of abuse

during her relationship with David Foster Wallace, reanimating concerns about Wallace's treatment of women and his place in the literary canon (Karr, Mary [@marykarrlit], "Deeply saddened by the allegations against #JunotDiaz & I support every woman brave enough to speak. The violence #DavidFosterWallace inflicted on me as a single mom was ignored by his biographer & @NewYorker as 'alleged' despite my having letters in his hand. But DFW was white"). Garber, "David Foster Wallace"; Paulson, "David Foster Wallace." See also the discussion of Wallace and Roth in Marsh, "Infinite Jerk."

34. After a 2017 *New York Times* report revealed that five women came forward about the comedian's misconduct, C.K. released a statement in which he admitted that "these stories are true" (Ryzik, Buckley, and Kantor, "Louis C.K. Is Accused by 5 Women of Sexual Misconduct"; Ducharme, "These Stories Are True").

35. McGrath, "No Longer Writing, Philip Roth Still Has Plenty to Say."

36. McGrath, "No Longer Writing, Philip Roth Still Has Plenty to Say."

37. McGrath, "No Longer Writing, Philip Roth Still Has Plenty to Say."

38. McGrath, "No Longer Writing, Philip Roth Still Has Plenty to Say."

39. Roth, *MLM*, 82–83.

40. Roth, *ST*, 241.

41. Roth, *PC*, 267.

42. Merkin, "Publicly, We Say #MeToo."

43. That victimizers are sometimes women or gay men is a point made by St. Félix, "One Year of #MeToo."

44. Scott, "My Woody Allen Problem."

45. Scott, "My Woody Allen Problem."

46. See also the critique of Scott made in Heer and Livingstone's "Woody Allen, #MeToo."

47. For some basic bibliography on New Criticism, see Wimsatt and Beardsley, "The Intentional Fallacy"; Brooks, *The Well Wrought Urn*; Wellek, "The New Criticism: Pro and Contra"; Wellek, "Literary Theory, Criticism and History"; and Raleigh, "The New Criticism." As for reader-response theory, a very useful introduction is the Bible and Culture Collective's *The Postmodern Bible*, ed. Aichele, 20–69. As for death-of-the-author theories, the foundational text is Barthes, *Image, Music, Text*, 142–48. A great follow-up is Gass, "The Death of the Author." Carlier and Watts, however, argue that most have misunderstood the satiric dimensions of Barthes's intervention and have read him in reverse (Carlier and Watts, "Roland Barthes's Resurrection of the Author"). For another death-of-the-author rumination, see Moxey, *The Practice of Persuasion*, 124–42.

48. Marghitu, "It's Just Art," 492. The "aesthetic alibi," as it was once called, can no longer acquit a perpetrator, as noted in Jay, "Force Fields," 19.

49. Cusk, "Can a Woman Who Is an Artist Ever Just Be an Artist?," 1.

50. Garber, "David Foster Wallace." Claire Dederer also riffs on "genius" in her open letter to Roman Polanski: "You are undeniably a genius. I wonder: Is your terrible history tied to your genius? Did your history make your work great? Does a genius get let off the hook? Are you great because you're sick? What does it even mean to be a genius?" (Dederer, *Love and Trouble*, 71).

51. Garber, "David Foster Wallace," In the #MeToo reckoning, great talent is sometimes spoken of in the same way as great wealth. It *may* have been earned. Or it may have been bestowed upon an individual through chance factors and social/gendered biases that predispose us to favor certain types of people (i.e., brooding, socially awkward, white male artists). The point is that exceptional talent, like a magnate's fortune, should never place one above the law. A somewhat different explanation for our tolerance of male misbehavior is made by Martha Nussbaum, who points out that geniuses, be they athletes or actors, make many people wealthy (Nussbaum, "Accountability in an Era of Celebrity").

52. Stewart-Kroeker, "What Do We Do with the Art of Monstrous Men?," 19.

53. Izadi, "Louis C.K.'s Movie Scrapped"; Stewart-Kroeker, "What Do We Do with the Art of Monstrous Men?," 12.

54. See Dederer's "What Do We Do with the Art of Monstrous Men?," which draws a link between Allen's life and cinema.

55. "All the Missing Girls," episode 5 of *Surviving R. Kelly*, dir. Nigel Bellis and Astral Finnie. At the 28:00-minute mark, we learn that the singer would bring Ms. Jones onstage and subject her to a simulated sex act performed for the fans. She then would theatrically sign a contract, the implication being that she had consented to these acts, signed away her rights, etc. The show reveals that, in real life, Kelly would make women sign similar contracts with false allegations against themselves (e.g., such as stealing), and these would be used as collateral toward various sex acts to which he subjected them.

56. Diemer, "Hiding Actualities," 4. Though Diemer's model would let Cosby's show stand since the misbehavior is not embodied in the artistic product.

57. Dederer, "What Do We Do with the Art of Monstrous Men?"

58. Dederer, "What Do We Do with the Art of Monstrous Men?"

59. Dederer, *Love and Trouble*, 69, 62.

60. Dederer, *Love and Trouble*, 226–31.

61. Hess, "How the Myth of the Artistic Genius Excuses the Abuse of Women."
62. Hess, "How the Myth of the Artistic Genius Excuses the Abuse of Women."
63. Morris, "Michael Jackson Cast a Spell."
64. Gay, *Bad Feminist*, 88.
65. Roth, *ST*, 64; Wake, "The Dying Animal."
66. Roth, *AL*, 44.
67. Roth, *AL*, 281.
68. Roth, *AL*, 281.
69. For some important studies of metafiction, see McCaffery, *The Metafictional Muse*; Boyd, *The Reflexive Novel*; Christensen, *The Meaning of Metafiction*; Hutcheon, *Narcissistic Narrative*; Scholes, *Fabulation and Metafiction*; and Waugh, *Metafiction*.
70. Roth, *HUMB*, 1.
71. Roth, *GW*, 103.
72. Roth, *GW*, 3.
73. Roth, *GW*, 94.
74. Roth, *GW*, 6.
75. The citations below come from the 2010 Anchor edition of the story.
76. Adichie, "Jumping Monkey Hill," 96
77. Adichie, "Jumping Monkey Hill," 113.
78. Adichie, "Jumping Monkey Hill," 108.
79. Adichie, "Jumping Monkey Hill," 100.
80. Adichie, "Jumping Monkey Hill," 100.
81. Adichie, "Jumping Monkey Hill," 103–5, 110–11. The intertexting with Adichie's story "Lagos, Lagos" are noted by Eisenberg, "'Real Africa' / 'Which Africa?,'" 8–24; and Tunca, "The Danger of a Single Short Story," 69–82.
82. Adichie, "Jumping Monkey Hill," 113–14.
83. Adichie, "Jumping Monkey Hill," 114.
84. Adichie, "Jumping Monkey Hill," 114.
85. Adichie, "Jumping Monkey Hill," 114. On the implications of this ending of the story, see Eisenberg, "'Real Africa' / 'Which Africa?,'" 16.
86. I simply observe that for both artists, there exists an acute awareness of how experiences generally deemed to be unpleasurable, objectionable, and inappropriate can nevertheless stimulate creativity. I made similar observations about Lena Dunham's debt to Roth in my article "When She Was Ambivalent."
87. Skidelsky, "The Interview"; Mustich, "Chimamanda Ngozi Adichie."
88. Among Roth's autofictional works, I would include *The Facts: A Novelist's Autobiography; Deception; Patrimony; Operation Shylock: A Confession; The Plot Against America;* and the short story "'I Always Wanted

You to Admire My Fasting'; Or, Looking at Kafka." Marjorie Worthington addresses some of these works in *The Story of "Me."* For other studies of autofiction, consult Worthington, "Fiction in the 'Post-Truth' Era"; Grell, "Pourquoi Serge Doubrovsky n'a pu éviter le terme d'autofiction?"; and Robin, "L'auto-théorisation d'un romancier."

89. Worthington, *The Story of "Me,"* 1. Worthington goes on to offer more nuanced and complex definitions of the term. She refers to the Rothian variety, following the lead of Gérard Genette, as "true autofiction" (11). In some cases he served up autofictional metafiction, like in *Operation Shylock: A Confession.*

90. Library of Congress, Philip Roth Papers, Box 19, Folder 10, "Lelchuk, Alan, 1974–1977." The letter is dated July 29, 1977. He continues: "Among other consequences here, by the way, may be the effect of this half-portrait upon those colleagues of mine who may read the book. It may very well confirm for them their own view of my failing and immoral character, and, on that basis, feel even more inclined to vote against me next year, when I am being 'reconsidered' at the school. This is just one example of a possible consequence to result from the portrait."

91. Roth, *POD*, 146–47.

92. On Lelchuk and Roth, see Mortara, "The Last Transatlantic Ambassador."

93. Library of Congress, Philip Roth Papers, Box 19, Folder 10, "Lelchuk, Alan, 1974–1977." Roth's letter back to Lelchuk is included in the archive—which is unusual. It is simply dated "Sunday." Roth continues: "I certainly didn't intend to upset you and I wish you weren't upset. . . . I think you are assuming much too quickly—and far too defensively—that you will be associated with Baumgarten, that you are clearly recognizable, etc. I don't view Baumgarten as a half or a quarter portrait of you."

94. Lelchuk, *Ziff,* 3. As for the payback, compare Roth's scene about Baumgarten (= Lelchuk) and a seventeen-year-old girl (in Roth, *POD*, 146–47), with Lelchuk's take on the exact same scene (*Ziff,* 30–37). In Lelchuk's version, though, the woman is of the age of consent, and the Roth-like character comes across as frightened and pathetic. The "fearless sexual trailblazer of the American novel," Lelchuk points out with gleeful spite, "had acted with . . . fear and timidity" (37).

95. Nadel, *Critical Companion to Philip Roth*, 104.

96. Pozorski, "Roth and Celebrity," 3; italics in original removed.

97. Pierpont, *Roth Unbound*, 4

98. Making a few excellent points about the type of biography Roth had in mind (i.e., about the work itself) vs. the more personally oriented form of biography that others had in mind is Miriam Jaffe-Foger, "Philip Roth: Death and Celebrity."

99. Library of Congress, Philip Roth Papers, Box 28, Folder 13, "Remnick, David, 1998–1999," letter from the *New Yorker* dated September 10, 1998.

100. McGrath, "Goodbye, Frustration."

101. Bonanos, "Philip Roth's Biographer."

102. McGrath, "Goodbye, Frustration"; Bonanos, "Philip Roth's Biographer." Perhaps this explains why Bailey possesses one of those two copies of Philip Roth's "Notes for My Biographer," likely a very juicy document.

103. Crouch, "The Biographer's Confessions."

104. Bonanos, "Philip Roth's Biographer."

105. Given the level of vitriol between Roth and Claire Bloom—"Notes for My Biographer" is said to be a challenge to Claire Bloom's aforementioned memoir—it is peculiar that Bailey took a swipe at her in an interview and mentioned "her undertaker's face." That, and his shade-throw to the first biographer, Ross Miller ("bless his heart"), might lead one to conclude that Bailey is fighting Roth's battles by proxy. Only time will tell (Bonanos, "Philip Roth's Biographer").

106. Kaprièlian, "In Which Philip Roth Announces."

107. Kaprièlian, "In Which Philip Roth Announces."

108. On Roth's determination to "control his posthumous representation and reputation," see Glass, "Zuckerman/Roth," 234.

109. C. Goldberg, "UConn Professor." Miller's enthusiasm for the project is evident in his interview with Christopher Goffard, "Philip Roth Unbound." See also Donadio, "Bio Engineering."

110. McGrath, "Philip Roth to Cooperate with New Biographer." On Roth's anger with Miller, as related by James Atlas (who himself was angling to be Roth's biographer), see Atlas, *Remembering Roth,* audiobook, time: 1:09:15–1:09:38.

111. Royal, "Paying Attention to the Man," 22–25; Jaffe-Foger, "Philip Roth: Death and Celebrity."

112. Taylor, *Here We Are,* 160. Another that is en route is by the historian Steven Zipperstein (also a confidante of Roth). See Zipperstein's "My Friend Philip"; see also Zipperstein, "Philip Roth's Forgotten Tape." At press time, there was no title for Zipperstein's forthcoming biography that is to be published by Yale University Press. Most promisingly, *Philip Roth: A Counterlife,* by Ira Nadel, will be released in 2021. Nadel is a leading Roth expert but not a Friend of Philip. See also Berlinerblau, "Do We Know Philip Roth?"

113. Milbauer and Watson, "An Interview with Philip Roth," 10.

114. Milbauer and Watson, "An Interview with Philip Roth," 10

115. Milbauer and Watson, "An Interview with Philip Roth," 10.

116. Krasnick, "Philip Roth."

117. Roth, "On *The Great American Novel*."

118. Throughout this book, I will think about Roth's entire fictional body of work as follows: I count twenty-eight novels, and twenty-five short stories, which makes for fifty-three discrete fictional products. I arrive at the number twenty-five by counting six stories in the 1959 collection *Goodbye, Columbus, and Five Short Stories*. To that, I add nineteen short stories, including his Bucknell juvenilia (see the list of abbreviations in this volume). In my reckoning of Roth's body of work, I do not include his collection of three separate novels, released in 1985 and entitled *Zuckerman Bound: A Trilogy and Epilogue*. According to Ira Nadel, the collection included "a concluding novella entitled 'Epilogue: Prague Orgy'" (Nadel, *Critical Companion to Philip Roth*, 258). *The Prague Orgy*, in turn, was released as a separate novella in 1985, which I count among the twenty-eight above.

119. Roth himself, in "On *Portnoy's Complaint*," speaks of being "strongly influenced by a sit-down comic named Franz Kafka" (18). The interview is replicated in Plimpton, "Philip Roth's Exact Intent," 39. Roth indirectly and jokingly refers to his reliance on James in "On *The Great American Novel*," 73.

120. Jacques Berlinerblau, Bethania Michael, and Heather Walters, "Intertexts and Influence: A Comprehensive Table of Intertexts in Philip Roth's Fiction, 1952–2010," *Philip Roth Studies*, 17, no. 2 (2021).

## 1. ROTH AND RACE

1. Take, for example, Eric Sundquist's *Strangers in the Land*, perhaps the single most comprehensive study of Black/Jewish relations, and one that leans heavily on readings of fiction. Although Sundquist mentions Roth often in his impressive study, he does not address the more problematic material we will cite below. The same occurs in Emily Miller Budick's *Blacks and Jews in Literary Conversation*. Ditto for Ethan Goffman, *Imagining Each Other*. The reasons for this oversight have nothing to do with the quality of the work of the scholars mentioned. Rather, these writers are not Roth specialists and understandably never got around to some of the more peripheral (but significant) material scrutinized below. The inability to read Roth comprehensively is more problematic when scholars draw broad inferences about Roth's engagement with racial issues on the basis of a limited sample size. See, for example, Gross, "American Fiction." Working almost solely from the portrait of the Black child in "Goodbye, Columbus," Gross is led to exaggerate Roth's good intentions. A special issue of *Philip Roth Studies* devoted to race also restricts itself to but a few works. Editor Dean Franco, however, is certainly correct that "we need a body of criticism that reads, analyzes, and critiques Roth and

race" (Franco, "Introduction: Philip Roth and Race," 85). Brett Ashley Kaplan is one of the few writers who notes that the body of evidence is larger than just a few famous texts. She speaks of the "skeletal sketching" of Black characters in Roth's novels versus the "careful fleshing out and detailing of white (mostly Jewish) characters" (Kaplan, "The American Berserk in *Sabbath's Theater*," 233). Kaplan is spot-on. Her view, however, that Roth does this "skeletal sketching" intentionally, as a way of commenting on how white privilege imagines that "race is itself peripheral," seems obviated by what we shall learn below.

Kaplan repeatedly makes similar arguments elsewhere and thus shields Roth from the type of critique I am advancing above (Kaplan, *Jewish Anxiety and the Novels of Philip Roth*, 85, 87). Making a similar point about how Roth may purposefully limit the scope of his Black characters to make a comment on racism is Jung-Suk Hwang, "Newark's Just a Black Colony," 14. Further, I disagree with Kaplan's assertion that "the racial dynamics in virtually all of Roth's subsequent works are evident in . . . 'Goodbye, Columbus'" (Kaplan, *Jewish Anxiety*, 14). See my periodization below.

2. Roth, GC, 3–136. Noticing the protective attitude of Neil toward the boy, as opposed to other library workers, like the Irishmen McKee, is Goldblatt, "The Whitening of the Jews," 89.
3. GC, 31, 74–75.
4. On PEN/Faulkner, see Nadel, *Critical Companion to Philip Roth*, 272.
5. On these issues more generally, see Johnson and Berlinerblau, *Blacks and Jews in America: An Introduction to Dialogue*.
6. On the "Grand Alliance," see Salzman, "Struggles in the Promised Land"; Glazer, "Jews and Blacks: What Happened to the Grand Alliance?" On the "Grand Coalition," see Drake, "African Diaspora and Jewish Diaspora: Convergence and Divergence."
7. See, for example, Greenberg, *Troubling the Waters*; Salzman and West, eds., *Struggles in the Promised Land*; Carson, "The Politics of Relations between African-Americans and Jews"; and Carson, "Blacks and Jews in the Civil Rights Movement."
8. Given the immensity of Roth's corpus, I am certain I missed a few examples here and there.
9. Similar references to African Americans can be found in the following short stories: "The Box of Truths" (1952), 10, 12 ("The Negro waiter . . ."); "The Fence" (1953), 20 ("She was a handsome Negro woman"); "Armando and the Fraud" (1953), 26 ("Hirsch had been wheeled through the store by a colored man"); "Heard Melodies Are Sweeter" (1958), 58 ("an all-Negro musical comedy adapted from Henry James . . ."); "Expect the Vandals" (1958), 215, 228 ("Pickaninny Blood"); "Novotny's Pain" (1962), 263,

272, 273 ("the Negro mess sergeant"); "Psychoanalytic Special" (1963), 108 ("She drove to the colored section"); "On the Air," (1970), entire text; "His Mistress's Voice" (1986), 159 ("Like a black girl and a white boy dating each other"); "I Always Wanted You to Admire My Fasting; or, Looking at Kafka" (1973), 157 ("And the poorest of Newark's Negroes shuffle meekly up and down the street").

10. See, for example, Gross, "American Fiction."

11. Roth, GC, 37; see also 31, 33–34, 59–60.

12. At least in his own eyes and those of wealthier Jews (Roth, GC, 74–75, 7, 40). Though there is condescension in the text. In a dream sequence, the captain (i.e., Neil Klugman) and his mate (i.e., the boy) are looking at "beautiful bare-skinned negresses" (74).

13. The point was made in Elèna Mortara's presentation, "About Meeting with Roth and Editing His Works in Italy."

14. On Roth's portrayal demonstrating the more liberal perspective of the Jewish Neil in contrast to his Irish colleague John McKee (GC, 34–35), see Byers, "Material Bodies and Performative Identities," 113. Byers rightly points out that "the nonwhite characters in *Goodbye, Columbus* are incomplete shadow selves—uneducated, poor, exploited, apolitical" (11).

15. Roth, DF.

16. Roth, DF, 166

17. Roth, DF, 166.

18. Roth, LG, 374.

19. Roth, LG, 374.

20. Roth, LG, 374.

21. Roth, LG, 624.

22. Roth, LG, 624.

23. The linkages between Blacks and Jews in the minds of those who hate them are discussed in Anti-Defamation League, "White Supremacists Embrace 'Race War'"; Ferber and Kimmel, "Reading Right"; and E. Green "Why the Charlottesville Marchers Were Obsessed with Jews." See also Mills, "Dark Ontologies," in *Blackness Visible*; and B. Smith, "Between a Rock and a Hard Place," 775.

24. Roth, IMAC, 48. This same derogatory coupling of Black and Jew in the mind of an eighteen-year-old white baseball player, Roland Agni, is seen in GAN, 297. The placing of Blacks and Jews in the same categories (of exclusion) is noted again in Roth, EG. Nathan Zuckerman's last love interest, Jamie Logan, went to Kinkaid in Houston, to which, according to her husband, Jews and Blacks were only recently admitted (Roth, EG, 79).

25. IMAC, 445.

26. Roth, WSWG, 243.

27. Roth, *WSWG*, 243.
28. Roth, *WSWG*, 243. Later it is insinuated that Ellie herself is dating this person (247).
29. Roth, *WSWG*, 243–44.
30. There is much merit to Derek Parker Royal's reading of this text as "an antipastoral tour de force," though the insensitive treatment of race that we are about to see suggests to me that Roth was not thinking very hard about how race figures in American pastorals (Royal, "Fouling Out," 159).
31. Roth describes him as a "paranoid fantasist" in "Reading Myself," 75.
32. Roth, *GAN*, 4. For more caricature, see the descriptions of the "the black bucks down in Barbados" whose dialect is made fun of as well (1).
33. Roth, *GAN*, 28; see also 41, 132, 148.
34. Roth, *GAN*, 149.
35. Roth, *GAN*, 151.
36. Roth, *GAN*, 170, 227–28.
37. Roth, *GAN*, 307.
38. Roth, *GAN*, 309.
39. Roth, *GAN*, 306–22.
40. Roth, *GAN*, 307, 308, 309, 311.
41. Roth, *GAN*, 314–22.
42. Roth, *GAN*, 318–19.
43. Nor is Roth exonerated for using the metafictional conceit of a letter to the editor to draw attention to his own unfunny, unoriginal, and unnecessary portrait of Africans and others. At the end of *The Great American Novel* Roth seems aware that he may have gone too far. Our narrator receives a letter that reads in part: "I find what I have read in your novel thoroughly detestable. It is a vicious and sadistic book of the most detestable sort, and your treatment of blacks, Jews, and women, not to mention the physically and mental handicapped is offensive in the extreme; in a word, sick" (Roth, *GAN*, 396).
44. Roth, "A Conversation with Philip Roth: Joyce Carol Oates/1974," 99.
45. Shostak, *Philip Roth—Countertexts, Counterlives*, 218.
46. Roth, *DEC*, 85–86.
47. Ivan draws the aforementioned link: "With the nigger it's his prick and with the Jew it's his questions" (Roth, *DEC*, 87).
48. Roth, *DEC*, 87.
49. Roth, *DEC*, 99–104.
50. Roth, *IMAC*, 91.
51. Roth, *IMAC*, 3. We learn that Zuckerman and Murray meet while the latter is enrolled for a course entitled "Shakespeare at the Millennium."
52. Roth, *IMAC*, 90–94.

53. Roth, *IMAC,* 90–94. Later on, Ira talks about an old Chicago friend, Earl, whom he describes as "the same kind of tramp working stiff as me" (94).

54. Roth, *IMAC,* 145. Ira continues his disquisition, telling Wondrous that by voting Democrat she has let her children and grandchildren down (146).

55. Roth, *IMAC,* 146.

56. Roth, *LG,* 224.

57. Brett Ashley Kaplan has suggested that "incidental black characters often initiate important moments in the plot and/or reveal crucial aspects of the more fleshed-out white characters" (Kaplan, *Jewish Anxiety,* 21). This is not the case in this scene, nor elsewhere.

58. Roth, *LG,* 224.

59. Roth, *ZU,* 224.

60. Roth, *AL,* 53.

61. Roth, *AL,* 53.

62. Roth, *PC,* 74, 130, 169.

63. Roth, *PC,* 130.

64. Roth, *PC,* 130.

65. Roth, *PC,* 107. Alex represents a vast tranche of post–World War II liberal Jews whose work as teachers, lawyers, social workers, civil rights activists, etc., drew them into close professional contact with African Americans. Roy Goldblatt, "The Whitening of the Jews," notices that Neil Klugman of "Goodbye, Columbus," is also engaged in this project of helping African Americans (91). See Franco, *Race, Rights, and Recognition,* 30–47, for an interesting discussion of how Roth based Portnoy's position on an existing rights-based commission.

66. Roth, *PC,* 13.

67. Roth, *PC,* 10.

68. Roth, *PC,* 75.

69. Roth, *PC,* Poles, (7), Irishmen (7), Puerto Ricans (160), Chinese (90), Italians (182), gays (125–26). There are too many insults of women, all gentiles, and Blacks to list here.

70. A similar example of a Jew demonstrating a false sense of respect and solidarity with Blacks is seen in *American Pastoral* as Swede Levov agonizes over his complicity in Newark's downfall (Roth, *AP,* 165–67).

71. Podhoretz, "My Negro Problem," 88.

72. Roth, *OTA,* 7–49.

73. Roth, "The Art of Fiction," 175.

74. Roth, *OTA,* 7–13.

75. Roth, *OTA,* 10.

76. Roth, *OTA,* 10.

77. Roth, *OTA,* 16.

78. Roth, OTA, 17.

79. Roth, OTA, 20.

80. See Jonathan Kaufman, "Blacks and Jews," 116; Diner, "Between Words and Deeds," 95. See also Salzman, "Struggles in the Promised Land," 1; Sobel and Sobel, "Negroes and Jews," 385; and Gutman, "Parallels in the Urban Experience."

81. Lester, "The Lives People Live," 168. For the single most comprehensive statement on all the similarities and differences between Blacks and Jews, see Mills, Blackness Visible, 83–86.

82. Diner, "Between Words and Deeds," 96.

83. Sundquist, Strangers in the Land, 346.

84. Roth, POD, 236.

85. Roth, CLF, 19.

86. Jonathan Kaufman, "Blacks and Jews," 116.

87. Diner, "Between Words and Deeds," 97. A similar point about the "pacific" approach of Jews (versus that of Italian Americans) is made in Reider, Canarsie, 43–54. See also Sobel and Sobel, "Negroes and Jews," 401.

88. Cheryl Greenberg has pointed out that in the North (and South) Jews "were more willing than most white Americans to serve Black clients and maintain stores in Black communities" ("I'm Not White, I'm Jewish," 40).

89. See Levine and Harmon, The Death of an American Jewish Community.

90. Lerner and West, Jews and Blacks, 162.

91. Gurock, The Jews of Harlem, 165–81, 214; Greenberg, "Negotiating Coalition," 479.

92. Baldwin, "Negroes Are Anti-Semitic." An intriguing counterstudy is Seth Forman's Blacks in the Jewish Mind, where it is argued that more attention should be paid to the remarkable support that Jews gave Blacks in the twentieth century. Julian Bond makes a point about "living in proximity without equality" (Bond, introduction to Strangers and Neighbors, 7).

93. On Newark in Roth's work, see Schechner, "Newark"; and Nadel, Critical Companion to Philip Roth, 301–3.

94. Interesting in this regard is Rabbi Jay Kaufman's 1969 essay "Thou Shalt Surely Rebuke Thy Neighbor." Kaufman spoke of "ethnic succession," or the process by which one immigrant ethnic group rises as it moves into another's neighborhood. Kaufman insinuates that Blacks may not be holding up their end of the bargain. Then again, most Blacks in America are not immigrants, and most faced unprecedented structural challenges in achieving their "ethnic succession."

95. Roth, AL, 39.

96. Roth, AL, 39.

97. Roth, *AL*, 39.

98. Roth, *ZU*, 155–56.

99. So much so that one scholar refers to it as "The Newark Trilogy" (Kimmage, *In History's Grip*, 4).

100. Levov continues: "I hired 'em! 'You're nuts, Levov'—this is what my friends in the steam room used to tell me—'What are you hiring schvartzes for? You won't get gloves, Levov, you'll get dreck. But hired 'em, treated them like human beings. . . . I'm by the pool and my wonderful friends look up from the paper and they tell me they ought to take the schvartzes and line 'em up and shoot them, and I'm the one who has to remind them that's what Hitler did to the Jews. And you know what they tell me, as an answer? 'How can you compare schvartzes to Jews?'" (Roth, *AP*, 163–64). On the July 1967 riots, see Kimmage, *In History's Grip*, 98–100. For an excellent discussion of Swede's take on Newark's Blacks, see Hwang "Newark's Just a Black Colony." Hwang argues provocatively that Roth seeks to undermine the views of Lou and Swede regarding Black rioters. This reading strikes me as plausible.

101. On goes Lou: "What is new, number one, is race. . . . Manufacturing is finished in Newark. Newark is finished. But, mark my words, Newark will be the city that never comes back" (Roth, *AP*, 345).

102. Roth, *CLF*, 40.

103. "The black kids prey on the elderly Jews . . . even in broad daylight. They bicycle in from Newark" (Roth, *PAT*, 125).

104. Roth, *IMAC*, 316.

105. Anti-Semites, we learn in *Operation Shylock*, find justification for their own hatred in Blacks' alleged hate of Jews: "The Jews don't have any friends at all. Even niggers hate Jews. . . . The niggers turn against Jews, everyone turns against Jews" (Roth, *OSH*, 254).

106. Roth, *CLF*, 124–25.

107. Schwartz, "Roth, Race, and Newark," 1.

108. Schwartz, "Roth, Race, and Newark," 9. Making a similar point about white flight and Newark is Jung-Suk Hwang "Newark's Just a Black Colony." On Black Newark and "the terrible conditions in the Central Ward," see Kevin Mumford, *Newark*, 23. Brad Tuttle, however, presents a slightly less dire picture of what life was like for African Americans in Newark—but dire nonetheless in *How Newark Became Newark*, 142–70.

109. Making this point is Karen Brodkin in *How Jews Became White Folks*, 25–52.

110. Hwang, "Newark's Just a Black Colony," 178.

111. See the excellent article of the late Derek Parker Royal, "Pastoral Dreams," 185–207. See also Gordon, "The Critique of Utopia"; and Brauner, *Philip*

*Roth*, 149. The "womb-dream" comment is from *The Counterlife* where Zuckerman develops the pastoral concept (323), and unspooled other great terms like "sanitized confusionless life" (322) or "strifeless unity" (323) to describe it; see also 317, 322.

112. Schwartz. "Roth, Race, and Newark," 1. Roth's obvious idealization of Newark is on display in Rothstein, "To Newark, with Love."

113. Though one critic reasonably argues that Roth's anti-PC bromides in this work might indicate that he didn't listen to people enough (Moore, "The Wrath of Athena"). A glance at table 1, in the appendix, indicates that Roth rarely cited Black writers and poets.

114. Roth, *HST*, 99.

115. Roth, *HST*, 20.

116. Hughes, "Passing." Though Silk went to the Village from Newark, as opposed to starting off in Harlem where the Hughes poem is situated.

117. Roth, *HST*, 109–10.

118. The exceptions being an employee at a "Norfolk whorehouse" (*HST*, 114), an African American woman whom he briefly dates (*HST*, 132), and his own family, whom he coldly leaves behind.

119. Glaser, "The Jew in the Canon," 1469.

120. Roth, *HST*, 318–19.

121. In an interview with Charles McGrath, Roth insists that Coleman had no affinity whatsoever with Judaism. His choice to embrace this religion was "strictly utilitarian" (McGrath, "Zuckerman's Alter Brain").

122. In the words of one scholar, they construe Professor Silk as a "sell-out, a self-hater, and a betrayer of [his] heritage" (Bluefarb, "*The Human Stain*," 223).

123. Roth, *HST*, 139.

124. Thus Timothy Parrish observes: "Zuckerman tells Coleman's story as a version of his own autobiography" ("Roth and Ethnic Identity," 139). Roth, too, freights Silk with many of his own peeves, passions, and preoccupations.

125. Brett Ashley Kaplan makes the argument that, in 1946, when he started passing as a Jew, he was "one person of color becoming another, slightly less oppressed person of color" ("Reading Race," 176).

126. Roth, *HST*, 120. Mollie Godfrey archly observes "The freedom Coleman pursues is not freedom from racism. . . . but freedom from racial solidarity itself" (Godfrey, "Passing as Post-Racial," 240).

127. Roth, *HST*, 324–25.

128. Roth, *HST*, 325.

129. See Parrish, "Roth and Ethnic Identity," 139. See also Parrish, "Becoming Black," for an important discussion of Ralph Ellison's influence on

Roth. Mark Schechner calls Silk "Roth's martyr to himself" (Schechner, "Roth's American Trilogy," 152). "History," as Matthew Wilson points out, "will have its revenge" (Wilson, "Reading *The Human Stain*," 148).

130. Roth, *HST,* 108.

131. Roth, *HST,* 108.

132. Roth, *HST,* 335.

133. On Coleman's desire to "opt out of his history . . . into a utopian realm of self-fashioning," see Wilson, "Reading *The Human Stain*," 142. See also Kirby, "Shades of Passing," 15–160.

134. Elam, "Passing in the Post-Race Era," 758, 755. See also Glaser, "The Jew in the Canon," 1469. See also Maslan, "The Faking of the Americans."

135. Elam, "Passing in the Post-Race Era," 756. Jennifer Glaser writes: "Roth's novel asks for a reinvestigation and progressive deconstruction of racial and ethnic categories to strip them of social and epistemological weight" (Glaser, "The Jew in the Canon," 1472). Glaser also makes the important observation that at the turn of the century, Roth had come "to embody the status quo he once sought to undermine" (1467). *The Human Stain*, she implies, took him way out of his comfort zone and gave him an opportunity to rebrand.

136. Kaplan, "Reading Race," 172.

137. Kaplan, "Reading Race," 172.

138. Gates made this point in an article about Anatole Broyard, who many believe is the model for Coleman Silk (Gates, *Thirteen Ways of Looking at a Black Man,* 208). For more affirmations of this being based on Broyard, see Faisst, "Delusionary Thinking, Whether White or Black or in Between," 121–37. See also Kaplan, "Reading Race," 175–76.

139. Franco, "Being Black, Being Jewish, and Knowing the Difference."

140. A somewhat similar desire to use the fiction to "reveal Roth's thinking about racial politics" is tried by Larry Schwartz in his analysis of *The Human Stain* (Schwartz, "Erasing Race," 66). The closest Roth comes to engaging biographical issues and race is an interview with Charles McGrath. He reveals that he had little interaction with the small Black population of Newark in the 1930s and 1940s. He also notes that his first, full-scale engagement with African Americans was in Chicago in the 1950s. There he dated a Black woman whose "pale" family on her mother's side got him thinking about questions of passing and "Self-transformation. Self-invention" (in McGrath, "Zuckerman's Alter Brain").

141. Roth, *CLF,* 78.

142. Roth, "Recollections from beyond the Last Rope," 277.

143. Roth, "Recollections from beyond the Last Rope," 277.

144. Roth, *IMC,* 93.

145. An excellent discussion of shifting perceptions of Jewish whiteness is found in Goldstein, *The Price of Whiteness: Jews, Race, and Identity*. For a review of the literature on Afro-Jews, see Johnson and Berlinerblau, *Blacks and Jews: An Introduction to Dialogue*, forthcoming.

146. See also Forman, *Blacks and the Jewish Mind*.

147. Roth, BT, 10–12.

148. Roth, BT, 10, 11.

149. Roth, BT, 11.

150. Then again, in 1962 Roth offers an understated but unambiguous denunciation of discrimination toward Blacks in the Midwest. The piece, entitled "Iowa: A Very Far Country Indeed," is quite clear-eyed about racism and white denials that such a thing actually exists (Roth, "Iowa," 242).

151. Roth shows cognizance of these tensions in Plimpton, "Philip Roth's Exact Intent," 38–39.

152. Michael Waltzer discusses this in "Blacks and Jews." Bond, introduction to *Strangers and Neighbors*, 6.

153. Bond, introduction to *Strangers and Neighbors*, 6; Greenberg, "Negotiating Coalition," 487–90; Carson, "Blacks and Jews in the Civil Rights Movement."

154. Dollinger, *Black Power, Jewish Power*. See also Sundquist, *Strangers in the Land*, 319–80.

155. Dollinger, *Black Power, Jewish Power*, 159. For an excellent analysis of how the rupture affected liberal Jews, see Feher, "The Schisms of '67."

156. See Johnson and Berlinerblau, *Blacks and Jews in America*, forthcoming. In *Race, Rights, and Recognition* Dean Franco touches on the Black-Jewish alliance and its relation to Roth's writing. For Franco the alliance "breaks down . . . over the very issues of communism, human rights, and support for American norms of democracy" (33). In the late 1960s, which is when *Portnoy's Complaint* was published, I believe the more salient issues would have been mutual accusations of racism and anti-Semitism, Black Power's anti-Zionist stance, and the bitter Ocean Hill–Brownsville controversy. Explicit disputes about "rights" came to the fore of the debate a little later, especially in rarefied legal arguments about affirmative action. I concur with Franco that Roth was drawing attention to hypocrisies and tensions within the Jewish American psyche as regards African Americans. When contextualized among other Roth writings of this period, however, I am critical of Roth's motivations in offering these portraits of Blacks. Franco asks the important question: "How is the political tension of racial politics in the late 1960s folded into *Portnoy's Complaint?*" (36). In my view, Roth articulated rather mainstream Jewish views on these tensions.

157. Interested readers might consult a blistering exchange between Roth and the poet LeRoi Jones on May 28, 1964, in the *New York Review of Books* (see the chapter epigraph) (L. Jones, "Channel X"). Jones was responding to Roth, "Channel X: Two Plays on the Race Conflict."

158. As Eric Sundquist put it: "Across the ideological spectrum, blacks and Jews alike withdrew the hand of brotherhood, sought to protect their own communal interests, and reverted at times to ugly stereotypes" (Sundquist, *Strangers in the Land,* 312). See also Feingold, "From Equality to Liberty," 111–13. B. Z. Sobel and May Sobel, in "Negroes and Jews," point to contemporaneous survey data indicating considerable prejudice toward Blacks on the part of Jews (397). The researchers make a point of distinguishing the views of elite Jewish leaders versus those of everyday Jews.

159. In exchange for cash and a promotion for Mrs. Silk, Fensterman wants Coleman to underperform on his exams and get a few Bs instead of As. Fensterman's son, Bert, would then graduate as valedictorian and Coleman as salutatorian (Roth, *HST,* 85–88).

160. Roth, *HST,* 97.

161. Roth, *PAA,* 72–73.

162. Roth, *PAA,* 72–73. Nor should we forget Stanley Crouch's critique of his friend's "absurdly reductive vision" and "ethnically self-absorbed book." Stanley Crouch is quick to note that in a country capable of pogroms, Blacks like Edward B. would also be in grave danger. Roth's dystopia inexplicably forgets "hysterical racism and violence toward black people" (S. Crouch, "Roth's Historical Sin").

163. Roth, *EG,* 262.

164. Roth, *EG,* 262.

165. Roth, *EG,* 262.

166. Roth, *EVR,* 174–80. Zuckerman Unbound ends with a similar replacement narrative. Nathan passes his old synagogue and comments, "it was now an African Methodist Episcopal church" (225).

167. Roth, *EVR,* 174. They speak often while at work about "Things in general. Life in general" (175).

168. Roth, *EVR,* 180.

### 2. OLD MEN, YOUNG WOMEN

1. Halliday, *Asymmetry,* 5.

2. Halliday, *Asymmetry,* 3–4. Notice how similar Ezra Blazer's pickup line is to that used by the unnamed Everyman in *Everyman* (Roth, *EVR,* 132).

3. Halliday, *Asymmetry,* 120.

4. Ezra Blazer resembles Philip Roth, at least in the first section of *Asymmetry*. In the third section, though, some biographical details are relayed that do not correspond to Roth's life. Blazer hails from Pittsburgh, not Roth's Newark (247). He won the Nobel Prize (247). He fathered two illegitimate children in France (262–63); whether this is true of Roth or not, I do not know. So far, no biographer has made the claim.

5. Wickenden, "Philip Roth in the #MeToo Era," podcast, time: 5:45–5:50.

6. Marriott, "Review." In spite of the real-life experience that she reprocessed into prose, Halliday insists that *Asymmetry* is mostly fictional. "It is a novel," she cautions, "and not a faithful account of our own story. Things that happened to me and to Philip do not happen in the book and vice versa" (Wickenden, "Philip Roth in the #MeToo Era," podcast, time: 5:54–6:00). Halliday acknowledges a relation between the dalliance with Roth and the art it spawned (i.e., the novel *Asymmetry*). At least she acknowledges that. Roth, as we shall see in the next chapter, refuses to do the same.

7. On what type of feminist statement this novel might be making, see Marsh, "Infinite Jerk."

8. McKenzie, *Age-Dissimilar Couples and Romantic Relationships*.

9. Table 2 was challenging to assemble. It is sometimes difficult to figure out how old a character is at a particular moment in Roth's narratives, hence the use of question marks.

10. The four novels, post-1974, where the theme does not appear are (1) *Zuckerman Unbound*, (2) *The Prague Orgy*, (3) *Indignation*, and (4) *Nemesis*.

11. Halliday, *Asymmetry*, 122.

12. Roth, *HST*, 1. Coleman dies/is murdered on his seventy-second birthday (319), says his sister Ernestine. Or, according to Zuckerman, on the evening before (344).

13. Roth, *HST*, 26.

14. Roth, *HST*, 6.

15. Roth, *HST*, 14.

16. Roth, *HST*, 28.

17. Roth, *HST*, 33.

18. Roth, *HST*, 230.

19. Roth, *HST*, 27.

20. Roth, *HST*, 232–33.

21. Roth, *IND*, 71.

22. Roth, *IND*, 71.

23. Roth, *IND*, 71

24. Roth, *DEC*, 181.

25. Roth, *DEC*, 87.
26. Roth, *DEC*, 120. Cooper, *Philip Roth and the Jews*, 231–32. Cooper also draws attention to the role of conversation in this work. As does Neelakantan, "Textualizing the Self," 59.
27. Roth, *DEC*, 194.
28. Shostak, *Philip Roth—Countertexts, Counterlives*, 69; see also Rogoff, "Philip Roth's Master Fictions," 506.
29. Shostak, *Philip Roth—Countertexts, Counterlives*, 69.
30. Roth, PSP, 108.
31. Roth, *IMAC*, 168. For more instances of Roth's emphasis on talk as being the core of a relationship, see Roth, *HUMB*, 50, 51. See also Roth, *NEM*, 168.
32. Roth, *CLF*, 254.
33. Molloy, "Philip Roth Told Us 5 Years Ago Which of His Books Are the Best."
34. Kelleter, "Portrait of the Sexist as a Dying Man," 272; Lauritzen, "Roth, Draper, Lil' Wayne."
35. Roth, *ST*, 3.
36. Roth, *ST*, 210.
37. Roth, *ST*, 211.
38. Roth, *ST*, 213; emphasis in original. In *CLF*, Nathan makes a similar reflection about how Henry's affair with Wendy is a form of art (35).
39. On the role of shamelessness in Roth's art, see Kelleter, "Portrait of the Sexist as a Dying Man," 264.
40. Brauner, *Philip Roth*, 130.
41. Roth, *ST*, 221.
42. In a personal communication, Roth's high school English teacher, Bob Lowenstein, whom he depicted in *I Married a Communist* as Murray Ringold, referred to the scene as "refried de Sade" (Library of Congress, Philip Roth Archives, Box 20, Folder 5, "Lowenstein, Robert: 1969, 1987–1995").
43. A similar criticism is advanced by Brauner, *Philip Roth*, 125.
44. Roth, *ST*, 240–41.
45. Scott, "Alter Alter Ego."
46. Roth, *DAN*, 10.
47. Roth, *DAN*, 2.
48. Roth, *DAN*, 5.
49. Kevin West, "Professing Desire," 235.
50. Roth, *DAN*, 29.
51. Roth, *DAN*, 102–3.

52. Even when he was with Consuela, he was afflicted by the fear that a young man—the type of young man he used to be—would seduce her away from him (Roth, *DAN*, 40; see also 38, 39, 40, 106).
53. Roth, *DAN*, 106.
54. Roth, *DAN*, 136.
55. Roth, *DAN*, 32–33; italics in original.
56. Roth, *DAN*, 99.
57. Roth, *DAN*, 98.
58. Ivanova, "My Own Foe from the Other Gender," 36.
59. As one critic observes, there is "an ironic distance in Roth's relationship to Kepesh, a distance that allows him to engage critically with the grotesqueness of American masculinity" (Sinykin, "This Is the Philip Roth Novel").
60. Roth, *DAN*, 156.
61. Judith Yaross Lee remarks that Kepesh is "an attractive character for the first time" (J. Lee, "Affairs of the Breast," 83).
62. Couples in which the partners are separated by only a few years, such as Roy Bassart and Lucy Nelson (*When She Was Good*), Dawn and Swede Levov (*American Pastoral*), or Bucky Cantor and Marcia Steinberg (*Nemesis*) are somewhat dull. Their conversations, I would add, are considerably less captivating. Then again, there are interesting couples to be found, like Neil Klugman and Brenda Patimkin in "Goodbye, Columbus" and Maureen Tarnopol and Peter in *My Life as a Man* (Maureen is actually a few years older than Peter).
63. Roth, *DAN*, 22.
64. There are more than a few fictional and nonfictional references to Roth himself cavorting with young women. His affair with the writer Janet Hobhouse appears to have been chronicled by her in *The Furies*. Roth's ex-wife Claire Bloom alleges, in *Leaving a Doll's House*, that her ex-husband had an inappropriate relationship with her daughter's best friend (225). Fictional accounts of Roth in action can be found in Lelchuk, *Ziff*. And, far less directly, John Updike, *The Complete Henry Bech*. Too, there are the scenes in *Deception* mentioned throughout this chapter.
65. Roth, *DEC*, 193.
66. Roth, *HUMB*, 59, 60, 130–31.
67. Roth, *HUMB*, 60.
68. Though Ira Ringold in *I Married a Communist* spirits twenty-four-year-old Pamela Solomon (a friend of his stepdaughter's) away from Little Italy in New York to his shack in Zinc Town for their occasional assignations. That affair is never snuffed out by his estranged wife.
69. Roth, *DAN*, 115.
70. Roth, *HST*, 261.

71. Roth, *HST,* 272.
72. Roth, *HST,* 277.
73. Roth, *HST,* 2.
74. Roth, *HST,* 2
75. Roth, *AL,* 86, 87, 94, 145.
76. Roth, *GW,* 69.
77. Roth, *CLF,* 111.
78. Roth, *HUMB,* 139.
79. Roth, *EG,* 36.
80. Roth, *EG,* 67.
81. Roth, *EG,* 292.
82. As Mark Schechner comments in Rodgers and Royal's "Grave Commentary," "where there is desire there is disaster" (9). See also Jaffe-Foger and Pozorski, "[A]nything but Fragile and Yielding," 87.

## 3. MISOGYNY AND AUTOBIOGRAPHY

1. Here, I am lifting a funny line from Kingsley Amis's *Lucky Jim* (2). Another denial is found in Hayman, "Philip Roth," 117.
2. Roth, "My Life as a Writer." See Davidson, "Talk with Philip Roth: Sara Davidson/1977," 102–13.
3. Roth, "Interview with *Le Nouvel Observateur,*" 100.
4. Roth, "Interview with *Le Nouvel Observateur,*" 100. Elsewhere, Roth remarks that his "writing process [is] a long way from the methods, let alone the purposes of autobiography" (Milbauer and Watson, "An Interview with Philip Roth," 1). As Timothy Parks observed, "Roth simply insists on a manifest gulf between himself and his supposed alter egos" (Parks, "How Best to Read Autofiction"). Roth makes the point again in Gray, "The Varnished Truths," 202–8. And again, Weber, "Life, Counterlife," 217. For some scholarly perspectives on this, see Rodenhurst, "Dis/simulation within Metafiction"; and Brauner, *Philip Roth,* 9–11.
5. For a review of this argument, see Durantaye, "How to Read Philip Roth," 317–18. He goes on to notice "the apparent bad faith" of Roth's many denials (320). On Zuckerman and Roth's similarities, see Masiero, *Philip Roth and the Zuckerman Books,* 31. As Jesse Tisch notes after studying Roth's personal correspondences, he "cleverly and omnivorously . . . exploited personal experiences" (Tisch, "The Philip Roth Archive").
6. The biographical data in this paragraph and the next is taken from Miller, "Chronology," 897–907.
7. Miller, "Chronology," 897–907. Making a similar point is Durantaye, "How to Read Philip Roth," 305.

8. For an excellent overview of psychoanalysis in Roth's work, see J. Berman, *The Talking Cure*, 239–69.

9. Roth, *PC*, 78.

10. Wickenden, "Philip Roth in the #MeToo Era," podcast, time: 9:55–10:02. David Gooblar opines: "The endless focus on whether Roth is or is not a misogynist has blotted from view nearly all other, more nuanced approaches to women in Roth" (Gooblar, "Introduction: Roth and Women").

11. Berlinerblau, "A Conversation with Cynthia Ozick," 23.

12. Allen, *The Necessary Blankness*, 96.

13. Gornick, "Radiant Poison." Gornick argues that the monstrosities emerged after *Portnoy's Complaint*. Interestingly, more than a few prominent critics evinced a similarly odd appreciation for *Portnoy's Complaint*. Kate Millet writes "Portnoy's long *kvetch* is a hilarious demonstration of . . . elaborate culture penis-worship" (Millet, *Sexual Politics*, 325). Thirty years earlier, Gornick made nearly the exact same charge as regards Roth's treatment of Maureen Tarnopol in *My Life as a Man* (Gornick, "Why Do These Men Hate Women?," 196). Judith Yaross Lee speaks of "Roth's habit of casting women as Madonnas, whores, or shrews, and then killing them off" (J. Lee, "Affairs of the Breast," 86). See also Quart, "The Rapacity of One Nearly Buried Alive."

14. Keller, "Philip Roth Hates Women."

15. Fox, "Philip Roth Hated Jewish Women."

16. Wickenden, "Philip Roth in the #MeToo Era," podcast, time: 10:30–10:36.

17. McKinley, "Testosterone and Sympathy," 94. McKinley was cross-referencing Adichie's comment in Marchese, "In Conversation."

18. Ivanova, "My Own Foe from the Other Gender," 32. In so doing, he advanced, in the words of Marshall Gentry, a "feminist subversion" of patriarchy (Gentry, "Newark Maid Feminism," 74). Dan Sinykin sees Roth creating heroes that "allow[s] him to engage critically with the grotesqueness of American masculinity" (Sinykin, "This Is the Philip Roth Novel"). See also Shostak, "Roth and Gender."

19. Daum, "In the Age of #MeToo."

20. Daum, "In the Age of #MeToo."

21. Daum, "In the Age of #MeToo." A Norwegian journalist, Ellen Lauritzen, reasons that "Roth's male characters may not always treat women the way society wants. But neither do many men in real life, which is what he is exploring. His bad boys might demean women, but most of all they demean themselves" (Lauritzen, "Roth, Draper, Lil' Wayne").

22. Though among Roth *specialists* the proportion is easily reversed.

23. Miller, "Chronology," 900.

24. Miller, "Chronology," 901. Ira Nadel, interestingly, dates their separation to 1963 in *A Critical Companion to Philip Roth,* 297. It is interesting how even top-flight scholars could disagree over something like this—it points to how little we know about this woman.
25. Miller, "Chronology," 901.
26. Roth, *MLM,* 191.
27. Roth, *MLM,* 198–99.
28. Roth, *MLM,* 196–97.
29. Roth, *MLM,* 155.
30. Roth, *MLM,* 283–84.
31. Roth, *MLM,* 328.
32. Roth, *MLM,* 334.
33. Kundera, "Some Notes on Roth's *My Life as a Man* and *The Professor of Desire*," 162.
34. Gornick, "Why Do These Men Hate Women?," 196. Roth responded to this piece, and not warmly, in "Interview with *Le Nouvel Observateur*," 101.
35. Quart, "The Rapacity of One Nearly Buried Alive," 595.
36. Interestingly, Roth once wrote a little-known short story about a weapons testing ground called "Expect the Vandals."
37. Cooper, *Philip Roth and the Jews,* 132.
38. In a neat twist, characters in *My True Story* actually complain to Peter that they think these two Zuckerman tales are kind of second-rate (*MLM,* 114–15, 119, 225, 228, 233).
39. Philip Ross, *MLM,* 34, 40, 44.
40. Philip Ross, *MLM,* 42.
41. Philip Ross, *MLM,* 82.
42. Philip Ross, *MLM,* 83.
43. Nadel, *Critical Companion to Philip Roth,* 297. Pierpont also argues that "*My Life as a Man* is the long-delayed work about his [Roth's] marriage" (Pierpont, *Roth Unbound,* 78–79).
44. Husband, "Female Hysteria and Sisterhood," 34.
45. Pierpont, *Roth Unbound,* 46.
46. Pierpont, *Roth Unbound,* 47.
47. Roth, *FAC,* 102–3, 107–8, 147–49. Speaking of Josie's/Maureen's/Maggie's fake pregnancy, he writes: "Probably nothing else in my work more precisely duplicates the autobiographical facts" (ibid., 107). See also Pierpont, *Roth Unbound,* 79, 104–5, 161.
48. Roth, *FAC,* 152.
49. Roth, *FAC,* 152.
50. Roth, *FAC,* 178. Then again, the real-life Maggie converted to Judaism. I was always impressed by the fact that she never, in Roth's She-Demoness

8

tales about her, expressed an anti-Semitic thought. There is so much more about this woman that we need to know.

51. Roth, *OSH,* 224.

52. Roth, *OSH,* 225.

53. Although more research needs to be conducted on the issue, I would assume that the following characters are based all, or in part, by Maggie: (1) Martha Reganhart in *Letting Go,* (2) Lucy Nelson in *When She Was Good,* (3) Maureen Tarnopol in *My Life as a Man,* (4) Lydia Ketterer in *My Life as a Man,* (5) Josie Jensen in *The Facts,* and (6) Jinx Possesski in *Operation Shylock.* Other Maggie sightings have been reported in Alan Cooper's, *Philip Roth and the Jews.* Cooper claims that versions of Maggie haunt (7) *Portnoy's Complaint,* and (8) *The Professor of Desire* (i.e., Helen Baird), 52, 67. She is also mentioned in (9) Roth, *Patrimony,* 107–8. It's an open question as to whether components of Maggie can be found in female characters in Philip Roth, *ST.*

54. Pierpoint, *Roth Unbound,* 323.

55. Nadel, *Critical Companion to Philip Roth,* 300. According to Claudia Roth Pierpoint, Ms. Mudge was "the antithesis of Maggie and in some ways the anecdote to her" (Pierpoint, *Roth Unbound,* 46). See also Cooper, *Philip Roth and the Jews,* 54.

56. Cooper, *Philip Roth and the Jews,* 54. On the glimpse of Mudge in *Everyman,* see Pierpoint, *Roth Unbound,* 287.

57. Pierpoint, *Roth Unbound,* 63, 104–5. Ira Nadel suggests "Paula Bates" in *The Facts* was the inspiration for a memorable scene in *When She Was Good* (Nadel, *Critical Companion to Philip Roth,* 87).

58. Roth, *FAC,* 88–89.

59. Pierpoint, *Roth Unbound,* 143, 154. She also notes that Janet Hobhouse is mistakenly assumed to be the model for Maria Zuckerman.

60. Pierpoint, *Roth Unbound,* 168. To understand how convoluted all these relationships were, please note the following. Claire Bloom believed that Maria Zuckerman was based on Janet Hobhouse (ibid.). What we learn reading Pierpoint, however, is that Hobhouse was the fake inspiration for Maria Zuckerman, and it was actually another woman.

61. Pierpoint, *Roth Unbound,* 194–95.

62. Pierpoint, *Roth Unbound,* 311.

63. Pierpoint, *Roth Unbound,* 311.

64. Pierpoint, *Roth Unbound,* 311. On Roth's act of vengeance against Bloom, see Hutchison, "Purity Is Petrefaction," 318; and Safer, "*Operation Shylock,*" 165n11. See also Thackray, "Roth Takes Novel Revenge."

65. Stroud, "The Dark Side of the Online Self," 168.

66. Roth, *CLF,* 220–39.

67. Roth, *CLF*, 238. In an earlier work Nathan Zuckerman's father's dying words to him were "bastard"—such was the anger he felt for a son who aired dirty laundry about his Jewish parents in a best-selling book (the novel that outraged Doc Zuckerman sure sounds like *Portnoy's Complaint*) (Roth, *ZU*, 193). A peculiar section of *My Life as a Man* shows similar empathy for those whose intimate secrets are repurposed for public consumption. Peter Tarnopol severs his relationship with his psychoanalyst upon finding out that the latter had used their therapy sessions as raw data for a scholarly article on narcissistic personality disorder in artists (Roth, *MLM*, 233–34).

68. B. Johnson, "Intimate Affairs," 256. Speaking of classic literature, Roth declares, "The serious, merciless invasion of privacy is at the heart of the fiction we value most highly" (Rothstein, "Philip Roth and the World of 'What If'?," 200). According to Jesse Tisch he acknowledged this invasiveness in his private correspondences as well (Tisch, "The Philip Roth Archive").

69. Roth received a letter from the Law Office of Goldberg and Hatterer on 4/13/1959 (Library of Congress, Philip Roth Papers, Box 12, Folder 13, "Gri-Gru miscellaneous," 1959–1999, n.d.). On Groffsky, see Goldsmith, "When Park Ave. Met Pop Art." See also Pierpoint, *Roth Unbound*, 30.

70. Cooper, *Philip Roth and the Jews*, 52.

71. J. Berman, *The Talking Cure*, 265.

72. PBS, "Philip Roth: Unmasked," time: 1:11:50—1:12:50.

73. He even pounded home this point in his fiction (see Roth, *ZU*, 168; Roth, *DEC*, 184).

74. Roth, *ZU*, 150.

75. Roth, "Interview with the *Paris Review*," 123–24.

76. Making the argument that Roth's writings on sex do not align with his autobiography is Jay Halio in "Eros and Death in Roth's Later Fiction," 200–201. But I am unconvinced by his argument. It's true that Roth is not a puppeteer like Mickey Sabbath, nor a media star like David Kepesh in *The Dying Animal*. But as for the salacious content of their lives, neither Halio nor I can confirm that this was not based on Roth's autobiography. As I said, we need to flip the paradigm (though see M. Smith, "Autobiography: False Confession").

77. Roth, *FAC*, 166.

78. Denham, *Sleeping with Bad Boys*, 203–10.

79. C. Bloom, *Leaving a Doll's House*.

80. Lelchuk, *Ziff*.

81. Halliday, *Asymmetry*.

82. Hobhouse, *The Furies,* 195.

83. Pierpont, *Roth Unbound,* 82.

84. Wickenden, "Philip Roth in the #MeToo Era," podcast, time: 4:02–4:05.

4. BEFORE WE CONCLUDE THAT ROTH'S FICTION IS MISOGYNISTIC

1. Leclerc, "Madame Bovary, c'est moi,' formule apocryphe."

2. Morrison, *Beloved,* 87.

3. Kraus, *I Love Dick,* 19.

4. Kraus, *I Love Dick,* 19.

5. To borrow the phrase that Mary-Jane Reed used to describe Alex Portnoy's eyes (Roth, *PC,* 210).

6. My conception of Nexus Roth seems to be roughly akin to Alan Cooper's idea of "Zuckerroth." Though maybe it encompasses more characters than just Zuckerman (Cooper, *Philip Roth and the Jews,* 210–51). The insinuation that there was something misogynistic about this operation surfaces in Rothstein, "From Philip Roth," 228.

7. Roth, *AL,* 171.

8. Roth, *AL,* 171.

9. Roth, *AL,* 171.

10. Reprinted as Vivian Gornick, "Why Do These Men Hate Women?" Roth acknowledged being called a misogynist and denied it in Davidson, "Talk with Philip Roth: Sara Davidson/1977," 105.

11. Roth, *DEC,* 107–8.

12. And I mean his actual youthful salad days, not the short story that appeared in *My Life as a Man.*

13. Bleich, "Eat Those Words, Philip Roth."

14. Keller, "Philip Roth Hates Women."

15. PBS, "Philip Roth: Unmasked," time: 21:50–22:00. We should also note that in the tumultuous aftermath of the breakup he decided to undergo psychoanalysis in 1962 (Nadel, *Critical Companion to Philip Roth,* 306–7).

16. There is very little scholarly work on these early stories. For one exception, see Fahy, "Filling the Love Vessel."

17. These would include five stories: "Philosophy, or Something Like That" (1952); "The Box of Truths" (1952); "The Fence" (1953); "Armando and the Fraud," (1953); and "The Final Delivery of Mr. Thorn" (1954). One gets a sulfur whiff of misogyny when "Armando and the Fraud" closes off with the protagonist inexplicably murmuring "I know that, I know that, slut!" (Roth, *ATF,* 32). For Philip Roth's critical assessment of his early Bucknell stories, see *FAC,* 59–60. PBS, "Philip Roth: Unmasked," time: 6:30–6:45.

18. These would include "The Day it Snowed" (1954); "The Contest for Aaron Gold" (1955); "Heard Melodies Are Sweeter" (1958); "Expect the Vandals" (1958); and "The Love Vessel" (1959). Only the latter story features an even remotely significant female character.
19. During this period, Roth wrote two novels: the mammoth *Letting Go* (1962) and *When She Was Good* (1967). In addition, he wrote four short stories: "The Good Girl" (1960); "The Mistaken" (1969); "The Psychoanalytic Special" (1963); "An Actor's Life for Me" (1964). It should also be noted that Roth was publishing many excerpts in the same period, some of which went on to figure in the 1969 *Portnoy's Complaint*. The most comprehensive list of these excerpts can likely be found in McDaniel, *The Fiction of Philip Roth*, 236–39.
20. See, for example, Husband, "Female Hysteria and Sisterhood"; Shostak, "Roth and Gender"; J. Jones and Nance, *Philip Roth*, 37–70; Baumgarten and Gottfried, *Understanding Philip Roth*, 60–76; and Halio, "Philip Roth Revisited," 37–66.
21. Roth, TGG, 100.
22. Roth, TGG, 99, 100, 101.
23. Roth, TGG, 101.
24. Roth, TGG, 99. Laurie is said to think about "other girls" who wind up "dreadfully unhappy" after agreeing to sit with men in "the backseats of cars" (100). These sorts of allusions are made throughout the story (101, 103).
25. Roth, TGG, 100, 101, 103.
26. Roth, TGG, 99, 100.
27. Roth, TGG, 99.
28. Roth, TGG, 99.
29. Roth, TGG, 00.
30. Roth, TGG, 101. See her references to Nancy, who "each month anxiously counted days on the calendar."
31. Roth, TGG, 101.
32. Roth, TGG, 102.
33. Roth, TGG, 102.
34. Roth, TGG, 103.
35. Roth, TGG, 103.
36. Denham, *Sleeping with Bad Boys*, 203–10.
37. Diamond, "Flavorwire Interview: Claudia Roth Pierpont." Making the argument more methodically is Brauner, "Getting in Your Retaliation First," 51.
38. Diamond, "Flavorwire Interview: Claudia Roth Pierpont."
39. Roth, PSP, 106.

40. Roth, PSP, 106.
41. Roth, PSP, 106.
42. Roth, PSP, 106.
43. Roth, PSP, 106.
44. Roth, PSP, 106.
45. Roth, PSP, 108. Roth is very cued in to the cluelessness of her husband, who imagines that after her psychoanalysis she will return to him.
46. Roth, PSP, 106.
47. Roth, PSP, 106.
48. Taylor, *Here We Are*, 48.
49. Roth, PSP, 106, 109.
50. Roth, PSP, 172.
51. Roth, PSP, 108.
52. Roth, HMV, 175. Parenthetically, I would note that I have my suspicions about the provenance of "His Mistress' Voice." Portions of the story seem not to be written by Roth at all. The sentences are uncharacteristically short, the cadence syncopated, and the flow uneven. To my ear, much of this story sounds like notebook transcriptions of *other* people's rants. This technique is evident in *Deception*.
53. See Ravits, "The Jewish Mother," 6.
54. Roth, GC.
55. Roth, *PC*, 12; Cohen, "Philip Roth's Would-be Patriarchs and Their Shikses and Shrews," 16. See also Fong, "Re-conceiving the Mother in Philip Roth's Life Writing."
56. Roth, *PC*, 121.
57. Roth, *PC*, 4, 121. On Roth's more complex portraits of Jewish mothers, see Wirth-Nesher, "The Artist Tales," 265.
58. Roth, *AL*, 41.
59. Roth, *AL*, 41.
60. Notice, for instance, how Aunt Gladys in "Goodbye, Columbus"—whose commitments to Judaism seem rather low level—saves food for "Poor Jews in Palestine" (Roth, GC, 6–7).
61. Roth, *PAA*, 40.
62. Roth, *PAA*, 292–98. "*Ma at work*" is how Marcus Messner, narrator of *Indignation*, describes the parent he has watched slave away in the family's kosher butcher shop (Roth, *IND*, 66). Two writers refer to her as "one of the strongest mother figures in recent literary history" (Jaffe-Foger and Pozorski, "[A]nything but Fragile and Yielding," 81).
63. Roth, *MLM*, 125, 205–9. On page 158, she is said to be nineteen years old; on page 124, she is twenty.
64. Roth, *AL*, 86–87.

65. Roth, *AL*, 94–106.

66. Roth, *NEM*, 165.

67. Roth, *NEM*, 260–61.

68. Roth, *NEM*, 259.

69. Roth, *CLF*, 324.

70. Roth, *CLF*, 204. A subcategory of a virtuous woman might also be "Dutiful Daughters," an excellent example being the kind and caring Phoebe of Roth, *EVR*, 120.

71. Roth, *PAA*, 318; see also 249.

72. For an interesting study of Hannah Portnoy and what it means for charges of misogyny in Roth's work, see Schweitzer, "The Story of 'Hannah P.'"

73. Keller, "Philip Roth Hates Women."

74. This seems to be what is occurring in the conflict between Brenda Patimkin and her mother in Roth, GC, 64. Above, we saw Laurie Bowen speak to Ms. Lasser about the same topic in Roth, TGG, 101–2.

75. As occurs between Ellie Sowerby and Lucy Nelson as they commiserate over the infidelity of Ellie's father, Julian (Roth, *WSWG*, 128–31). The same story features discussions between Lucy and Kitty Egan about Catholicism (71–80). Also, Ginny and Lucy seem to have some type of symbiotic relationship (10). With its female protagonist, *When She Was Good* probably has more woman-to-woman conversations than any other work by Roth. In Roth, *HST*, 239, Faunia Farley discusses a crow with a female attendant at an animal shelter.

76. Roth, HMV, 166. Of interest here is Fahy, "Filling the Love Vessel," 117–26. In terms of occasional exceptions to this rule, we might look at the bickering between Martha Reganhart and Sissy in *Letting Go*.

77. Husband, "Female Hysteria and Sisterhood," 40.

78. Bechdel, *Dykes to Watch Out For*, 22–23.

79. B. D. Johnson, "Intimate Affairs," 256.

80. B. D. Johnson, "Intimate Affairs," 256.

81. These would include *Portnoy's Complaint, The Great American Novel, My Life as a Man,* and *The Professor of Desire.*

82. Mannes, "A Dissent," 39.

83. H. Lee, "Life *is* And," 265.

84. Jaffe-Foger and Pozorski, "[A]nything but Fragile and Yielding," 83, 93. See also Vanderhoof, "Me and the Monkey."

85. Garber, "David Foster Wallace."

86. Roth, *IND*, 72, 65.

87. Roth, *IND*, 173.

88. Roiphe, "The Naked and the Conflicted."

89. Lauritzen, "Roth, Draper, Lil' Wayne."

90. Very important in this regard is Ivanova, "My Own Foe from the Other Gender." And see Grant, "Breast Man."
91. Meyers, "Why Did I Cry for Philip Roth?"
92. Meyers, "Why Did I Cry for Philip Roth?"

## 5. YOU MUST CHANGE YOUR LIFE!

1. Roth, "Interview with *The Paris Review*," 142. Roth mentions this again in Sanoff, "Writers Have a Third Eye," though Roth argues that the desire for "self-renewal and transformation" is a phenomenon that strikes people in middle age.
2. Roth, *HST*, 256.
3. Roth, *EG*, 166.
4. Roth, *DEC*, 85.
5. Roth, *CLF*, 39. Anyone except a holocaust survivor, as Dr. Zuckerman realizes.
6. Eliot, *Silas Marner*; Hardy, *The Mayor of Casterbridge*; Fitzgerald, *The Great Gatsby*.
7. Fitzgerald, *The Great Gatsby*, 98.
8. This important point is noted by Aarons, "Reading Roth/Reading Ourselves," 28.
9. Roth, ALM, 123.
10. Roth, ALM, 123.
11. Roth, ALM, 123–24.
12. Roth, AL, 233.
13. Roth, AL, 103.
14. Roth, AL, 109, 187.
15. Roth, AL,172.
16. Roth, AL, 214.
17. Roth, AL, 171, 196.
18. Roth, AL, 263.
19. Roth, *WSWG*, 32; italics in original.
20. Roth, *HST*, 47.
21. In this section on reinvention I won't mention Ira Ringold (Iron Rinn) of *I Married a Communist*, even though Roth keeps parsing him as a character who sought self-reinvention. Frankly, I think Roth does a poor job with this change narrative. In numerous asides we are told that Ira was obsessed with reinventing himself. For example, "How drunk on metamorphosis could he get, the heroic reinvention of himself he called Iron Rinn?" (*IMAC*, 301). Yet, I don't see much in the way of reinvention, or even basic character development in Iron Rinn; he seems to be the same

troubled, excessive person throughout the entire novel. He just becomes more of himself until he explodes. I think Roth confuses Ira's desire for self-change with his desire to change the world. We learn that Ira's real interest was the latter: "But change was what Ira lived for. *Why* he lived. Why he lived *strenuously*. It is the essence of the man that he treats everything as a challenge to his will. He must always make the effort. He must change everything. For him that was the purpose of being in the world. Everything he wanted to change was here" (*IMAC*, 84). Exactly! Ira wants to change *the world*, not himself. It is for this reason that I don't see his case as exemplifying the theme of reinvention examined in this section.

22. Roth, EP, in *GC*.
23. The author comments on this story, and the rash, in a 1971 piece, "The Story of Three Stories," 214.
24. Roth, EP, 210.
25. Roth, EP, 218.
26. J. Jones and Nance, *Philip Roth*, 5.
27. Roth, EP, 207–8.
28. Roth, ELF.
29. For some interesting background on Woodenton, see Gittleman, "The Pecks of Woodenton, Long Island, Thirty Years Later"; and Fink, "Fact, Fiction, and History in Philip Roth's 'Eli, the Fanatic.'"
30. Roth, ELF, 289.
31. Roth, ELF, 271.
32. Roth, ELF, 297.
33. Roth, AL, 28.
34. Roth, AL, 14.
35. Roth, *AL*, 40. In *Zuckerman Unbound*, we learn that Nathan's father's last words to him were "bastard." Doc Zuckerman's anger was also on account of *Carnovsky* (Roth, *ZU*, 199).
36. Roth, *IND*, 148. Roth again lets us see what his characters cannot in Indignation. Marcus Messner's mother contemplating a divorce exclaims: "Darling, is this what they call a personality change. . . . All I know is that something has made my husband into a different person."
37. Roth, *HUMB*, 1.
38. Roth, *HUMB*, 27.
39. Roth, *HUMB*, 43.
40. Roth, *HUMB*, 52.
41. Roth, *HUMB*, 51.
42. We also learn that Pegeen is something of a change agent—at least one of her jilted lovers, Louis Renner, believes so: "She turned her Montana lover into a man. She's turned me into a beggar. Who knows what

she's turning you into. She leaves a trail of disaster. Where does the power come from?" (*HUMB*, 87).

43. A few explicable metamorphosis narratives not mentioned above can be found in Roth, *MLM*, 7, 25.

44. See his 1973 hybrid essay/short story "'I Always Wanted You to Admire My Fasting'; or, Looking at Kafka," and the 1974 *My Life as a Man*.

45. The broad contours of this change are noted in Statlander, *Philip Roth's Postmodern American Romance*, 3.

46. Roth, *BRE*, 4, 26, 49.

47. Roth, *BRE*, 13.

48. Roth, *BRE*, 13, 14.

49. Roth, *BRE*, 77.

50. Nadel, *Critical Companion to Philip Roth*, 9.

51. Roth, *BRE*. That he is imagining it is implied on page 53. That he is having a dream is suggested on page 54. That Kepesh is experiencing a psychological collapse is intimated on pages 55, 56, 59, 60, 68, and 73. On pages 86 and 88, it seems that he is merely giving a lecture.

52. Though the first instance of this occurs in Roth, *MLM*.

53. Roth, *CLF*, 1–49.

54. Roth, *CLF*, 59.

55. Roth, *CLF*, 61.

56. Roth, *CLF*, 129–40.

57. Roth, *CLF*, 204–5.

58. Roth, *CLF*, 225–28.

59. Roth, *CLF*, 239–54.

60. Roth, *CLF*, 312.

61. Shostak, "Introduction: Roth's America," 8. In fact in his notes on the drafts, Roth wrote a reminder to himself: "START ANEW WITH EACH CHAPTER. Never take advantage of momentum." The incompleteness of the sketches is not by accident (Shostak, *Philip Roth—Countertexts, Counterlives*, 198).

62. The five autofictional pieces are "'I Always Wanted You to Admire My Fasting': Or, Looking at Kafka" (1973), *The Facts* (1988), *Deception* (1990), *Patrimony* (1991), and then later on as a childhood version of himself in *The Plot Against America* (2004).

63. For an example, see Doubrovsky, *Fils*. For discussion of its definitions and its migration as a concept into Anglophone studies, see Dix, ed., *Autofiction in English*. The collection does feature a few references to Roth, especially in Womble, "Roth Is Roth as Roth." See also Mortimer, "Autofiction as Allofiction."

64. There are actually three Philip Roths. We must consider the "real" Philip Roth who appears in the novel to be distinct from the real Philip Roth who wrote it.

65. Roth, *OSH,* 77–78.

66. Roth, *OSH,* 101, 252.

67. Roth, *OSH,* 30–33, 40–48.

68. Roth, *OSH,* 13.

69. Roth, *OSH,* [399]. Though it is perhaps not irrelevant that this "Note" appears on a page with no number—a page that comes after the final page of the book—page 398.

70. A few lines later even *that* assertion is qualified (and undermined) by the statement "This confession is false" (Roth, *OSH,* 399). The perceptive reader might notice that, on page 361, Roth raised the possibility of issuing a disclaimer. The disclaimer we see on page 361 is identical to the one on the last page of the book with the exception of the words "This confession is false." That is probably the strongest argument for proving that Roth is referring to the disclaimer itself as being false, and not to *Operation Shylock: A Confession* as being false. In a word, mind games! What is false? The claim that Roth worked for the Mossad? Or, the disclaimer that this is "a work of fiction" (which would imply that he *did* work for the Mossad)? What is going on here? On *OSH,* see Worthington's "Fiction in the Post-Truth Era," 477.

71. Kakutani, "Of a Roth within a Roth within a Roth." Esther Fein, "Philip Roth Sees Double," refers to *Operation Shylock* as, "a novel that frequently exhausts the reader's desire to know evermore about characters answering to the name, 'Philip Roth.'"

72. Updike, "Recruiting Raw Nerves," 298; C. Bloom, *Leaving a Doll's House,* 192–204.

73. Royce, "Metempsychosis," 556. Royce goes on to note that this a heretical idea within Christianity. In another version "the doctrine of the transmigration of souls, teaches that the same soul inhabits in succession the bodies of different beings, both men and animals" (Maher, "Metempsychosis," 234).

74. See Senn, "Met Whom What?," 110.

75. Ovid, *Metamorphoses,* lines 158–59, p. 377.

76. Lefèvre, "Métempsycose," 39.

77. Jacques Berlinerblau, Bethania Michael, and Heather Walters, "Intertexts and Influence: A Comprehensive Table of Intertexts in Philip Roth's Fiction, 1952–2010," *Philip Roth Studies,* 17, no. 2 (2021).

78. In *A la recherche de temps perdu,* the French original reads: "Puis elle commençait à me devenir inintelligible, comme après la métempsycose

les pensées d'une existence antérieure" (Proust, *A la recherche du temps perdu*, 3). If I am correct, then he would have overlooked the reference to "la métempsycose" since the cognate does not appear in the famous C. K. Scott Moncrieff English translation. There, the line is rendered—or botched—as follows: "Then it would begin to seem unintelligible, as the thoughts of a former existence must be to a reincarnate spirit" (Proust, *Swann's Way*, 9).

79. Joyce, *Ulysses*, 52.

80. Joyce, *Ulysses*, 52–53.

81. Joyce, *Ulysses*, 53.

82. For some studies on metempsychosis, see Wicke, "Who's She When She's at Home?"; Levy, "The Mimesis of Metempsychosis in *Ulysses*," 367. See also Corrigan, *American Metempsychosis*; and Gillespie, "Literary Afterlives."

83. Roth, *OSH*, 202.

84. Roth, *OSH*, 180.

85. Roth, *OSH*, 237. James Ramey refers to "intertextual metempsychosis" or "the transmigration of characters from ancient to modern texts" in "Intertextual Metempsychosis in *Ulysses*" (97).

86. Roth, *OSH*, 244; italics mine.

87. Roth, *OSH*, 224.

88. Roth, *OSH*, 224, 225. By the end of the scene Roth bickers with his "resurrected wife," complaining, "Can't you even return from *death* without screaming about the morality of your position versus the immorality of mine" (225).

89. The reader is also advised to look at a dream sequence in which Roth imagines that the souls of everyone on earth are draining into the body of Ivan of Treblinka. Roth mentions "metempsychosis" explicitly in this passage, though what he is getting at is difficult to discern (Roth, *OSH*, 207–8). A metempsychotic moment might be implied in *LG*, 473.

90. Roth, *CLF*, 312.

91. Roth, *NEM*, 244.

92. Roth, *NEM*, 275–80.

93. Compare this transfer of selves in the context of Jainism with a conversation about Buddhism in Roth, *ST*, 197.

94. Roth, *PSP*, 106, 109.

95. Roth, *PAA*.

96. Roth, *CLF*, 147; see also 142.

97. A sort of collective metamorphosis also occurs in *The Great American Novel* where the hapless and hopeless baseball team the Ruppert Mundys suddenly starts winning because they imbibe spiked cereal (Roth, *GAN*, 325–26, 328). They later transform into a violent and nasty bunch

because of the Communist subterfuge of their manager, Gil Gamesh (372, 380). Other collective transformations include the desire for sexual transformation noted in Roth, *DAN*, 54. And the desire for "violence" and "thirst for self-transformation" which gripped 1960s radicals discussed in Roth, *AP*, 254.

98. The only explicit and detailed scholarly engagement with the idea that transformation lies at the core of Roth's work can be found in Kartiganer, "Fictions of Metamorphosis." Though the analytical lines Kartiganer follows are very different from the ones adduced above.

99. Sartre, *Existentialism and Human Emotions*, 15. Very little has been written about the influence of existentialist philosophy on Roth's thought. My hunch is that it was more influential than we currently know. The point of contact likely would have been Roth's formation at Bucknell and the University of Chicago in the 1950s, when these European ideas were washing up on American shores. For some interesting studies of existentialist themes in Roth, see Hayes, "With an Accomplice No Less Brilliant than Jean Genet"; James Duban, "Sartrian Nothingness"; Duban, "From Negative Identity"; and Duban, "Juice or Gravy?" 75.

100. Rilke, "Archaïscher Torso Apollos," 172.

101. Roth quoted those words on the final page of *The Breast*, 89. A few years later the mantra appears again in *The Ghost Writer* (27). He even considered using this phrase as the title for what eventually became *The Counterlife* (Shostak, *Philip Roth—Countertexts, Counterlives*, 204).

102. Shostak, *Philip Roth—Countertexts, Counterlives*, 187.

103. Roth, LAK, 164.

## 6. GO FLUX YOUR SELF!

1. Roth, *LG*, 21.

2. Roth, *LG*, 234–38. For an unusual take on the interpersonal dynamics of scholars at different ranks, see Berlinerblau, *Campus Confidential*.

3. These happenings begin on *LG*, 408.

4. Roth, *LG*, 435.

5. Roth, *LG*, 435.

6. Roth, *LG*, 435. Notice that in *The Counterlife*, Nathan speaks in similar terms of "Henry's Henryness" (Roth, CLF, 119).

7. Roth, *LG*, 435.

8. Roth, *LG*, 435.

9. Roth, *LG*, 435.

10. Schubert, "Cooley, Charles Horton." On Cooley's lineage in the history of Symbolic Interaction, see Blumer, *Symbolic Interactionism*, 1. Although

he taught at the University of Michigan, Cooley is reckoned as a member of the Chicago school. On his association with the Chicago school, see Musolf, "The Chicago School," 96. On Cooley as an influence on Symbolic Interaction, see Bruce and Yearley, "Looking Glass Self, Symbolic Interaction," 177. The same point is made in Jacobsen, "Introduction: Instigators of Interactionism," 6–7. Cooley was fond of literature and invoked it when trying to encapsulate his theories. For the "Looking Glass Self," he cited Goethe: "Only in man does man know himself; life alone teaches each one what he is." See also his discussions of Hamlet and others in *Human Nature and the Social Order*, 181.

11. Steinmetz, "American Sociology before and after World War II," 328.

12. Schubert, "Cooley, Charles Horton." "Cooley considered the development of the self to be a process of interaction between it and the surrounding world" (ibid., 153–54). Or, as other commentators put it: "We can only come to know ourselves indirectly, by imaginatively projecting ourselves into the viewpoint of significant and generalized others as they react to, and judge us" (Puddephatt, "George Herbert Mead," 104).

13. Atkinson and Delamont, "Qualitative Research Traditions," 47.

14. Roth, *LG*, 435. I am not sure what to make of a passage in *Sabbath's Theater* where Sabbath discovers that which "was inexorably himself." Why Sabbath achieves this essentialist recognition is still perplexing to me (Roth, *ST*, 184). Then again, there is the intimation in this text that Sabbath's self is somehow broken or "barely what you would call a self" (ibid., 198).

15. These dates are taken from Miller, "Chronology," 897–907.

16. Oddly, Maureen Tarnopol in *My Life as a Man* recognizes this idea when she notes in a diary: "It's hard to sketch my own personality really, since personality implies the effect one has on others, and it's difficult to know truly what that effect is" (Roth, *MLM*, 312).

17. Of collateral interest to this discussion is Safer, "The Double," 167. Safer notes that Roth "uses the concept of the double to reassert postmodern skepticism about identity of the self."

18. As Zadie Smith put it, he splayed "echoes, shadows, inversions, fragments" of the "real" Philip Roth across the page in novel after novel (Z. Smith, "The I Who Is Not Me," 345).

19. Roth, *CLF*, 320.

20. Roth, *CLF*, 145.

21. Roth, *CLF*, 320.

22. Roth, *CLF*, 320.

23. Roth, *CLF*, 320. Perhaps the most sensitive and subtle reader of *The Counterlife* is the late Derek Parker Royal, who drew the following possibility to our attention: "Roth . . . is suggesting that a literal text is very

much like the 'text' of the self, a multifaceted and non-linear project that is always ongoing." Royal continues, "This notion of self as performance permeates Roth's later fiction" (Royal, "Postmodern Jewish Identity," 427, 437). Of interest is Swede Levov's recognition that he too is "masquer- ading as the ideal man." Roth speaks of "the huge pretense of living as himself." As we shall see below, there is heroism in the recognition of one's constant playacting (Roth, *AP*, 174). Also notice that Delphine Roux "refused to take the prescribed view of herself. She seemed to herself to have subverted herself in the altogether admirable effort to *make* herself" (Roth, *HST*, 272). The writer E. I. Lonoff, for his part, believes he has no self, that it "happens not to exist." Do all writers suffer from this ontologi- cal affliction? (Roth, *GW*, 41).

24. Roth, *POD*, 12. Even in the aughts this idea was on Roth's mind. In *The Dying Animal*, David Kepesh complains that his male friends are "dil- igently presenting a counterfeit image of their lives" (Roth, *DAN*, 115).

25. Roth, *CLF*, 138.

26. That Roth may have been influenced by Goffman has been insinu- ated in passing by a handful of writers. Though to the best of my knowl- edge, the argument has never been developed beyond a sentence. Among those perceptive scholars are Gelbart, "[Sticking] to a Plan Completely"; Goodheart, "Writing and the Unmaking of the Self"; and Leeke, *The Counterlife of Knight Errant Christie McKay*, 299–300. See also Posnock, *Philip Roth's Rude Truth*, 19. That Goffman himself may have been influ- enced by Sartrean existentialism is interesting in terms of my observation in the previous chapter that Roth may have also been impacted by Sartre's writings (Lofland, "Early Goffman," 46–47). That parsing Goffman under the rubric "Symbolic Interactionism" and equating him with the Chicago school is inaccurate is a point made by Williams, "Appraising Goffman," 350. Also reflecting on the proper categorization of Goffman in relation to the Chicago school and Interactionism are Atkinson and Housley, *Interac- tionism*, 12–13. On this point, see Jacobsen, "Erving Goffman," 208–13.

27. On the wide impact of Goffman's work, see Ditton, "Editor's Introduc- tion"; and G. Smith, "Erving Goffman." See also Giddens, "On Reread- ing *The Presentation of Self in Everyday Life*." It's likely that Roth read Goffman, and he might have even enjoyed the read. Marshall Berman probably overshot the runway (and the continent) when he insisted that Goffman "comes closer than any living writer to being the Kafka of our time" (M. Berman, "Weird but Brilliant Light on the Way We Live Now"). Much of Goffman's writing, *contra* Berman, is painstakingly technical and dense. Still, his prose was not without its sinister charms—sinister charms that would be congenial to someone like Philip Roth.

28. For a quick overview of his life and character and work, see Jacobsen, "Erving Goffman."

29. Goffman, *Stigma,* 10.

30. His most famous example coming from the preening character Preedy in William Sansom's 1956 novel *A Contest of Ladies* (Goffman, *The Presentation of Self in Everyday Life,* 16–17).

31. Williams, "Appraising Goffman," 356.

32. Alexander, *Twenty Lectures,* 232–33.

33. Dawe, "The Underworld-View of Erving Goffman," 252–53.

34. Berlinerblau, "The Productive Obscene"; Howe, "Philip Roth Reconsidered."

35. Goffman, *The Presentation of Self in Everyday Life,* 17.

36. Goffman, *The Presentation of Self in Everyday Life,* 245.

37. An excellent collection of essays on the subject can be found in Brissett and Edgley, eds., *Life as Theater.* Edgley, "The Dramaturgical Genre." See also Tseëlon, "Is the Presented Self Sincere?"; and Petit, "The Con Man as Model Organism." Though Goffman was very cautious in pointing out his references to theater were metaphorical.

38. Roth, *CLF,* 320–21.

39. Roth reiterated this position in *Operation Shylock:* "Amazing, that something as tiny, really, as a self should contain contending subselves—and that these subselves should themselves be constructed of subselves, and on and on and on" (Roth, *OSH,* 152). This meshes well with the conclusion of two eminent theorists of dramaturgy that "having more than one self is a performative necessity!" (Brissett and Edgley, eds., *Life as Theater,* 18).

40. On this subtle, but important, point, see Messinger, Sampson, and Towne, "Life as Theater."

41. See also N. Gross, "Pragmatism," 200.

42. Roth, *CLF,* 324.

43. Roth, *CLF,* 324. See also page 314, where Maria Zuckerman intimates that this is actually Nathan's "irreducible core." Similar observations about British anti-Semitism are made in Roth's *DEC,* 99–106.

44. On some of these issues pertaining to Roth's Judaism, see Parrish, "Roth and Ethnic Identity." I feel compelled to note that Roth drew this very correlation between his authentic self and being Jewish. In an aside he made in a 1971 essay, he drew a link between "a sense of self, which for lack of a better term is frequently called 'Jewishness'" (Roth, "The Story of Three Stories," 214). So maybe Roth always viewed his Jewish identity as something that superseded the self's capacity for impersonation. In any case, this has yet to make logical sense. Elsewhere, Roth intimates that a lover in the throes of passion may represent an essential state of the self:

"the lover does, in fact, feel more deeply implicated in his own life than at any moment in memory—the true self at its truest, moored by every feeling to its own true home!" (Roth, *POD*, 254).

45. Budick, "Roth and Israel," 69.
46. Rodgers, *Philip Roth*, 136.
47. Roth, *BRE*, 43–44. A similar example of a mind expressing its uncertainties about itself as a mind can be found in Roth, *EG*, 162.
48. Z. Smith, *Changing My Mind*, 278. A similar observation is made about the self-consciousness of Roth's protagonists in H. Lee "You Must Change Your Life," 149.
49. Roth, *CLF*, 205. Compare this declaration to that found in Roth, *EG*, 31.
50. See Kremer, "Philip Roth's Self-Reflexive Fiction." Although not directly related to the self's consciousness of the self that I am identifying in Roth's protagonists, Brian Stonehill provides a seminal study of self-consciousness in fiction (Stonehill, *The Self-Conscious Novel*). Also of interest is the oddly entitled article by Fusillo, "Self-Reflexivity in Ancient Novel."
51. Roth, *WSWG*, 250.
52. Roth, *LG*, 528.
53. Roth, *LG*, 528.
54. Roth, *MLM*, 334. Roth tried exegeting the line, and it still doesn't make sense to me (see Roth, "A Conversation with Philip Roth: Joyce Carol Oates/1974," 95).
55. Roth, *CJ*, 147.
56. Roth, *CJ*, 147–48. A similar howl is mouthed by Walter Appel, who says to himself, "*OK—I am naked! In the light! In the window! I am doing this!*" (Roth, *ALM*, 137).
57. As Bonnie Lyons notes, for Roth "the notion of a unified self is another comforting but groundless idea" (Lyons, "En-Countering Pastorals," 122).
58. Roth, *GC*, 100.
59. Roth, *GC*, 100.
60. Roth, *GC*, 100.
61. Roth, *IND*, 54–55.
62. Roth, *WSWG*, 56–60.
63. Roth, *MLM*, 297.
64. Roth, *OSH*, 60.
65. Roth, *CLF*, 43.
66. Roth, *CLF*, 44. He also meets Shimmy Kirsch, a citadel of thoughtlessness as far as Zuckerman is concerned. Sizing the dull man up, he complains "No questions, no excuses, none of this who-am-I, what-am-I, where-am-I crap, not a grain of self-mistrust" (37).
67. Roth, *CLF*, 140.

68. Roth, *OSH*, 334.

69. Debra Shostak notes that one of Roth's early titles for *Operation Shylock* was "You Are Not Yourself" (Shostak, "The Diaspora Jew," 728).

70. Interestingly, Nathan Zuckerman at his lowest point in *The Anatomy Lesson* is simply exhausted by self-scrutiny and wants out: "But that sounded to Zuckerman like all a man could want, an end to the search for the release from self" (Roth, *AL*, 274).

71. Roth, *AP*, 329. Those squares also change, but with far less self-reflection. In an underappreciated passage from *American Pastoral*, Swede Levov ruminates on the less kinetic minds among us: "What was astonishing to him was how people seem to run out of their own being, run out of whatever the stuff was that made them who they were and, drained of themselves, turned into the sort of people they would once would have felt sorry for. It was as though while their lives were rich and full they were secretly sick of themselves and couldn't wait to dispose of their sanity and their health and all sense of proportion so as to get down to that other self, the *true* self, who was a wholly deluded fuck up."

72. This point comes out very strongly in *I Married a Communist*. Referring to Ira Ringold, we read "[B]ecause everything that lives is in movement. Because purity is petrifaction. Because purity is a lie." Notice the dislike of stasis articulated in this comment. Also notice how kinetic Ira is: "His passion was to be someone he didn't know how to be. He never discovered his life . . . he looked for it everywhere. . . . He couldn't find it anywhere" (Roth, *IMAC*, 318–19).

73. H. Lee, *Philip Roth*, 83.

74. Roth, *BRE*, 82.

75. Some of these ideas are explored by other Roth scholars, though from different angles. Timothy Parrish comes to this conclusion as well, though his reasoning is different than my own above. He writes: "For Roth, the self takes its form through experimentation and should be perceived as a type of fiction" (Parrish, "Introduction: Roth at Mid-Career," 2; see also Parrish, "Roth and Ethnic Identity," 130). Another way of looking at the issue is offered by Brett Ashley Kaplan, who speaks of "Roth's concept of the self's ability to create and live by its own fictions" (Kaplan, "Reading Race," 182). "Freedom exists," writes the Roth critic Debra Shostak, "in the capacity to invent counterlives" (Shostak, *Philip Roth—Countertexts, Counterlives*, 204).

## 7. FICTION IS TRUTH! (RIGHT?)

1. Roth, *POD*, 11.

2. Roth, *PO*, 10–24.

3. Roth, *ST,* 102. Later in the work, Sabbath points out that "everything *is* acted," 290.

4. Roth, *IND,* 193–94.

5. Roth, *LAK,* 163. As if there could be any doubt concerning how much Roth thought about this artform, see his 1964 story "An Actor's Life for Me." It features Walter Appel, a failed playwright who gravitates to a business job in the theater, dates an unstable actress, and loses his mind by story's end (Roth, ALM).

6. Roth, *POD,* 123–26; Roth, *HST,* 61.

7. That artist would be Sandy Roth in Roth, *PAA,* 155. Notice that in *AP* (321), Bill Orcutt was an "abstract painter." Foul-mouthed Uncle Asher in *LG* is one as well (83), as is the character of Dick (218).

8. Roth, *GW,* 36. I'm not quite sure what Roth's precise views on puppetry were, but it seems like the apt vocation for a person as demented as Mickey Sabbath—a sixty-four-year-old man who plunders dresser drawers and sniffs the underwear of teenage girls. David Kepesh of *The Dying Animal* considers pornography "a fallen art form." "It's not just make-believe," he complains, "it's patently insincere" (Roth, *DA,* 41).

9. Roth, *DA,* 22.

10. Roth, *HST,* 209.

11. Roth, *HST,* 209.

12. Roth, *HST,* 209, 210.

13. Roth, "Imagining Jews," 251–52.

14. Roth, *Shop Talk,* 40–77, 90–100.

15. See Jacques Berlinerblau, Bethania Michael, and Heather Walters, "Intertexts and Influence: A Comprehensive Table of Intertexts in Philip Roth's Fiction, 1952–2010," *Philip Roth Studies,* 17, no. 2 (2021).

16. Safer, "The Double," 58.

17. Those that do not fulfill this criterion are: (1) *When She Was Good,* (2) *Portnoy's Complaint,* (3) *Our Gang,* (4) *Sabbath's Theater,* (5) *The Plot Against America,* and (6) *Everyman.*

18. Roth, *MLM,* 97.

19. Roth, *MLM,* front matter.

20. He claims, not entirely convincingly, that the sexual dimension fully set in when Monica was sixteen years old (Roth, *MLM,* 82–83). Too complex to note here is that the two Nathans in these two short stories are not precisely the same Nathan.

21. Roth, *MLM,* 83–87.

22. Roth, *MLM,* 334.

23. Though this Nathan Zuckerman is a different fellow from the one(s) we met in *My Life as a Man.*

24. Roth, *FAC*, 4.

25. Here is something to think about: Nathan is now, inexplicably, ten years younger than Philip Roth, even though in other Zuckerman novels they are always the same age, both born in 1933 (Roth, *FAC*, 186).

26. Roth, *FAC*, 161.

27. Roth, *FAC*, 188.

28. Roth, *FAC*, 185.

29. Roth, *FAC*, 165.

30. Roth, *FAC*, 172.

31. Claudia Roth Pierpoint makes the observation, "The implicit lesson of *The Facts* is that the only way to reach the truth is through fiction" (Pierpont, *Roth Unbound*, 162).

32. Roth, *OSH*, 58. This was clearly a paradox that Roth thought about throughout his life. In the 1959 "Defender of the Faith," he writes: "Long ago, someone had taught Grossbart the sad rule that only lies can get the truth" (Roth, DF, 194).

33. Roth, *FAC*, 171. For some interesting observations on this, see Faisst, "'Delusionary Thinking.'"

34. See, for example, Roth, *AP*, 64.

35. Roth, *AP*, 35.

36. Roth, *GW*, 1. Many of the issues raised in this section are explored in detail in Berlinerblau, "Imagine That!"

37. Roth, *GW*, 105.

38. Roth, *GW*, 16–17.

39. The 1995 Vintage International reprint doesn't even have a "3" at its head; the author, I argued elsewhere, removed the "3" on purpose to make us feel that this is not a "chapter," but some ghostly intrusion into the book (Berlinerblau, "Imagine That!").

40. Roth, *GW*, 122–55.

41. Roth, *GW*, 157

42. Roth, *GW*, 169.

43. Roth, *EG*, 156.

44. Library of Congress, Philip Roth Papers, Box 92, Folder 5, The Ghost Writer, Drafts Copy B, Set I, 1978, Nov NZ. "They will not take your defilement lightly . . . I love you Anne" "Then fuck me, damn it" (Library of Congress, Philip Roth Papers, Box 93, Folder 1, The Ghost Writer, Drafts Copy 3, Set II, undated). And here he adds, "defile me, will you, please?" James Atlas, in his audiobook *Remembering Roth*, claims that he urged Roth to tone down the erotic dimensions of Anne Frank's portraiture in *GW*. She was, Atlas insisted, "not a figure to be tampered with." I do

not know if Atlas read the version that I read in the Library of Congress (Atlas, *Remembering Roth,* audiobook, time 19:30–20:02).

45. Library of Congress, Philip Roth Papers, Box 92, Folder 5, The Ghost Writer, Drafts Copy B, Set I, 1978, Nov NZ.
46. Roth, *AP,* 14.
47. Roth, *AP,* 3.
48. Roth, *AP,* 15.
49. Roth, *AP,* 17–18.
50. Roth, *AP,* 21–39.
51. Roth, *AP,* 23.
52. Roth, *AP,* 30.
53. Roth, *AP,* 30.
54. Roth, *AP,* 39.
55. Roth, *AP,* 60–77.
56. Roth, *AP,* 73.
57. Roth, *AP,* 68–69.
58. The other materials that Zuckerman uses to re-create the story include some visits to Swede and Merry's old haunts (Roth, *AP,* 75–76).
59. Roth, *AP,* 74. Nathan describes the writerly challenge that confronts him, ruminating about inhabiting Swede and struggling to "disappear into him" (Roth, *AP,* 74).
60. Roth, *AP,* 89.
61. Roth, *AP,* 84, 89.
62. Roth, *AP,* 90–92.
63. Every now and then, Zuckerman reminds us, subtly, that this is a fiction. He offers us paragraphs with headings like "Conversation #12 about New York." Here, sixteen-year-old Merry and Swede argue about her trips to Manhattan and many other matters. My guess is that these are notebook entries, sketches that Zuckerman wrote as a fictionalist and in a postmodern way inserted into the text (Roth, *AP,* 104–13). On page 215 Zuckerman refers to "another *book,*" presumably different from the present one that he is writing and we are reading. Then there are two endings mentioned above. These are the only signs we receive from Zuckerman that he is still "in the book" (421).
64. Roth, *AP,* 423.
65. Masiero, *Philip Roth and the Zuckerman Books,* 148, 152; Royal, "Pastoral Dreams," 189.
66. Roth, *IMAC,* 223.
67. Roth, *HST,* 225–34.
68. Roth, *HST,* 68–71.

69. That Zuckerman is reconstructing these encounters is clear from the following passages (Roth, *HST*, 63, 304, 337–41).
70. Schwartz, "Erasing Race," 73.
71. Roth, *OSH*, 364–73. Notice how, starting on page 364, Roth explicitly tells us he's going to imagine a letter from Jinx.
72. Fishman, "Success in Circuit Lies," 145, argues that Aharon Appelfeld in *Operation Shylock* holds the position that "an author is forced to fictionalize in order to tell the truth."
73. Norman Podhoretz suggests that Glucksman's "aestheticist creed" approximates Roth's own view on the supremacy of prose and poetry (Podhoretz, "The Adventures of Philip Roth," 30).
74. Roth, *IMAC*, 219–20.
75. Roth, *IMAC*, 218.
76. Roth, *IMAC*, 220.
77. On this point, see Connolly, *Philip Roth and the American Liberal Tradition*, 90.
78. Roth, *IMAC*, 219.
79. Roth, *IMAC*, 218.
80. Roth, *IMAC*, 223–24
81. Roth, *IMAC*, 224.
82. Roth, *GAN*, 400.
83. Roth, *GAN*, 400.
84. Roth, *CLF*, 306.
85. Arguing that truth, for Roth, can be "never fully reached or defined" is Jason Siegel, "*The Plot Against America*," 132.
86. Timothy Parks makes a similar observation when he notes: "Actually most people don't *write* fictitious versions of their lives at *any* time, though they may invent such versions in conversation or reflection. Roth seems to be conflating, or confusing, the novelist's activity with the individual's construction of a personal history" (Parks, "How Best to Read Autofiction").
87. As Stanley Trachtenberg says, "Only through the ambiguities of fiction, then, can reality acquire a redeeming truth" (Trachtenberg, "In the Egosphere," 327). See also Pia Masiero, *Philip Roth and the Zuckerman Books*, who argues that Roth sees the imagination as an "instrument to grasp truth" (50).

CONCLUSION

1. Worthington, *The Story of "Me,"* 59.
2. Dodd, "History or Fiction," 62.
3. Roth, *MLM*, 100; italics in original.

4. Library of Congress, Box, 26, Folder 12, "Ozick, Cynthia 1969–1979, 1983–1998."

5. To borrow Debra Shostak's excellent term (Shostak, *Philip Roth—Countertexts, Counterlives*, 158). See also Shostak, "Philip Roth's Fictions of Self-Exposure."

6. Taylor, *Here We Are*, 162.

7. Library of Congress, Philip Roth Papers, Box 34, Folder 3, "Sil-Sk Miscellaneous 1975–1993." Roth cribbed the *American Pastoral* high school reunion scene from his actual high school reunion down to the categories of ages, of children, grandchildren, etc., as well as the "In Memoriam" page (see Roth, *AP*, 51).

8. Philip Roth, *CLF*, 58.

9. Philip Roth, *ZU*, 38.

10. Glass, "Zuckerman/Roth," 223.

11. The term "front man" comes from Philip Roth, *FAC*, 165.

12. Kanye West, "Famous."

13. An important discussion of autofiction in popular culture can be found in Worthington, "Fiction in the 'Post-Truth' Era." Maslan, "The Faking of the Americans," 382–83. Also note the distinction Maslan draws between "fictional autobiography" and "fictional memoir" (ibid., 383n17).

14. On this shift away from reclusivity, see O'Grady, "The Shadows."

15. Diemer, "Hiding Actualities," 3–4.

16. Similarly for "meta-art," which has been in force for decades (see Christensen, *The Meaning of Metafiction*, 1).

17. Dederer, "What Do We Do with the Art of Monstrous Men?"

18. See the discussion of Taylor, *Here We Are*, 159.

19. Roth, *HST*, 17–21.

20. Roth, *FAC*, 170.

21. Roth, *FAC*, 171, 173.

22. Sarah Stewart-Kroeker, "What Do We Do with the Art of Monstrous Men?," 12.

23. The summation below represents all the texts I did *not* use in developing my arguments about Roth's obsession with the self (and there are more). Thus, what is below represents perhaps one-tenth of all of the references he made to this problematic. My point being: this was no minor concern for Philip Roth, and we need a biographer to explain to us why that is.

    *Selves that became other selves: PAA*, 253 ("the fresh excitement of desire had transformed his existence"); *AP*, 29 ("this man . . . had been transformed into an impulsive, devitalized being"); *AP*, 329 ("To get down to that other self, the *true* self."); *AP*, 88 ("He'd invoked in me . . . the strongest fantasy I had of being someone else"); *AP*, 187 ("the heroic renewal began with the face-lift"); *PAT*, 122 ("he'll never be himself again, though maybe he can be something close to himself"); *CLF*, 239 ("he met me and suddenly he felt this horrible urge to quit his life and be another person"); *HST*, 25 ("this was not even another man, this was another *soul*"); *HMV*, 172 ("I wanted to divest myself of everything cheap . . . to clean myself out"); *POD*, 60 ("David. You're hopelessly intent on being what you're not"); *POD*, 263 ("fear of transformations yet to come").

    *Double or triple or quadruple existences*: *PAA*, 183 ("he was leading a double existence!"); *PAA* 358 ("my precocious brother was three different boys in the course of twenty-four months"); *HST*, 47 ("It was enough to feel the thrill of leading a double life"); *HST*, 130 ("to be possessed of a double, or a triple, or a quadruple personality?"); *ST*, 34 ("the stories of her second life. Her *third* life"), *ST*, 146 ("Nikki had another life. Everybody has another life"); *DAN*, 153 ("In every calm and reasonable person, there is a hidden second person"); *GW*, 113 ("That would require a second existence"); *IND*, 148 ("Darling. Is this what they call a personality change? . . . I am completely confused about whether he is one man or two!").

24. For an interesting rumination on forgiveness in light of #MeToo, see Penny, "The Horizon of Desire."
25. Fein, "Philip Roth Sees Double"; see also David Remnick, "Into the Clear." A review of these arguments from Roth can be found in Shipe, "Twilight of the Superheroes."
26. J. Brown, "The Plot Against America."
27. T. Brown, "Philip Roth Unbound."
28. T. Brown, "Philip Roth Unbound." And again in Haven, "An Interview with Philip Roth." To invoke our Fictional Supremacist metaphor of chapter 7, Roth chanted (alone and with pessimism), "Screens will not replace us!"
29. Waldman, "One Year of #MeToo."

# WORKS CITED

Aarons, Victoria. "Reading Roth/Reading Ourselves: Looking Back." *Philip Roth Studies* 15 (2019): 27–32.

Adams, Maurianne, and John Bracey. *Strangers and Neighbors: Relations between Blacks and Jews in the United States.* Amherst: University of Massachusetts Press, 1999.

Adichie, Chimamanda Ngozi. "Jumping Monkey Hill." *Granta*, October 2, 2006. https://granta.com/jumping-monkey-hill/.

———. "Jumping Monkey Hill." In *The Thing around Your Neck*, 95–114. New York: Anchor, 2010.

Alexander, Jeffrey. *Twenty Lectures: Sociological Theory since World War II.* New York: Columbia University Press, 1987.

"All the Missing Girls." Episode 5 of *Surviving R. Kelly*, directed by Nigel Bellis and Astral Finnie.

Allen, Mary, *The Necessary Blankness: Women in Major American Fiction in the Sixties.* Urbana: University of Illinois Press, 1976.

Amis, Kingsley. *Lucky Jim.* New York: New York Review Books, 2012.

Anderson, Monica, and Skye Toor. "How Social Media Users Have Discussed Sexual Harassment since #MeToo Went Viral." *Pew Research Center*, October 11, 2018. https://www.pewresearch.org/fact-tank/2018/10/11/how-social-media-users-have-discussed-sexual-harassment-since-metoo-went-viral/.

Anti-Defamation League. "White Supremacists Embrace 'Race War.'" *ADL*, January 8, 2020. https://www.adl.org/blog/white-supremacists-embrace-race-war.

Associated Press. "A Timeline of Roman Polanski's 4-Decade Underage Sex Case." May 3, 2018. https://apnews.com/e087fdee79e74caf99caa27edd8a8887/A-timeline-of-Roman-Polanski's-4-decade-underage-sex-case.

Atkinson, Paul, and Sara Delamont. "Qualitative Research Traditions." In *The Sage Handbook of Sociology*, edited by Craig Calhoun, Chris Rojek, and Bryan Turner, 40–60. London: Sage, 2005.

Atkinson, Paul, and William Housley. *Interactionism: An Essay in Sociological Amnesia.* London: Sage, 2003.

Atlas, James. *Remembering Roth.* Narrated by Atlas. Audiobook. Audible, 2018.

Avishai, Bernard. *Promiscuous: Portnoy's Complaint and Our Doomed Pursuit of Happiness.* New Haven, CT: Yale University Press, 2012.

Bailey, Blake. *Cheever: A Life.* New York: Vintage, 2010.

Baldwin, James. "Negroes Are Anti-Semitic Because They're Anti-White." In *Blacks and Jews: Alliances and Arguments,* edited by Paul Berman, 31–41. New York: Delacorte, 1994.

Barthes, Roland. *Image, Music, Text.* London: Fontana, 1977.

Baumgarten, Murray, and Barbara Gottfried. *Understanding Philip Roth.* Columbia: University of South Carolina Press, 1990.

Bechdel, Alison. *Dykes to Watch Out For.* Ithaca, NY: Firebrand, 1986.

Berlinerblau, Jacques. *Campus Confidential: How College Works, Or Doesn't, for Professors, Parents, and Students.* New York: Melville House, 2017.

——. "A Conversation with Cynthia Ozick: An Interview by Jacques Berlinerblau." *Program for Jewish Civilization Occasional Papers in Literature and the Arts* (Fall 2008). https://georgetown.app.box.com/s/of0smjz7dpfhn5zjkvxu.

——. "Do We Know Philip Roth?" *Chronicle of Higher Education,* April 7, 2014. https://www.chronicle.com/article/Do-We-Know-Philip-Roth-/145671.

——. "'Imagine That!' Philip Roth's Threshold Scenes: The Case of 'Femme Fatale.'" *Philip Roth Studies* 10 (2014): 35–57.

——. "Judaism and Secularism." In *The Cambridge Handbook to Philip Roth,* edited by Magdalene McKinley. Forthcoming from Cambridge University Press.

——. "The Productive Obscene: Philip Roth and the Profanity Loop." In *Profane: Sacrilegious Expression in a Multicultural Age,* edited by Christopher Grenda, Chris Beneke, and David Nash, 57–81. Oakland: University of California Press, 2014.

——. "Review of Philip Roth and the American Liberal Tradition." *Philip Roth Studies* 14 (2018): 97–99. https://muse.jhu.edu/article/705457.

——. "When She Was Ambivalent: Lena Dunham, *Girls,* and Philip Roth." *Melville House,* March 10, 2017. https://www.mhpbooks.com/lena-dunham-girls-and-philip-roth/.

Berlinerblau, Jacques, Bethania Michael, and Heather Walters. "Intertexts and Influence: A Comprehensive Table of Intertexts in Philip Roth's Fiction, 1952–2010." *Philip Roth Studies* 17, no. 2 (2021).

Berman, Jeffrey. *The Talking Cure: Literary Representations of Psychoanalysis.* New York: New York University Press, 1985.

Berman, Marshall. "Weird but Brilliant Light on the Way We Live Now." *New York Times,* February 27, 1972.

Berman, Paul. *Blacks and Jews: Alliances and Arguments.* New York: Delta, 1995.

The Bible and Culture Collective. *The Postmodern Bible.* Edited by George Aichele. New Haven, CT: Yale University Press, 1995.

Bleich, Sondra G. "Eat Those Words, Philip Roth." *New York Times,* July 26, 1981. https://www.nytimes.com/1981/07/26/nyregion/eat-those-words-philip-roth.html.

Bloom, Claire. *Leaving a Doll's House: A Memoir.* Boston: Little, Brown, 1996.

Bloom, James. "Philip Roth's Lover's Quarrel." In *Roth and Celebrity,* edited by Aimee Pozorski, 29–45. Lanham, MD: Lexington, 2014.

Bluefarb, Sam. "*The Human Stain:* A Satiric Tragedy of the Politically Incorrect." In *Playful and Serious: Philip Roth as a Comic Writer,* edited by Ben Siegel and Jay Halio, 222–28. Newark: University of Delaware Press, 2010.

Blumer, Herbert. *Symbolic Interactionism: Perspective and Method.* Berkeley: University of California Press, 1986.

Bonanos, Christopher. "Philip Roth's Biographer Has a Hair-Raising Claire Bloom Story to Share." *Vulture,* May 29, 2018. https://www.vulture.com/2018/05/philip-roth-biographer-has-a-hair-raising-claire-bloom-story.html.

Bond, Julian. Introduction to *Strangers and Neighbors: Relations between Blacks and Jews in the United States,* edited by Maurianne Adams and John Bracey, 1–13. Amherst: University of Massachusetts Press, 1999.

Boyd, Michael. *The Reflexive Novel: Fiction as Critique.* Lewisburg, PA: Bucknell University Press, 1983.

Brauner, David. "'Getting in Your Retaliation First': Narrative Strategies in *Portnoy's Complaint.*" In *Philip Roth: New Perspectives on an American Author,* edited by Derek Parker Royal, 43–57. Westport, CT: Praeger, 2005.

———. *Philip Roth.* Manchester: Manchester University Press, 2007.

Brissett, Dennis, and Charles Edgley, eds. *Life as Theater: A Dramaturgical Sourcebook.* 2nd ed. New Brunswick, NJ: Transaction, 2006.

Brodkin, Karen. *How Jews Became White Folks and What That Says about Race in America.* New Brunswick, NJ: Rutgers University Press, 2010.

Brooks, Cleanth. The Well Wrought Urn. New York: Harcourt, Brace, 1968.

Brown, Jeffrey. "The Plot Against America Author Philip Roth to Continue Pushing Envelope." *PBS News Hour,* November 10, 2004. https://www.pbs.org/newshour/show/the-plot-against-america-author-philip-roth-to-continue-pushing-envelope.

Brown, Tina. "Philip Roth Unbound: This Is How I Write." *Daily Beast,* October 30, 2009. https://www.thedailybeast.com/philip-roth-unbound-interview-transcript.

Bruce, Steve, and Steven Yearley. "Looking Glass Self, Symbolic Interaction." In *The Sage Dictionary of Sociology.* London: Sage, 2006.

Brühwiler, Claudia Franziska. "Serving His Tour as an 'Exasperated Liberal and Indignant Citizen': Philip Roth, A Public Intellectual?" In *A Political Companion to Philip Roth,* edited by Brühwiler and Lee Trepanier, 41–63. Lexington: University Press of Kentucky, 2017.

Budick, Emily Miller. *Blacks and Jews in Literary Conversation.* Cambridge: Cambridge University Press, 1998.

——. "Roth and Israel." In *The Cambridge Companion to Philip Roth,* edited by Timothy Parrish, 68–81. Cambridge: Cambridge University Press, 2007.

Bugbee, Stella, "Everyone Loses When We Widen the Feminist Generation Gap." *New York Magazine,* January 6, 2018. https://www.thecut.com/2018/01/daphne-merkin-new-york-times-metoo.html.

Buhle, Paul, and Robin Kelley. "Allies of a Different Sort: Jews and Blacks in the American Left." In *Struggles in the Promised Land: Towards a History of Black-Jewish Relations in the United States,* edited by Jack Salzman and Cornel West, 197–229. New York: Oxford University Press, 1997.

Burke, Tarana. "#MeToo Was Started for Black and Brown Women and Girls: They're Still Being Ignored." *Washington Post,* November 9, 2017. https://www.washingtonpost.com/news/post-nation/wp/2017/11/09/the-waitress-who-works-in-the-diner-needs-to-know-that-the-issue-of-sexual-harassment-is-about-her-too/.

Byers, Michele. "Material Bodies and Performative Identities: Mona, Neil, and the Promised Land." *Philip Roth Studies* 2 (2006): 102–20.

Carlier J. C., and C. T. Watts. "Roland Barthes's Resurrection of the Author and Redemption of Biography." *Cambridge Quarterly* 29 (2000): 386–93.

Carson, Clayborne, Jr. "Blacks and Jews in the Civil Rights Movement." In *Strangers and Neighbors: Relations between Blacks and Jews in the United States,* edited by Maurianne Adams and John Bracey, 574–89. Amherst: University of Massachusetts Press, 1999.

——. "The Politics of Relations between African-Americans and Jews." In *Blacks and Jews: Alliances and Arguments,* edited by Paul Berman, 131–43. New York: Delacorte, 1994.

CBS/AP. "More than 12M 'Me Too' Facebook Posts, Comments, Reactions in 24 Hours." *CBS News,* October 17, 2017. https://www.cbsnews.com/news/metoo-more-than-12-million-facebook-posts-comments-reactions-24-hours/.

Christensen, Inger. *The Meaning of Metafiction: A Critical Study of Selected Novels by Sterne, Nabokov, Barth and Beckett.* Bergen, Norway: Universitetsforlaget, 1981.

Churchwell, Sarah. "Pushing Back: Why It's Time for Women to Rewrite the Story." *The Guardian,* February 17, 2018, "Books" sec. https://www.the

guardian.com/books/2018/feb/17/pushing-back-why-its-time-for-women
-to-rewrite-the-story.

Cohen, Sarah Blacher. "Philip Roth's Would-be Patriarchs and Their Shikses and Shrews." *Studies in American Jewish Literature* 1 (1975): 16–22.

Connolly, Andy. *Philip Roth and the American Liberal Tradition.* Lanham, MD: Lexington, 2017.

Cooley, Charles Horton. *Human Nature and the Social Order.* New York: Schocken, 1964.

Cooper, Alan. "*Indignation:* The Opiates of the Occident." In *Playful and Serious: Philip Roth as a Comic Writer,* edited by Ben Siegel and Jay Halio, 255–68. Newark: University of Delaware Press, 2010.

———. *Philip Roth and the Jews.* New York: State University of New York Press, 1996.

Corrigan, John Michael. *American Metempsychosis: Emerson, Whitman, and the New Poetry.* New York: Fordham University Press, 2012.

Cowley, Jason. "The Nihilist." *Atlantic,* May 1, 2001. https://www.theatlantic .com/magazine/archive/2001/05/the-nihilist/302197/.

Crouch, Ian. "The Biographer's Confessions." *New Yorker,* February 27, 2014. https://www.newyorker.com/books/page-turner/the-biographers -confessions.

Crouch, Stanley. "Roth's Historical Sin." *Salon,* October 11, 2004. https://www .salon.com/2004/10/11/crouch_9/.

Cruse, Harold. "My Jewish Problem and Theirs." In *Black Anti-Semitism and Jewish Racism,* edited by Nat Hentoff, 143–88. New York: Schocken, 1972.

Cusk, Rachel. "Can a Woman Who Is an Artist Ever Just Be an Artist?" *New York Times,* November 19, 2019. https://www.nytimes.com/2019/11/07 /magazine/women-art-celia-paul-cecily-brown.html.

Daum, Meghan. "In the Age of #MeToo, Philip Roth Offers an Unlikely Blueprint for Feminists." *Los Angeles Times,* May 25, 2018. https://www.latimes.com /opinion/op-ed/la-oe-daum-philip-roth-and-women-20180525-story.html.

Davidson, Sara. "Talk with Philip Roth: Sara Davidson/1977." In *Conversations with Philip Roth,* edited by George Searles, 100–107. Jackson: University Press of Mississippi, 1992.

Dawe, Alan. "The Underworld-View of Erving Goffman." *British Journal of Sociology* 24 (1973): 246–53.

Dederer, Claire. *Love and Trouble: A Midlife Reckoning.* New York: Knopf, 2017.

———. "What Do We Do with the Art of Monstrous Men?" *Paris Review,* November 20, 2017. https://www.theparisreview.org/blog/2017/11/20/art -monstrous-men/.

Denham, Alice. *Sleeping with Bad Boys: A Juicy Tell-all of Literary New York in the Fifties and Sixties.* N.p.: Book Republic Press, 2006.

Diamond, Jason. "Flavorwire Interview: Claudia Roth Pierpont on Philip Roth's Life, Work, and Misunderstood Women." *Flavorwire,* October 24, 2013. https://www.flavorwire.com/421693/flavorwire-interview-claudia -roth-pierpont-on-philip-roths-life-work-and-misunderstood-women.

Dickstein, Morris. "My Life as a Man." *New York Times,* June 2, 1974.

Diemer, Derek M. "Hiding Actualities: Whether Art Should Exist Independent of the Artist." *American University Intellectual Property Brief* 11, no. 2. https://papers.ssrn.com/sol3/papers.cfm?abstract_id=3515628.

Diner, Hasia. "Between Words and Deeds: Jews and Blacks in America, 1880–1935." In *Struggles in the Promised Land: Towards a History of Black-Jewish Relations in the United States,* edited by Jack Salzman and Cornel West, 87–106. New York: Oxford University Press, 1997.

Ditton, Jason. "Editor's Introduction: A Bibliographic Exegesis of Goffman's Sociology." In *The View from Goffman,* edited by Ditton, 1–23. New York: St. Martin's, 1980.

Dix, Hywel, ed. *Autofiction in English.* Cham, Switzerland: Palgrave Macmillan. 2018.

Dodd, Philip. "History or Fiction: Balancing Contemporary Autobiography's Claims." *Mosaic: An Interdisciplinary Critical Journal* 20 (1987): 61–69.

Dollinger, Marc. *Black Power, Jewish Power: Reinventing the Alliance in the 1960s.* Waltham, MA: Brandeis University Press, 2018.

Donadio, Rachel. "Bio Engineering." *New York Times,* November 3, 2007. https://www.nytimes.com/2007/11/04/books/review/Donadio-t.html.

Doubrovsky, Serge. *Fils.* Paris: Éditions Galilée, 1977.

Drake, John Gibbs St. Clair. "African Diaspora and Jewish Diaspora: Convergence and Divergence." In *Jews in Black Perspectives: A Dialogue,* edited by Joseph Washington, 19–41. Rutherford, NJ: Associated University Presses, 1984.

Duban, James, "From Negative Identity to Existential Nothingness: Philip Roth and the Younger Jewish Intellectuals." *Partial Answers: Journal of Literature and the History of Ideas* 13 (2015): 43–55.

———. "'Juice or Gravy?': Philosophies of Composition by Roth, Poe, and Sartre." *Philip Roth Studies* 12 (2016): 71–82.

———. "Sartrian Nothingness: Roth's *The Ghost Writer, The Anatomy Lesson, Zuckerman Unbound, The Prague Orgy,* and *Exit Ghost." Philip Roth Studies* 10 (2014): 11–34.

Ducharme, Jamie. "'These Stories Are True': Read Louis C.K.'s Response to Claims He Masturbated in Front of Women." *Time,* November 10, 2017. https://time.com/5019384/louis-ck-apologizes-full-statement/.

Durantaye, Leland de la. "How to Read Philip Roth, or the Ethics of Fiction and the Aesthetics of Fact." *Cambridge Quarterly* 39 (2010): 303–30.

Edgley, Charles. "The Dramaturgical Genre." In *Handbook of Symbolic Inter-actionism,* edited by Larry Reynolds and Nancy Herman-Kinney, 141–72. Lanham, MD: Altamira, 2003.

Eisenberg, Eve. "'Real Africa'/'Which Africa?': The Critique of Mimetic Realism in Chimamanda Ngozi Adichie's Short Fiction." In *ALT 31: Writing Africa in the Short Story: African Literature Today,* edited by Ernest Emenyonu et al., 8–24. Woodbridge, Suffolk, UK: Boydell and Brewer, 2013.

Elam, Michele. "Passing in the Post-Race Era: Danzy Senna, Philip Roth, and Colson Whitehead." *African American Review* 41 (2007): 749–68.

Eliot, George. *Silas Marner.* London: Penguin Classics, 1996.

Fahy, Tony. "Filling the Love Vessel: Women and Religion in Philip Roth's Uncollected Short Fiction." *Shofar* 19 (2000): 117–26.

Faisst, Julia. "'Delusionary Thinking, Whether White or Black or in Between': Fictions of Race in Philip Roth's *The Human Stain.*" *Philip Roth Studies* 2 (2006): 121–37.

Farrow, Dylan. "An Open Letter from Dylan Farrow." *New York Times,* February 1, 2014. https://kristof.blogs.nytimes.com/2014/02/01/an-open-letter-from-dylan-farrow/.

Farrow, Ronan. "From Aggressive Overtures to Sexual Assault: Harvey Weinstein's Accusers Tell Their Stories." *New Yorker,* October 10, 2017. https://www.newyorker.com/news/news-desk/from-aggressive-overtures-to-sexual-assault-harvey-weinsteins-accusers-tell-their-stories.

Feher, Michel. "The Schisms of '67: On Certain Restructurings of the American Left, from the Civil Rights Movement to the Multiculturalist Constellation." In *Blacks and Jews: Alliances and Arguments,* edited by Paul Berman, 262–85. New York: Delacourt, 1994.

Fein, Esther. "Philip Roth Sees Double: And Maybe Triple, Too." *New York Times,* March 9, 1993.

Feingold, Henry. "From Equality to Liberty: The Changing Political Culture of American Jews." In *The Americanization of the Jews,* edited by Robert Seltzer and Norman Cohen, 97–118. New York: New York University Press, 1995.

Ferber, Abby L., and Michael Kimmel. "Reading Right: The Western Tradition in White Supremacist Discourse." *Sociological Focus* 33 (2002): 193–213.

Fileborn, Bianca, and Rachel Loney-Howes. "Introduction: Mapping the Emergence of #MeToo." In *#MeToo and the Politics of Social Change,* edited by Fileborn and Loney-Howes, 1–11. London: Palgrave Macmillan, 2019.

Fink, Steven. "Fact, Fiction, and History in Philip Roth's 'Eli, the Fanatic.'" *MELUS* 39 (2014): 89–111.

Fishman, Sylvia Barack. "Success in Circuit Lies: Philip Roth's Recent Explorations of American Jewish Identity." *Jewish Social Studies* 3 (1997): 132–55.

Fitzgerald, F. Scott. *The Great Gatsby.* New York: Scribner, 2004.

Fong, Tony. "Re-conceiving the Mother in Philip Roth's Life Writing." *Philip Roth Studies* 8 (2012).

Forman, Seth. *Blacks in the Jewish Mind: A Crisis of Liberalism*. New York: New York University Press, 1998.

Fox, Tamar. "Philip Roth Hated Jewish Women." *Alma,* May 23, 2018. https://www.heyalma.com/philip-roth-hated-jewish-women/.

Franco, Dean. "Being Black, Being Jewish, and Knowing the Difference: Philip Roth's 'The Human Stain'; Or, It Depends on What the Meaning of 'Clinton' Is." *Studies in American Jewish Literature* 23 (2004): 88–103.

———. "Introduction: Philip Roth and Race." *Philip Roth Studies* 2 (2006): 83–85.

———. *Race, Rights, and Recognition: Jewish American Literature since 1969.* Ithaca, NY: Cornell University Press, 2012.

Furman, Andrew. "A New 'Other' Emerges in American Jewish Literature: Philip Roth's Israel Fiction." *Contemporary Literature* 36 (1995): 633–53.

Fusillo, Massimo. "Self-Reflexivity in Ancient Novel." *Revue Internationale de Philosophie* 63 (2009): 165–76.

Garber, Megan. "David Foster Wallace and the Dangerous Romance of Male Genius." *Atlantic,* May 9, 2018. https://www.theatlantic.com/entertainment/archive/2018/05/the-world-still-spins-around-male-genius/559925/.

Garcia, Sandra. "The Woman Who Created #MeToo Long Before Hashtags." *New York Times,* October 20, 2017. https://www.nytimes.com/2017/10/20/us/me-too-movement-tarana-burke.html.

Gass, William H. "The Death of the Author." *Salmagundi,* no. 65 (2015): 3–26.

Gates, Henry Louis, Jr. *Thirteen Ways of Looking at a Black Man.* New York: Random House, 1997.

Gay, Roxane. *Bad Feminist.* New York: Harper Perennial, 2014.

———, ed. *Not That Bad: Dispatches from Rape Culture.* New York: HarperCollins, 2018.

Gelbart, Amy. "'[Sticking] to a Plan Completely': Performance, Affective Adaptation, Memory, Pretend Play and Suicide in Philip Roth's *The Humbling.*" In *Roth after Eighty: Philip Roth and the American Literary Imagination,* edited by David Gooblar and Aimee Pozorski, 149–65. Lanham, MD: Lexington, 2016.

Gentry, Marshall Bruce. "Newark Maid Feminism in Philip Roth's *American Pastoral.*" *Shofar: An Interdisciplinary Journal of Jewish Studies* 19 (2000): 74–83.

———. "Ventriloquists' Conversations: The Struggle for Gender Dialogue in E. L. Doctorow and Philip Roth." *Contemporary Literature* 34, no. 3 (1993): 512–37.

Giddens, Anthony. "On Rereading *The Presentation of Self in Everyday Life*: Some Reflections." *Social Psychology Quarterly* 72 (2009): 290–95.

Gieseler, Carly. *The Voices of #MeToo: From Grassroots Activism to a Viral Roar.* Lanham, MD: Rowman and Littlefield, 2019.

Gilbert, Sophie, "The Movement of #MeToo: How a Hashtag Got Its Power." *Atlantic,* October 16, 2017. https://www.theatlantic.com/entertainment /archive/2017/10/the-movement-of-metoo/542979/.

Gillespie, Stuart. "Literary Afterlives: Metempsychosis from Ennius to Jorge Luis Borges." In *Classical Literary Careers and Their Reception,* edited by Philip Hardine and Helen Moore, 209–25. Cambridge: Cambridge University Press, 2010.

Gittleman, Sol. "The Pecks of Woodenton, Long Island, Thirty Years Later: Another Look at 'Eli, the Fanatic.'" *Studies in American Jewish Literature* 8 (1981): 138–42.

Glaser, Jennifer. "The Jew in the Canon: Reading Race and Literary History in Philip Roth's 'The Human Stain.'" *PMLA* 123 (2008): 1465–78.

Glass, Loren. "Zuckerman/Roth: Literary Celebrity between Two Deaths." *PMLA* 129 (2014): 223–36.

Glazer, Nathan. "Jews and Blacks: What Happened to the Grand Alliance?" In *Jews in Black Perspectives: A Dialogue,* edited by Joseph Washington, 105–12. Rutherford, NJ: Associated University Presses, 1984.

Godfrey, Mollie. "Passing as Post-racial: Philip Roth's *The Human Stain,* Political Correctness, and the Post-Racial Passing Narrative." *Contemporary Literature* 58 (2017): 233–61.

Goffard, Christopher. "Philip Roth Unbound." *Tampa Bay Times,* July 4, 2004. www.sptimes.com/2004/O7/04/Floridian/Philip_Roth_unbound.shtml.

Goffman, Erving. *The Presentation of Self in Everyday Life.* 1959. London: Penguin, 1990.

———. *Stigma: Notes on the Management of Spoiled Identity.* Englewood Cliffs, NJ: Prentice Hall, 1963.

Goffman, Ethan. *Imagining Each Other: Blacks and Jews in Contemporary American Literature.* Albany: State University of New York Press, 2000.

Goldberg, Carole. "UConn Professor Chosen to Write Philip Roth Biography." *Hartford Courant,* June 20, 2004. https://www.courant.com/news /connecticut/hc-xpm-2004-06-20-0406200526-story.html.

Goldberg, Emma. "Do Works by Men Toppled by #MeToo Belong in the Classroom?" *New York Times,* October 7, 2019. https://www.nytimes.com /2019/10/07/us/metoo-schools.html.

Goldblatt, Roy. "The Whitening of the Jews and the Changing Face of Newark." *Philip Roth Studies* 2 (2006): 86–101.

Goldsmith, Barbara. "When Park Ave. Met Pop Art." *Vanity Fair,* January 1, 2003.

Goldstein, Eric. *The Price of Whiteness: Jews, Race, and Identity.* Princeton, NJ: Princeton University Press, 2006.

Gooblar, David. "Introduction: Roth and Women." *Philip Roth Studies* 8, no. 1 (2012): 7–15.

Goodheart, Eugene. "Writing and the Unmaking of the Self." *Contemporary Literature* 29 (1988): 438–53.

Goodman, Shayna. 2014. "Why I Did Not 'Like' Philip Roth's New York Times Interview." *Lilith Magazine.* May 25, 2014. https://www.lilith.org/blog /2014/03/why-i-did-not-like-philip-roths-new-york-times-interview/.

Gordon, Andrew. "The Critique of Utopia in Philip Roth's *The Counterlife* and *American Pastoral.*" In *Turning up the Flame: Philip Roth's Later Novels,* edited by Jay Halio and Ben Siegel, 151–59. Newark: University of Delaware Press, 2005.

Gornick, Vivian. "Radiant Poison." *Harper's,* September 2008. https://harpers .org/archive/2008/09/radiant-poison/.

———. "Why Do These Men Hate Women?" Reprinted in *Essays in Feminism,* 189–99. New York: Harper and Row, 1978.

Grant, Linda. "Breast Man." *The Guardian,* June 30, 2001. https://www .theguardian.com/books/2001/jun/30/fiction.philiproth.

Gray, Paul. "The Varnished Truths." In *Conversations with Philip Roth,* edited by George Searles, 202–8. Jackson: University Press of Mississippi, 1992.

Green, Emma. "Why the Charlottesville Marchers Were Obsessed with Jews." *Atlantic,* August 15, 2017.

Green, Martin. Introduction to *A Philip Roth Reader.* New York: Farrar, Straus and Giroux, 1980.

Greenberg, Cheryl. "'I'm Not White—I'm Jewish': The Racial Politics of American Jews." In *Race, Color, Identity: Rethinking Discourses about "Jews" in the Twenty-First Century,* edited by Efraim Sicher, 35–55. New York: Berghahn, 2013.

———. "Negotiating Coalition: Black and Jewish Civil Rights Agencies in the Twentieth Century." In *Strangers and Neighbors: Relations between Blacks and Jews in the United States,* edited by Maurianne Adams and John Bracey, 476–94. Amherst: University of Massachusetts Press, 1999.

———. *Troubling the Waters: Black-Jewish Relations in the American Century.* Princeton, NJ: Princeton University Press, 2006.

Grell, Isabelle. "Pourquoi Serge Doubrovsky n'a pu éviter le terme d'*autofiction?*" *Genèse et Autofiction.* J-L. Jeanelle et C. Violet (dir.), 2006. Louvain-la-Neuve: Academia Bruylant, 39–51.

Gross, Barry. "American Fiction, Jewish Writers, and Black Characters: The Return of the 'Human Negro' in Philip Roth." *MELUS* 11 (1984): 5–22.

Gross, Neil. "Pragmatism, Phenomenology, and Twentieth-Century American Sociology." In *Sociology in America: A History*, edited by Craig Calhoun, 183–224. Chicago: University of Chicago Press, 2007.

Gurock, Jeffrey. *The Jews of Harlem: The Rise, Decline, and Revival of a Jewish Community*. New York: New York University Press, 2016.

Gutman, Herbert. "Parallels in the Urban Experience." In *Jews in Black Perspectives: A Dialogue*, edited by Joseph Washington, 98–104. Rutherford, NJ: Associated University Presses, 1984.

Halio, Jay. "Eros and Death in Roth's Later Fiction." In *Turning up the Flame: Philip Roth's Later Novels*, edited by Halio and Ben Siegel, 200–206. Newark: University of Delaware Press, 2005.

———. *Philip Roth Revisited*. New York: Twayne, 1992.

Halliday, Lisa. *Asymmetry*. New York: Simon and Schuster, 2018.

Hardy, Thomas. *The Mayor of Casterbridge*. New York: Barnes and Noble Books, 2004.

Haven, Cynthia. "An Interview with Philip Roth: 'The Novelist's Obsession Is with Language.'" *Stanford University: The Book Haven*, February 3, 2014. https://bookhaven.stanford.edu/2014/02/an-interview-with-philip-roth-the-novelists-obsession-is-with-language/.

Hayes, Patrick. "'With an Accomplice No Less Brilliant than Jean Genet': A Comparative Approach to Roth's Autofiction." In *Roth after Eighty: Philip Roth and the American Literary Imagination*, edited by David Gooblar and Aimee Pozorski, 43–60. Lanham, MD: Lexington, 2016.

Hayman, Ronald. "Philip Roth: Should Sane Women Shy Away from Him at Parties?" In *Conversations with Philip Roth*, edited with George Searles, 113–19. Jackson: University Press of Mississippi, 1992.

HBO. "Winona Ryder, Zoe Kazan and John Turturro to Star in David Simon's 'The Plot Against America.'" https://www.hbo.com/hbo-news/the-plot-against-america-david-simon.

Heer, Jeet, and Josephine Livingstone. "Woody Allen, #MeToo, and the Separation of Art from Artist." *New Republic*, February 2, 2018. https://newrepublic.com/article/146876/woody-allen-metoo-separation-art-artist.

Hentoff, Nat, James Baldwin, Earl Rabb, Rabbi Jay Kaufman, Rabbi Alan W. Miller, Judge William H. Booth, and Walter Karp. *Black Anti-Semitism and Jewish Racism*. New York: Schocken, 1972.

Hess, Amanda. "How the Myth of the Artistic Genius Excuses the Abuse of Women." *New York Times*, November 10, 2017. https://www.nytimes.com/2017/11/10/arts/sexual-harassment-art-hollywood.html.

Hjalmarson, Birgitta. "Philip Roth and #MeToo." January 2019. http://birgittahjalmarson.net/2019/01/19/phillip-roth-and-metoo/.

Hobhouse, Janet. *The Furies*. New York: New York Review Books, 2004.

Horowitz, Mikhail. "Philip Roth Is Laid to Rest in Annandale." *HV1*, May 29, 2018. https://hudsonvalleyone.com/2018/05/29/philip-roth-is-laid-to-rest-in-annandale/.

Howe, Irving. "Philip Roth Reconsidered." "Commentary." December 1972. https://www.vanityfair.com/news/2003/01/larry-rivers.

Hughes, Langston. "Passing." *Phylon* 11 (1950): 15–15.

Husband, Julie. "Female Hysteria and Sisterhood in *Letting Go* and *When She Was Good*." In *Philip Roth: New Perspectives on an American Author*, edited by Derek Parker Royal, 25–41. Praeger: Westport, CT, 2005.

Hutcheon, Linda. *Narcissistic Narrative: The Metafictional Paradox*. Waterloo, Ontario: Wilfrid Laurier University Press, 1980.

Hutchison, Anthony. "'Purity Is Petrefaction': Liberalism and Betrayal in Philip Roth's *I Married a Communist*." *Rethinking History* 9 (2005): 315–27.

Hwang, Jung-Suk. "'Newark's Just a Black Colony': Race in Philip Roth's *American Pastoral*." *Twentieth Century Literature* 64 (2018): 161–90.

Ivanova, Velichka. "My Own Foe from the Other Gender: (Mis)representing Women in *The Dying Animal*." *Philip Roth Studies* 8 (2012): 31–44.

Izadi, Elahe. "Louis C.K.'s Movie Scrapped, FX and Netflix Cut Ties after Allegations of Sexual Misconduct." *Washington Post*, November 10, 2017. https://www.washingtonpost.com/news/arts-and-entertainment/wp/2017/11/09/louis-c-k-accused-of-sexual-misconduct-in-new-bombshell-new-york-times-report/.

Jacobsen, Michael Hviid. "Erving Goffman—Exploring the Interaction Order through Everyday Observations and Imaginative Metaphors." In *The Interactionist Imagination: Studying Meaning, Situation and Micro-Social Order*, edited by Jacobsen, 195–232. London: Palgrave Macmillan, 2017.

——. "Introduction: Instigators of Interactionism—A Short Introduction to Interactionism in Sociology." In *The Interactionist Imagination: Studying Meaning, Situation and Micro-Social Order*, edited by Jacobsen, 1–35. London: Palgrave Macmillan, 2017.

Jaffe-Foger, Miriam. "Philip Roth: Death and Celebrity." In *Roth and Celebrity*, edited by Aimee Pozorski, 67–85. Lanham, MD: Lexington, 2014.

Jaffe-Foger, Miriam, and Aimee Pozorski. "'[A]nything but Fragile and Yielding': Women in Roth's Recent Tetralogy." *Philip Roth Studies* 8 (2012): 81–94.

Jay, Martin. "Force Fields." *Salmagundi* 93 (1992): 13–25.

Johnson, Brian D. "Intimate Affairs." In *Conversations with Philip Roth*, edited by George Searles, 254–58. Jackson: University Press of Mississippi, 1992.

Johnson, Terrence, and Jacques Berlinerblau. *Blacks and Jews in America: An Introduction to Dialogue*. Forthcoming from Georgetown University Press.

Jokinen, Tom. "Last of the Great Male Narcissists?" *Hazlitt,* December 12, 2012. https://hazlitt.net/feature/last-great-male-narcissists.

Jones, Judith, and Guinevera Nance. *Philip Roth.* New York: Frederick Ungar, 1981.

Jones, LeRoi. "Channel X." *New York Review of Books,* July 9, 1964. https://www.nybooks.com/articles/1964/07/09/channel-x-1/.

Jordan, Tina. "Why Aren't People Buying Much Fiction These Days?" *New York Times,* November 16, 2018. https://www.nytimes.com/2018/11/16/books/review/low-sales-fiction-best-seller.html.

Joyce, James. *Ulysses.* Edited by Hans Walter Gabler. New York: Vintage, 1986.

Kafka, Franz. "A Fratricide." In *The Basic Kafka,* 146–48. New York: Pocket Books, 1979.

Kakutani, Michiko, "Books of the Times: A Man Adrift, Living on Sexual Memories." *New York Times,* May 8, 2001. https://www.nytimes.com/2001/05/08/books/books-of-the-times-a-man-adrift-living-on-sexual-memories.html.

———. "Of a Roth within a Roth within a Roth." *New York Times,* March 4, 1993.

———. "A Postwar Paradise Shattered from Within." *New York Times,* April 15, 1997.    https://www.nytimes.com/1997/04/15/books/a-postwar-paradise-shattered-from-within.html.

Kantor, Jodi, and Megan Twohey. "Harvey Weinstein Paid off Sexual Harassment Accusers for Decades." *New York Times,* October 5, 2017. https://www.nytimes.com/2017/10/05/us/harvey-weinstein-harassment-allegations.html.

Kaplan, Brett Ashley. "The American Berserk in *Sabbath's Theater* (1995)." In *A Political Companion to Philip Roth,* edited by Claudia Franziska Brühwiler and Lee Trepanier, 220–37. Lexington: University Press of Kentucky, 2017.

———. "Double-Consciousness and the Jewish Heart of Darkness: The Counterlife *and* Operation Shylock." In *Roth and Celebrity,* edited by Aimee Pozorski, 133–53. Lanham, MD: Lexington, 2012.

———. *Jewish Anxiety and the Novels of Phillip Roth.* New York: Bloomsbury, 2015.

———. "Reading Race and the Conundrums of Reconciliation in Philip Roth's *The Human Stain.*" In *Turning up the Flame: Philip Roth's Later Novels,* edited by Jay Halio and Ben Siegel, 172–93. Newark: University of Delaware Press, 2005.

Kaprièlian, Nelly. "In Which Philip Roth Announces His Retirement (In English)." *Paris Review,* November 13, 2012. https://www.theparisreview.org/blog/2012/11/13/in-which-philip-roth-announces-his-retirement-in-english/.

———. "Philip Roth: Némésis sera mon dernier livre." *Les Inrockuptibles,* July 10, 2012.    https://www.lesinrocks.com/2012/10/07/livres/livres/philip-roth-nemesis-sera-mon-dernier-livre/.

Kartiganer, Donald. "Fictions of Metamorphosis: From *Goodbye, Columbus* to *Portnoy's Complaint.*" In *Reading Philip Roth,* edited by Asher Milbauer and Donald Watson, 82–104. London: Macmillan, 1988.

Kaufman, Jonathan. "Blacks and Jews: The Struggle in the Cities." In *Struggles in the Promised Land: Towards a History of Blacks-Jewish Relations in the United States,* edited by Jack Salzman and Cornell West, 107–21. New York: Oxford University Press, 1997.

Kaufman, Rabbi Jay. "Thou Shalt Surely Rebuke Thy Neighbor." In *Black Anti-Semitism and Jewish Racism,* edited by Nat Hentoff, 43–76. New York: Schocken, 1972.

Keller, Julia. "Philip Roth Hates Women." *Chicago Tribune,* June 1, 2006. https://www.chicagotribune.com/news/ct-xpm-2006-06-01-0605310232-story.html.

Kelleter, Frank. "Portrait of the Sexist as a Dying Man: Death, Ideology, and the Erotic in Philip Roth's 'Sabbath's Theater.'" *Contemporary Literature* 39 (1998): 262–302.

Kimmage, Michael. "The Newark Trilogy." In *History's Grip: Philip Roth's Newark Trilogy.* Stanford, CA: Stanford University Press, 2012.

Kirby, Lisa. "Shades of Passing: Teaching and Interrogating Identity in Roth's *The Human Stain* and Fitzgerald's *The Great Gatsby.*" *Philip Roth Studies* 2 (2006): 15–160.

Krasnick, Martin. "Philip Roth: 'It No Longer Feels a Great Injustice That I Have to Die.'" *The Guardian,* December 14, 2005.

Kraus, Chris. *I Love Dick.* Los Angeles: Semiotexte, 2006.

Kremer, Lillian. "Philip Roth's Self-Reflexive Fiction." *Modern Language Studies* 28 (1998): 57–72.

Kundera, Milan. "Some Notes on Roth's *My Life as a Man* and *The Professor of Desire.*" In *Reading Philip Roth,* edited by Asher Milbauer and Donald Watson, 162–67. London: Macmillan, 1988.

Lauritzen, Ellen Sofie. "Roth, Draper, Lil' Wayne: A Feminist Case for Embracing Sexist Art." *Talking Points Memo,* March 12, 2015. https://talkingpointsmemo.com/theslice/philip-roth-draper-lil-wayne-a-feminist-case-for-embracing-sexist-art.

Leclerc, Yvan. "'Madame Bovary, c'est moi,' formule apocryphe." Centre Flaubert. https://flaubert.univ-rouen.fr/ressources/mb_cestmoi.php.

Lee, Hermione. *Contemporary Writers.* London: Methuen, 1982.

———. "'Life *is* And': Philip Roth in 1990." In *Conversations with Philip Roth,* edited by George Searles, 259–66. Jackson: University Press of Mississippi, 1992.

———. "'You Must Change Your Life': Mentors, Doubles and Literary Influences in the Search for Self." In *Modern Critical Views: Philip Roth,* edited by Harold Bloom, 149–62. New York: Chelsea House, 1986.

Lee, Judith Yaross. "Affairs of the Breast: Philip Roth and David Kepesh." In *Playful and Serious: Philip Roth as a Comic Writer,* edited by Ben Siegel and Jay Halio, 68–91. Newark: University of Delaware Press, 2010.

Leeke, Philip. "The Counterlife of Knight Errant Christie McKay and The Trials of Philip Roth: Writing as Ordeal and Punishment." Ph.D. diss., University of Manchester, 2013.

Lefèvre, Ch. "Métempsycose." In *Catholicisme: Hier-Aujourd'hui-Demain, Tome Neuvième: Messianisme-Œcuménisme,* 35–46. Paris: Letouzey et Ané, 1982.

Leibovitz, Liel. "The Grapes of Roth." *Tablet Magazine,* November 15, 2011. https://www.tabletmag.com/sections/arts-letters/articles/the-grapes-of-roth.

Lelchuk, Alan. *Ziff: A Life?* New York: Carroll and Graf, 2003.

Lerner, Michael, and Cornel West. *Jews and Blacks: A Dialogue on Race, Religion, and Culture in America.* New York: Penguin, 1996.

Lester, Julius. "The Lives People Live." In *Blacks and Jews: Alliances and Arguments,* edited by Paul Berman, 164–77. New York: Delacorte, 1994.

Leung, Rebecca, and Robert Williams. "#MeToo and Intersectionality: An Examination of the #MeToo Movement through the R. Kelly Scandal." *Journal of Communication Inquiry,* 43 (2019): 349–71.

Levine, Hillel, and Lawrence Harmon, *The Death of An American Jewish Community: A Tragedy of Good Intentions.* New York: Free Press, 1992.

Levy, Eric. "The Mimesis of Metempsychosis in Ulysses." *Philological Quarterly* 81 (2002): 359–77.

Lofland, John. "Early Goffman: Style, Structure, Substance, Soul." In *The View from Goffman,* edited by Jason Ditton, 24–51. New York: St. Martin's, 1980.

Loney-Howes, Rachel. "The Politics of the Personal: The Evolution of Anti-Rape Activism from Second-Wave Feminism to #MeToo." In *MeToo and the Politics of Social Change,* edited by Bianca Fileborn and Rachel Loney-Howes, 21–35.

Long, Heather. "The World's Top Economists Just Made the Case for Why We Still Need English Majors." *Washington Post,* October 19, 2019. https://www.washingtonpost.com/business/2019/10/19/worlds-top-economists-just-made-case-why-we-still-need-english-majors/.

Lopez, Linette, and Chris Snyder. "Tarana Burke on Why She Created the #MeToo Movement—and Where It's Headed." *Business Insider,* December 13, 2017. https://www.businessinsider.com/how-the-metoo-movement-started-where-its-headed-tarana-burke-time-person-of-year-women-2017-12.

Lyons, Bonnie. "En-Countering Pastorals in *The Counterlife.*" In *Philip Roth: New Perspectives on an American Author,* edited by Derek Parker Royal, 119–27. Westport, CT: Praeger, 2005.

Maher, Michael. "Metempsychosis." In *The Catholic Encyclopedia,* vol. 10: *Mass–Newman,* edited by Charles Herbermann et al., 234–37. New York: Appleton, 1911.

Malamud, Bernard. "Angel Levine." In *The Complete Stories,* 158–66. New York: Noonday, 1997.

Mannes, Marya. "A Dissent from Marya Mannes." *Saturday Review,* February 22, 1969.

Marchese, David. "In Conversation: Chimamanda Ngozi Adichie the Novelist on Being a 'Feminist Icon,' Philip Roth's Humanist Misogyny, and the Sadness in Melania Trump." *Vulture,* July 9, 2018. https://www.vulture.com/2018/07/chimamanda-ngozi-adichie-in-conversation.html.

Marghitu, Stefania. "'It's Just Art': *Auteur* Apologism in the Post-Weinstein Era." *Feminist Media Studies* 18 (2018): 491–94. https://www.tandfonline.com/doi/full/10.1080/14680777.2018.1456158.

Marriott, James. 2018. "Review: Asymmetry by Lisa Halliday—a Tale of Love and Roth." *The Times,* February 17, 2018, "Saturday Review" sec. https://www.thetimes.co.uk/article/review-asymmetry-by-lisa-halliday-a-tale-of-love-and-roth-cthcjj5qm.

Marsh, Laura. "Infinite Jerk." *New Republic,* February 12, 2020. https://newrepublic.com/article/156550/infinite-jerk.

Masiero, Pia. *Philip Roth and the Zuckerman Books: The Making of a Storyworld.* Amherst: Cambria, 2011.

Maslan, Mark. "The Faking of the Americans: Passing, Trauma, and National Identity in Philip Roth's *The Human Stain.*" *Modern Language Quarterly* 66 (September 2005): 365–89.

McCaffery, Larry. *The Metafictional Muse: The Works of Robert Coover, Donald Barthelme, and William H. Gass.* Pittsburgh: University of Pittsburgh Press, 1982.

McCann, Sean. "Training and Vision: Roth, DeLillo, Banks, Peck, and the Postmodern Aesthetics of Vocation." *Twentieth Century Literature* 53 (2007): 298–326.

McDaniel, John. *The Fiction of Philip Roth.* Haddonfield, NJ: Haddonfield House, 1974.

McGrath, Charles. "Goodbye, Frustration: Pen Put Aside, Roth Talks." *New York Times,* November 17, 2012. https://www.nytimes.com/2012/11/18/books/struggle-over-philip-roth-reflects-on-putting-down-his-pen.html.

———. "No Longer Writing, Philip Roth Still Has Plenty to Say." *New York Times,* January 16, 2018, "Books" sec. https://www.nytimes.com/2018/01/16/books/review/philip-roth-interview.html.

———. "Philip Roth to Cooperate with New Biographer." *New York Times,* September 5, 2012. https://artsbeat.blogs.nytimes.com/2012/09/05/philip-roth-to-cooperate-with-new-biographer/.

———. "Zuckerman's Alter Brain." *New York Times,* May 7, 2000. http://movies2
.nytimes.com/books/00/05/07/reviews/000507.07mcgrat.html.

McKenzie, Lara. *Age-Dissimilar Couples and Romantic Relationships: Ageless
Love?* New York: Palgrave Macmillan, 2015.

McKinley, Maggie. "'I Wanted to Be Humanish: Manly, a Man': Morality,
Shame, and Masculinity in Philip Roth's *My Life as a Man.*" *Philip Roth
Studies* 9, no. 1 (2013): 89–101.

———. "Testosterone and Sympathy." *Philip Roth Studies* 15 (2019): 92–97.

Mendes, Kaitlynn, J. Ringrose, and Jessalynn Keller. "#MeToo and the Promise and Pitfalls of Challenging Rape Culture through Digital Feminist
Activism." *European Journal of Women's Studies* 25 (2018). https://journals
.sagepub.com/doi/abs/10.1177/1350506818765318?journalCode=ejwa#.

Merkin, Daphne. "Publicly, We Say #MeToo. Privately, We Have Misgivings."
*New York Times,* January 5, 2018. https://www.nytimes.com/2018/01/05
/opinion/golden-globes-metoo.html.

Messinger, Sheldon, Harold Sampson, and Robert Towne. "Life as Theater:
Some Notes on the Dramaturgic Approach to Social Reality." *Sociometry*
25 (1962): 98–110.

Meyers, Helene. "Why Did I Cry for Philip Roth?" *Lilith Magazine,* May 24,
2018. https://www.lilith.org/blog/2018/05/why-did-i-cry-for-philip-roth/.

Michel, Pierre. "Philip Roth's Reductive Lens." *Revue des Langues Vivantes* 42
(1976): 509–19.

Milbauer, Asher, and Donald Watson. "An Interview with Philip Roth." In *Reading
Philip Roth,* edited by Milbauer and Watson, 1–16. London Macmillan, 1988.

Miller, Ross. "Chronology." In *Philip Roth: Novels & Stories, 1959–1962: "Goodbye, Columbus and Five Short Stories," and "Letting Go,"* 897–907. New York:
Library of America, 2005.

Millett, Kate. *Sexual Politics.* New York: Columbia University Press, 2016.

Mills, Charles. *Blackness Visible: Essays on Philosophy and Race.* Ithaca, NY:
Cornell University Press, 1998.

Molloy, Tim. "Philip Roth Told Us 5 Years Ago Which of His Books Are the
Best." *The Wrap,* May 23, 2018. https://www.thewrap.com/philip-roth-told
-us-which-of-his-books-are-the-best/.

Moore, Laurie. "The Wrath of Athena." *New York Times,* May 7, 2000.

Morley, Catherine. "'My Kinsmen, My Precursors': Philip Roth, Epic, Influence, and Bardic Proclivities." In *Roth after Eighty: Philip Roth and the American Literary Imagination,* edited by David Gooblar and Aimee Pozorski,
109–26. Lanham, MD: Lexington, 2016.

Morris, Wesley. "Michael Jackson Cast a Spell. 'Leaving Neverland' Breaks It."
*New York Times,* February 28, 2019. https://www.nytimes.com/2019/02/28
/arts/television/michael-jackson-leaving-neverland.html.

Morrison, Toni, *Beloved*. New York: Plume, 1987.

Mortara, Elèna. "About Meeting with Roth and Editing His Works in Italy." Paper delivered at the "Roth Remembered" conference, April 7, 2019, New York.

———. "The Last Transatlantic Ambassador of American Literature? Philip Roth (Un)Masked as Ziff by Alan Lelchuk." In *Ambassadors: American Studies in a Changing World*, edited by Massimo Bacigalupo and Gregory Dowling, 220–31. Rapallo: Azienda Grafica Busco Edizioni, 2006.

Mortimer, Armine Kotin. "Autofiction as Allofiction: Doubrovsky's 'L'Après-vivre.'" *L'Espirit Crèateur* 49 (2009): 22–35.

Moxey, Keith. *The Practice of Persuasion: Paradox and Power in Art History*. Ithaca, NY: Cornell University Press, 2001.

Mumford, Kevin. *Newark: A History of Race, Rights, and Riots in America*. New York: New York University Press, 2007.

Musolf, Gil Richard. "The Chicago School." In *Handbook of Symbolic Interactionism*, edited by Larry Reynolds and Nancy Herman-Kinney, 91–117. Lanham, MD: Altamira, 2003.

Mustich, James. "Chimamanda Ngozi Adichie: A Conversation with James Mustich." June 29, 2009. Barnes and Noble. https://www.barnesandnoble.com/review/chimamanda-ngozi-adichie.

Nadel, Ira. *Critical Companion to Philip Roth: A Literary Reference to His Life and Work*. New York: Facts on File, 2011.

Neelakantan, G. "Textualizing the Self: Adultery, Blatant Fictions, and Jewishness in Philip Roth's *Deception*." In *Turning up the Flame: Philip Roth's Later Novels*, edited by Jay Halio and Ben Siegel, 58–67. Newark: University of Delaware Press, 2005.

Newlin, James. "Living on the Edge: Deconstruction, The Limits of Readability, and Philip Roth's *The Counterlife*." *Philip Roth Studies* 8 (2012): 161–77.

North, Anna. "The #MeToo Movement and Its Evolution, Explained." *Vox*, October 11, 2018. https://www.vox.com/identities/2018/10/9/17933746/me-too-movement-metoo-brett-kavanaugh-weinstein.

Nussbaum, Martha. "Accountability in an Era of Celebrity." In *Ideas That Matter: Democracy, Justice, Rights*, edited by Debra Satz and Annabelle Lever. University Press Scholarship Online. August 2019. https://www-universitypressscholarship-com.proxy.library.georgetown.edu/view/10.1093/oso/9780190904951.001.0001/oso-9780190904951.

Nwanevu, Osita. "The 'Cancel Culture' Con." *New Republic*, September 23, 2019. https://newrepublic.com/article/155141/cancel-culture-con-dave-chappelle-shane-gillis.

O'Grady, Megan. "The Shadows." *New York Times*, April 13, 2020. https://www.nytimes.com/interactive/2020/04/13/t-magazine/artist-recluse.html.

Onwuachi-Willig, Angela. "What about #UsToo?; The Invisibility of Race in the #MeToo Movement." *Yale Law Journal Forum,* June 18, 2018, 105–20. https://scholarship.law.berkeley.edu/facpubs/3024/.

Ovid. *Metamorphoses.* In *Ovid in Six Volumes,* translated by Frank Justus Miller. Cambridge, MA: Harvard University Press, 1984.

Paley, Grace. "Zagrowsky Tells." In *Grace Paley: The Collected Stories,* 348–64. New York: Farrar, Straus and Giroux, 1994.

Parks, Timothy. "How Best to Read Autofiction." *New York Review of Books,* May 25, 2018. https://www.nybooks.com/daily/2018/05/25/how-best-to-read-auto-fiction/.

Parrish, Timothy. "Becoming Black: Zuckerman's Bifurcating Self in *The Human Stain.*" In *Philip Roth: New Perspectives on an American Author,* edited by Derek Parker Royal, 209–23. Westport, CT: Praeger, 2005.

———. "Introduction: Roth at Mid-Career." In *The Cambridge Companion to Philip Roth,* edited by Parrish, 1–8. Cambridge: Cambridge University Press, 2007.

———. "Roth and Ethnic Identity." In *The Cambridge Companion to Philip Roth,* edited by Parrish, 127–41. Cambridge: Cambridge University Press, 2007.

Paulson, Steve. "David Foster Wallace in the #MeToo Era: A Conversation with Clare Hayes-Brady." *Los Angeles Review of Books,* September 10, 2018. https://lareviewofbooks.org/article/david-foster-wallace-in-the-metoo-era-a-conversation-with-clare-hayes-brady/.

PBS. "Philip Roth: Unmasked." *American Masters,* March 29, 2013.

Penny, Laurie. "The Horizon of Desire and We're All Mad Here: Weinstein, Women, and the Language of Lunacy and the Unforgiving Minute." In *The Best American Magazine Writing,* edited by Sid Hold, 93–120. New York: Columbia University Press, 2019.

Petit, Michael. "The Con Man as Model Organism: The Methodological Roots of Erving Goffman's Dramaturgical Self." *History of Human Sciences* 24 (2011): 138–54.

Phillips, Kristine. "Pulitzer Prize-Winning Author Junot Diaz Accused of Sexual Misconduct, Misogynistic Behavior." *Washington Post,* May 6, 2018. https://www.washingtonpost.com/news/arts-and-entertainment/wp/2018/05/05/pulitzer-prize-winning-author-junot-diaz-accused-of-sexual-misconduct-misogynistic-behavior/.

Pierpoint, Claudia Roth. *Roth Unbound: A Writer and His Books.* New York: Farrar, Straus and Giroux, 2013.

Pierson, Brendan. "Harvey Weinstein Loses Bid to Have Rape Trial Moved out of New York City." *Reuters,* October 3, 2019. https://www.reuters.com/article/us-people-harvey-weinstein/harvey-weinstein-loses-bid-to-have-rape-trial-moved-out-of-new-york-city-idUSKBN1WI26D.

Plimpton, George. "Philip Roth's Exact Intent: George Plimpton/1969." In *Conversations with Philip Roth*, 35–50. Jackson: University Press of Mississippi, 1992.

Podhoretz, Norman. "The Adventures of Philip Roth." *Commentary*, October 1998.

———. "My Negro Problem—And Ours." In *Blacks and Jews: Alliances and Arguments*, edited by Paul Berman, 76–96. New York: Delacorte, 1994.

Popova, Milena. *Sexual Consent*. Cambridge, MA: MIT Press, 2019.

Posnock, Ross. *Philip Roth's Rude Truth: The Art of Immaturity*. Princeton, NJ: Princeton University Press, 2006.

Pozorski, Aimee. "Roth and Celebrity: An Introduction." In *Roth and Celebrity*, edited by Pozorski, 1–10. Lanham, MD: Lexington, 2014.

Proust, Marcel. *A la recherche du temps perdu I*. Paris: Gallimard, 1954.

———. *Swann's Way*. Translated by C. K. Scott Moncrieff. London: Penguin, 1957.

Puddephatt, A. J. "George Herbert Mead: The Evolution of Mind, Self and Society through Interaction." In *The Interactionist Imagination: Studying Meaning, Situation and Micro-Social Order*, edited by Michael Hviid Jacobsen, 95–119. London: Palgrave Macmillan, 2017.

Quart, Barbara Koenig. "The Rapacity of One Nearly Buried Alive." *Massachusetts Review* 24 (1983): 590–608.

Raleigh, John Henry. "The New Criticism as an Historical Phenomenon." *Comparative Literature* 11 (1959): 21–28.

Ramey, James. "Intertextual Metempsychosis in *Ulysses:* Murphy, Sinbad, and the 'U.P.: up' Postcard." *James Joyce Quarterly* 45 (2007): 97–114.

Ransom, Jan. "Harvey Weinstein Is Found Guilty of Sex Crimes in #MeToo Watershed." *New York Times*, February 24, 2020. https://www.nytimes.com/2020/02/24/nyregion/harvey-weinstein-trial-rape-verdict.html?searchResultPosition=9.

Ravits, Martha. "The Jewish Mother: Comedy and Controversy in American Popular Culture." *MELUS* 25 (2000): 3–31.

Reider, Jonathan. *Canarsie: The Jews and Italians of Brooklyn Against Liberalism*. Cambridge, MA: Harvard University Press, 1985.

Remnick, David. "Grace Paley, Voice from the Village." *Washington Post*, April 14, 2015.

———. "Into the Clear: Philip Roth Puts Turbulence in Its Place." *New Yorker*, May 8, 2000.

———. "Philip Roth in the #MeToo Era." *New Yorker*, Politics and More Radio Hour, July 23, 2018. https://www.newyorker.com/podcast/political-scene/philip-roth-in-the-metoo-era.

Rilke, Rainer Maria. "Archaïscher Torso Apollos." In *Rainer Maria Rilke: New Poems*, translated by Len Krisak. Woodbridge: Boydell and Brewer, 2015.

Robin, Régine. "L'auto-théorisation d'un romancier: Serge Doubrovsky." *Études françaises* 33 (1997): 45–59. https://id.erudit.org/iderudit/036052ar.

Rodenhurst, Nigel. "Dis/simulation within Metafiction: Hiding and Disguising as Literary Compulsion in the Fiction of Philip Roth." In *Roth and Celebrity*, edited by Aimee Pozorski, 155–73. Lanham, MD: Lexington, 2014.

Rodgers, Bernard, Jr. *Philip Roth*. Boston: Twayne, 1978.

Rodgers, Bernard, Jr., and Derek Parker Royal. "Grave Commentary: A Roundtable Discussion on Everyman." *Philip Roth Studies* 3 (2007): 3–25.

Rogoff, Jay. "Philip Roth's Master Fictions." *Southern Review* 45 (2009): 497–55.

Roig-Franzia, Manuel. "Bill Cosby Convicted on Three Counts of Sexual Assault." *Washington Post*, April 26, 2018. https://www.washingtonpost.com/lifestyle/style/bill-cosby-convicted-on-three-counts-of-sexual-assault/2018/04/26/d740ef22-4885-11e8-827e-190efaf1f1ee_story.html.

Roiphe, Katie. 2009. "The Naked and the Conflicted—Sex and the American Male Novelist." *New York Times*, December 31, 2009, "Sunday Book Review" sec. https://www.nytimes.com/2010/01/03/books/review/Roiphe-t.html.

Romano, Aja. "Why We Can't Stop Fighting about Cancel Culture." *Vox*, December 30, 2019. https://www.vox.com/culture/2019/12/30/20879720/what-is-cancel-cultureexplained-history-debate.

Rosewarne, Lauren. "#MeToo and the Reasons to Be Cautious." In *#MeToo and the Politics of Social Change*, edited by Bianca Fileborn and Rachel Loney-Howes, 171–84. London: Palgrave Macmillan, 2019.

Roth, Philip. "An Actor's Life for Me." In *Playboy Stories: The Best of 40 Years of Short Fiction*, edited by Alice Turner, 121–41. New York: Dutton, 1984.

———. *American Pastoral*. New York: Vintage International, 1998.

———. *The Anatomy Lesson*. New York: Vintage International, 1996.

———. "The Art of Fiction LXXXIV: Philip Roth, Hermione Lee/1984." In *Conversations with Philip Roth*, edited by George Searles, 162–87. Jackson: University Press of Mississippi, 1992.

———. *The Breast*. 1972. New York: Vintage International 1994.

———. "Channel X: Two Plays on the Race Conflict." *New York Review of Books*, May 28, 1964. https://www.nybooks.com/articles/1964/05/28/channel-x-two-plays-on-the-race-conflict/.

———. "A Conversation with Philip Roth: Joyce Carol Oates/1974." In *Conversations with Philip Roth*, edited by George Searles, 89–99. Jackson: University Press of Mississippi, 1992.

———. *The Counterlife*. New York: Vintage International, 1996.

———. *Deception*. New York: Vintage International, 1990.

———. "Defender of the Faith." In *Goodbye, Columbus and Five Short Stories*, 161–200. New York: Vintage International, 1993.

——. *The Dying Animal*. New York: Vintage International, 2002.

——. *Everyman*. New York Vintage International, 2006.

——. *Exit Ghost*. Ontario: Penguin, 2008.

——. "Expect the Vandals." *Esquire*, December 1958, 208–28.

——. *The Facts: A Novelist's Autobiography*. New York: Vintage International, 1997.

——. "The Fence." *Et Cetera*, May 1953, 18–23.

——. *The Ghost Writer*. New York: Vintage International, 1995.

——. "The Good Girl." *Cosmopolitan*, May 1960, 98–103.

——. *The Great American Novel*. New York: Vintage International, 1995.

——. "His Mistress's Voice." *Partisan Review* 53 (1986): 155–76.

——. *The Human Stain*. New York: Vintage International, 2000.

——. *The Humbling*. New York: Vintage International, 2010.

——. "'I Always Wanted You to Admire My Fasting'; Or, Looking at Kafka." In *A Philip Roth Reader*, 147–66. New York: Farrar, Straus and Giroux, 1980.

——. *I Married a Communist*. New York: Vintage International, 1999.

——. "Imagining Jews." In *Reading Myself and Others*, 251–52. New York: Vintage International, 2001.

——. *Indignation*. Boston: Houghton Mifflin, 2008.

——. "Interview with *Le Nouvel Observateur*" (1981), by Alain Finkielkraut. In *Reading Myself and Others*, 98–110. New York: Vintage International, 2001.

——. "Interview with *The Paris Review*." In *Reading Myself and Others*, 119–48. New York: Vintage International, 2001.

——. "Iowa: A Very Far Country Indeed." *Esquire*, December 1962.

——. *Letting Go*. New York: Vintage International, 1997.

——. *My Life as a Man*. New York: Vintage International, 1974.

——. "My Life as a Writer: Interview with Daniel Sandstrom" *New York Times*, March 2, 2014. https://www.nytimes.com/2014/03/16/books/review/my -life-as-a-writer.html.

——. "The National Pastime." *Cavalier* 15 (May 1965): 16, 54.

——. *Nemesis*. Boston: Houghton Mifflin Harcourt, 2010.

——. "On *Portnoy's Complaint*." In *Reading Myself and Others*, 65–80. New York: Vintage International, 2001.

——. "On the Air." *New American Review* 10 (1970): 7–49.

——. "On *The Great American Novel*." In *Reading Myself and Others*, 65–80. New York: Vintage International, 2001.

——. *Operation Shylock*. New York: Vintage International, 1994.

——. *The Plot Against America*. New York: Vintage International, 2005.

——. *Portnoy's Complaint*. New York: Vintage International, 1994.

——. *The Prague Orgy*. New York: Vintage International, 1996.

——. *The Professor of Desire*. New York: Vintage International, 1994.

——. "The Psychoanalytic Special." *Esquire,* November 1963.

——. "Reading Myself: Philip Roth/1973." In Conversations with Philip Roth, edited by George Searles, 63–76. Jackson: University Press of Mississippi, 1992.

——. "Recollections from beyond the Last Rope." In *For Our Time: 24 Essays by 8 Contemporary Americans,* edited by Barry Gross, 274–84. New York: Dodd, Mead, 1970.

——. *Sabbath's Theater.* New York: Vintage International, 1996.

——. *Shop Talk: A Writer and His Colleagues and Their Work.* New York: Vintage International, 2002.

——. "The Story of Three Stories." In *Reading Myself and Others,* 212–15. New York: Vintage International, 2001.

——. *When She Was Good.* New York: Vintage International, 1995.

——. *Zuckerman Bound: A Trilogy and Epilogue, 1979–1985.* New York: Library of America, 2007.

——. *Zuckerman Unbound.* New York: Vintage International, 1995.

Rothstein, Mervyn. "From Philip Roth, 'The Facts,' as He Remembers Them." In *Conversations with Philip Roth,* edited by George Searles, 226–29. Jackson: University Press of Mississippi, 1992.

——. "Philip Roth and the World of 'What If'?'" In *Conversations with Philip Roth,* edited by George Searles, 198–201. Jackson: University Press of Mississippi, 1992.

——. "To Newark, with Love. Philip Roth." *New York Times,* March 29, 1991. https://www.nytimes.com/1991/03/29/books/to-newark-with-love -philip-roth.html.

Royal, Derek Parker. "Fouling Out the American Pastoral: Rereading Philip Roth's *The Great American Novel.*" In *Upon Further Review: Sports in American Literature,* edited by Michael Cocchiarale and Scott Emmert, 157–68. Westport, CT: Praeger, 2004.

——. "Pastoral Dreams and National Identity in *American Pastoral* and *I Married a Communist.*" In *Philip Roth: New Perspectives on an American Author,* edited by Royal, 185–207. Westport, CT: Praeger, 2005.

——. "Paying Attention to the Man behind the Curtain: Philip Roth and the Dynamics of Written and Unwritten Celebrity." In *Roth and Celebrity,* edited by Aimee Pozorski, 11–28. Lanham, MD: Lexington, 2014.

——. "Postmodern Jewish Identity in Philip Roth's *The Counterlife.*" *Modern Fiction Studies* 48 (2002): 422–43.

——. "Roth, Literary Influence and Postmodernism." In *The Cambridge Companion to Philip Roth,* edited by Timothy Parrish, 22–34. Cambridge: Cambridge University Press, 2007.

Royce, J. E. "Metempsychosis." In *New Catholic Encyclopedia,* vol. 9: *Mab–Mor.* 2nd ed. Detroit: Thomson Gale, 2003.

Ryzik, Melena, Cara Buckley, and Jodi Kantor. "Louis C.K. Is Accused by 5 Women of Sexual Misconduct." *New York Times,* November 9, 2017. https://www.nytimes.com/2017/11/09/arts/television/louis-ck-sexual-misconduct.html?smid=tw-share&_r=0.

Safer, Elaine. "The Double, Comic Irony, and Postmodernism in Philip Roth's Operation Shylock." *MELUS* 21 (1996): 157–72.

———. *Mocking the Age: The Later Novels of Philip Roth.* Albany: State University of New York Press, 2006.

———. "*Operation Shylock:* Double Double Jewish Trouble." In *Philip Roth: New Perspectives on an American Author,* edited by Derek Parker Royal, 153–67. Westport, CT: Praeger, 2005.

Salzman, Jack. "Struggles in the Promised Land." In *Struggles in the Promised Land: Towards a History of Black-Jewish Relations in the United States,* edited by Salzman and Cornel West, 1–19. New York: Oxford University Press, 1997.

Salzman, Jack, Adina Back, and Gretchen Sullivan Sorin. *Bridges and Boundaries: African Americans and American Jews.* New York: G. Braziller in association with the Jewish Museum, 1992.

Salzman, Jack, and Cornel West, eds. *Struggles in the Promised Land: Towards a History of Black-Jewish Relations in the United States.* New York: Oxford University Press, 1997.

Sanoff, Alvin. "Writers Have a Third Eye." In *Conversations with Philip Roth,* edited by George Searles, 209–13. Jackson: University Press of Mississippi, 1992.

Sartre, Jean-Paul. *Existentialism and Human Emotions.* New York: Philosophical Library, 1957.

Schechner, Mark. "Newark: The Shtetl." In *Roth after Eighty: Philip Roth and the American Literary Imagination,* edited by David Gooblar and Aimee Pozorski, 167–79. Lanham, MD: Lexington, 2016.

———. "Roth's American Trilogy." In *The Cambridge Companion to Philip Roth,* edited by Timothy Parrish, 142–57. Cambridge: Cambridge University Press, 2007.

Scholes, Robert. *Fabulation and Metafiction.* Urbana: University of Illinois Press, 1979.

Schubert, Hans-Joachim. "Cooley, Charles Horton." In *Encyclopedia of Social Theory, Volume One,* edited by George Ritzer, 150–55. Thousand Oaks, CA: Sage, 2005.

Schwartz, Larry. "Erasing Race in Philip Roth's *Human Stain.*" *Philip Roth Studies* 7 (2011): 65–81.

———. "Roth, Race, and Newark." *Cultural Logic: A Journal of Marxist Theory & Practice* 8 (2005): 1–21. https://ojs.library.ubc.ca/index.php/clogic/article/view/191860/188829.

Schweitzer, Ivy. "The Story of 'Hannah P.': Recovering Portnoy's Sister." In *Shofar, An Interdisciplinary Journal of Jewish Studies* 31 (2012): 70–92.

Scott, A. O. "Alter Alter Ego." *New York Times,* May 27, 2001. https://archive.nytimes.com/www.nytimes.com/books/01/05/27/reviews/010527.27scottt.html?0525bk.

———. "My Woody Allen Problem." *New York Times,* January 31, 2018. https://www.nytimes.com/2018/01/31/movies/woody-allen.html.

Sehgal, Parul. "#MeToo Is All Too Real. But to Better Understand It, Turn to Fiction." *New York Times,* May 1, 2019. https://www.nytimes.com/2019/05/01/books/novels-me-too-movement.html.

Senn, Fritz. "Met Whom What?" *James Joyce Quarterly* 30 (1992): 109–13.

Shipe, Matthew. "Twilight of the Superheroes: Philip Roth, Celebrity, and the End of Print Culture." In *Roth and Celebrity,* edited by Aimee Pozorski, 101–18. Lanham, MD: Lexington, 2014.

Shostak, Debra. "The Diaspora Jew and the 'Instinct for Impersonation': Philip Roth's 'Operation Shylock.'" *Contemporary Literature* 38 (1997): 726–54.

———. "Introduction: Roth's America." In *Philip Roth: American Pastoral, The Human Stain, The Plot Against America,* edited by Shostak, 1–14. London: Continuum, 2011.

———. *Philip Roth—Countertexts, Counterlives.* Columbia: University of South Carolina Press, 2004.

———. "Philip Roth's Fictions of Self-Exposure." In *Turning up the Flame: Philip Roth's Later Novels,* edited by Jay Halio and Ben Siegel, 21–57. Newark: University of Delaware Press, 2005.

———. "Roth and Gender." In *The Cambridge Companion to Philip Roth,* edited by Timothy Parish, 111–26. Cambridge: Cambridge University Press, 2007.

Siegel, Jason. "*The Plot against America:* Philip Roth's Counter-Plot to American History." *MELUS* 37 (2012): 131–54.

Sinykin, Dan. "This Is the Philip Roth Novel That Explains Philip Roth. And Our Moment." *Washington Post,* May 24, 2018. https://www.washingtonpost.com/news/posteverything/wp/2018/05/24/this-is-the-philip-roth-novel-that-explains-philip-roth-and-our-moment/?noredirect=on&utm_term=.699eadce4449.

Skidelsky, William. "The Interview: Chimamanda Ngozi Adichie." *The Guardian,* April 4, 2009. https://www.theguardian.com/books/2009/apr/05/chimamanda-ngozi-adichie-interview.

Smith, Barbara. "Between a Rock and a Hard Place: Relationships between Black and Jewish Women." In *Strangers and Neighbors: Relations between*

*Blacks and Jews in the United States,* edited by Maurianne Adams and John Bracey, 765–88. Amherst: University of Massachusetts Press, 1999.

Smith, Greg. "Erving Goffman." In *The Wiley-Blackwell Companion to Major Social Theorists,* vol. 2: *Contemporary Social Theorists,* edited by George Ritzer and Jeffrey Stepnisky, 125–54. West Sussex: Wiley Blackwell, 2011.

Smith, Margaret. "Autobiography: False Confession?" In *Turning up the Flame: Philip Roth's Later Novels,* edited by Jay Halio and Ben Siegel, 99–114. Newark: University of Delaware Press, 2005.

Smith, Zadie. *Changing My Mind: Occasional Essays.* New York: Penguin, 2010.

——. "The I Who Is Not Me." In *Feel Free,* 333–47. New York: Penguin, 2018.

Sobel, B. Z., and May Sobel, "Negroes and Jews: American Minority Groups in Conflict." In *The Ghetto and Beyond: Essays on Jewish Life in America,* 384–408. New York: Random House, 1969.

Spanke, Jeff. "Magnificent Things and Terrible Men: Teaching Sherman Alexie in the Age of #MeToo." *English Education* 51 (2018): 101–8. https://secure .ncte.org/library/NCTEFiles/Resources/Journals/EE/0511_oct2018 /EE0511Oct18Magnificent.pdf.

St. Félix, Doreen. "One Year of #MeToo: We Need a More Inclusive Language of Abuse and Victimhood." *New Yorker,* October 10, 2018. https:// www.newyorker.com/culture/culture-desk/one-year-of-metoo-we-need-a -more-flexible-language-of-abuse-and-victimhood.

Statlander, Jane. *Philip Roth's Postmodern American Romance: Critical Essays on Selected Works.* New York: Peter Lang, 2011.

Steinmetz, George. "American Sociology before and after World War II: The (Temporary) Settling of a Disciplinary Field." In *Sociology in America: A History,* edited by Craig Calhoun, 314–66. Chicago: University of Chicago Press, 2007.

Stewart-Kroeker, Sarah. "'What Do We Do with the Art of Monstrous Men?' Betrayal, and the Feminist Ethics of Aesthetic Involvement." *De Ethica. A Journal of Philosophical, Theological, and Applied Ethics* (2019): 1–24.

Stonehill, Brian. *The Self-Conscious Novel: Artifice in Fiction from Joyce to Pynchon.* Philadelphia: University of Pennsylvania Press, 1988.

Stroud, Scott. "The Dark Side of the Online Self: A Pragmatist Critique of the Growing Plague of Revenge Porn." *Journal of Mass Media Ethics* 29 (2014): 168–83.

Sundquist, Eric J. "Black Power, Jewish Power." In *Strangers in the Land: Blacks, Jews, Post-Holocaust America,* by Sundquist. Cambridge, MA: Belknap Press of Harvard University Press, 2008.

——. *Strangers in the Land: Blacks, Jews, Post-Holocaust America.* Cambridge, MA: Belknap Press of Harvard University Press, 2008.

Synikin, Dan. "This Is the Philip Roth Novel That Explains Philip Roth. And Our Moment." *Washington Post.* May 24, 2018. https://www.washingtonpost .com/news/posteverything/wp/2018/05/24/this-is-the-philip-roth-novel -that-explains-philip-roth-and-our-moment/.

Taylor, Benjamin. *Here We Are: My Friendship with Philip Roth.* New York: Penguin, 2020.

Thackray, Rachelle. "Roth Takes Novel Revenge on Ex-Wife Claire Bloom." *The Independent,* October 11, 1998.

Tisch, Jesse. "The Philip Roth Archive." *Tablet Magazine,* May 22, 2020. https:// www.tabletmag.com/sections/arts-letters/articles/philip-roth-letters.

Trachtenberg, Stanley. "'In the Egosphere': Philip Roth's Anti-Bildungsroman." *Papers and Language & Literature* (Spring 1989): 326–41.

Traister, Rebecca. "Why the Harvey Weinstein Sexual-Harassment Allegations Didn't Come Out until Now." *The Cut,* October 5, 2017. https://www.thecut .com/2017/10/why-the-weinstein-sexual-harassment-allegations-came -out-now.html.

Tseëlon, Erfat. "Is the Presented Self Sincere? Goffman, Impression Management and the Postmodern Self." *Theory, Culture and Society* 9 (1992): 115–28.

Tunca, Daria. "The Danger of a Single Short Story: Reality, Fiction and Metafiction in Chimamanda Ngozi Adichie's 'Jumping Monkey Hill.'" *Journal of Postcolonial Writing* 54 (2018): 69–82.

Tuttle, Brad. *How Newark Became Newark: The Rise, Fall, and Rebirth of an American City.* New Brunswick, NJ: Rivergate, 2009.

Updike, John. *The Complete Henry Bech: Twenty Stories.* New York: Knopf, 2001.

———. "Recruiting Raw Nerves." In *More Matter: Essays and Criticism,* 291–99. New York: Knopf, 1999.

Vanderhoof, Erin. "Me and the Monkey: How Philip Roth Created Literature for Female Dirtbags, Too." *Vanity Fair,* May 24 2018. https://www.vanityfair .com/style/2018/05/how-philip-roth-created-literature-for-female -dirtbags-too.

Wake, Bob. "The Dying Animal—Philip Roth." *CultureVulture,* May 9, 2001. https://culturevulture.net/books-cds/the-dying-animal-philip-roth/.

Waldman, Katy. "One Year of #MeToo: 'He Said, She Said' Is a Literary Problem, Too." *New Yorker,* October 10, 2018. https://www.newyorker.com /books/page-turner/one-year-of-metoo-he-said-she-said-is-a-literary -problem-too.

Waltzer, Michael. "Blacks and Jews: A Personal Reflection." In *Struggles in the Promised Land: Towards a History of Black-Jewish Relations in the United*

*States,* edited by Jack Salzman and Cornel West, 401–9. New York: Oxford University Press, 1997.

Waugh, Patricia. *Metafiction: The Theory and Practice of Self-Conscious Fiction.* Abingdon, UK: Routledge, 1984.

Weber, Katherine. "Life, Counterlife." In *Conversations with Philip Roth,* edited by George Searles, 214–19. Jackson: University Press of Mississippi, 1992.

Wellek, René. "Literary Theory, Criticism and History." *Sewanee Review* 68 (1960): 1–19.

———. "The New Criticism: Pro and Contra." *Critical Inquiry* 4 (1978): 611–24.

West, Kanye. "Famous." *Genius.* https://genius.com/Kanye-west-famous-lyrics.

West, Kevin R. "Professing Desire: The Kepesh Novels." In *Philip Roth: New Perspectives on an American Author,* edited by Derek Parker Royal, 225–39. Westport, CT: Praeger, 2005.

Wicke, Jennifer. "'Who's She When She's at Home?' Molly Bloom and the Work of Consumption." *James Joyce Quarterly* 28 (1991): 749–63.

Wickenden, Dorothy. "Philip Roth in the #MeToo Era." *New Yorker* (podcast), July 23, 2018. https://www.newyorker.com/podcast/political-scene/philip-roth-in-the-metoo-era.

Williams, Simon Johnson. "Appraising Goffman." *British Journal of Sociology* 37 (1986): 348–69.

Wilson, Matthew. "Reading *The Human Stain* through Charles W. Chestnutt: The Genre of the Passing Novel." *Philip Roth Studies* 2 (2006): 138–50.

Wimsatt, W. K., Jr., and M. C. Beardsley. "The Intentional Fallacy." *Sewanee Review* 54, no. 3 (1946): 468–88.

Wirth-Nesher, Hana. "The Artist Tales of Philip Roth." *Prooftexts* 3 (1983): 263–72.

———. "Roth's Autobiographical Writings." In *The Cambridge Companion to Philip Roth,* edited by Timothy Parrish, 158–72. Cambridge: Cambridge University Press, 2007.

Womble, Todd. "Roth Is Roth as Roth: Autofiction and the Implied Author." In *Autofiction in English,* edited by Hywel Dix, 219–36. Cham, Switzerland: Palgrave Macmillan, 2018.

Worthington, Marjorie. "Fiction in the 'Post-Truth' Era: The Ironic Effects of Autofiction." *Critique: Studies in Contemporary Fiction* 58 (2017): 471–83.

———. *The Story of "Me": Contemporary American Autofiction.* Lincoln: University of Nebraska Press, 2018.

Zax, Talya. "Philip Roth Is Immersing Himself in Jewish History, and Doesn't Know How to Respond to #MeToo." *The Forward,* January 16, 2018. https://forward.com/culture/392200/philip-roth-new-york-times-plot-against-america-metoo/.

Zipperstein, Steven J. "My Friend Philip." *Jewish Quarterly*, August 14, 2018. https://www.jewishquarterly.org/2018/07/my-friend-philip/.

———. "Philip Roth's Forgotten Tape: The Beginnings of The Great American Writer." *The Forward*, May 28, 2018. https://forward.com/culture /books/401928/philip-roths-forgotten-tape-the-beginnings-of-the-great -american-writer/.

# INDEX